BV 825 .A4 1964

THE OVERSEAS MISSION SOCIETY
MOUNT SAINT ALBAN
WASHINGTON, D. C. 20016

FROM THE LIBRARY OF
THE INSTITUTE FOR
WORSHIP STUDIES
FLORIDA CAMPUS

THE
LITURGY IN
ENGLISH

THE
LITURGY IN ENGLISH

EDITED BY
BERNARD WIGAN
Vicar of Mark Beech, Kent

SECOND EDITION

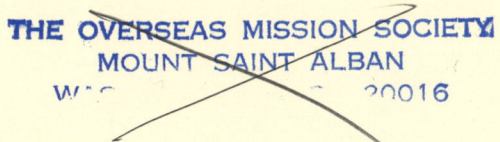

LONDON
OXFORD UNIVERSITY PRESS
NEW YORK   TORONTO
1964

Oxford University Press, Amen House, London E.C.4

GLASGOW NEW YORK TORONTO MELBOURNE WELLINGTON
BOMBAY CALCUTTA MADRAS KARACHI LAHORE DACCA
CAPE TOWN SALISBURY NAIROBI IBADAN ACCRA
KUALA LUMPUR HONG KONG

Selection, arrangement, and editorial matter
© *Oxford University Press 1962, 1964*

First edition 1962
Second edition 1964

PRINTED IN GREAT BRITAIN

G. C. W.

PATRINO ET PATRONO

D.D.

B. J. W.

PREFACE

THIS book is intended to take the place of a useful work which has been out of print for some years: *Anglican Liturgies* edited by J. H. Arnold (1939). But in several ways its scope is wider than that of Dr. Arnold's book, and an attempt has been made to indicate this by the change of title. It is, in fact, a new book, which depends upon the earlier work only for the text of the Ceylon Liturgy. There are four principal differences between the old and the new:

1. The Anglican liturgies that existed in 1939 are here printed in greater number; and, of course, several new liturgies have been issued in the last twenty years.
2. In certain cases notes have been added showing how the present text of a liturgy differs from its earlier forms.
3. In five appendixes have been grouped material which it seemed a waste of space to print repeatedly in each liturgy: Prefaces, Offertory Sentences, Post-communions, Introits and Graduals, and provisions for Supplementary Consecration. It is hoped that this arrangement will also facilitate their study.
4. Lastly, some liturgies which are composed in English, but which are not Anglican, have been included. In 1939 Anglicans could still believe that they held the initiative in the matter of vernacular liturgy. In 1960 this is not the case; English-speaking Protestant communions, which are developing a liturgical worship, now look to older models than the Book of Common Prayer. Three specimens of these modern liturgies are included; and they are preceded by the provision for the Lord's Supper of the *Directory of Public Worship*, which was imposed in place of the Prayer Book under the Commonwealth. The inclusion of this short text completes the series of eucharistic rites of post-Reformation England.

There are other texts which it would have been a convenience to include in this volume. And, were the editor resident in another part of the world, no doubt he would have chosen other non-Anglican liturgies. But there comes a moment when any book of this kind is in danger of breaking the price-barrier, and the reader is asked to be content with what is provided.

If some of the texts in this book are in English but not Anglican, others are Anglican but not in English. As is indicated in the notes prefixed to certain chapters, some Anglican liturgies have been compiled away from England in the local vernacular and have not before been printed in English. In one case no translation at all appears to exist.

The following points should be added about the methods used in presenting these texts:

1. In chapters which give, with the aid of notes, an historical edition, the text printed is the standard of the present day. The notes give the variations from this text of earlier recensions and of recensions used elsewhere. This is the reverse of the normal method, in which the *oldest* text is printed and the critical apparatus records deviations from it. But it seems to be unquestionably the right method in these chapters, where the object is to illustrate the history of the present text. For the same reason variants are grouped by liturgies and not by references to the text above.
2. In Appendix A (Proper Prefaces), on the other hand, the variants of every liturgy are given in reference to each passage of the text, for here the aim is not the reconstruction of a rite but the study of the search for perfection in the wording of the texts.
3. Except in Appendix A, trivial variants have usually been ignored, especially in liturgies composed in foreign vernaculars, whose English version has no liturgical authority.
4. In the introductory notes to each chapter the source of the text has been indicated, with some account of its history, and (where possible) a clear statement of its canonical authority in December 1960.
5. Several liturgies have a large number of lengthy rubrics prefixed. It is to be feared that absolute consistency has not been achieved; but the aim has been to include those that refer to the performance of the rite and to exclude those that define the qualifications of the Minister and communicants, or are of a more general character.
6. The attempt has been made to distinguish clearly between optional and mandatory features of the Anglican liturgies.

7. When the compilation of this book was begun, it was intended to present the texts in a typographically uniform manner. Two circumstances have led to the abandonment of this ideal: several of the texts have meanwhile been the subject of considerable revision; and the editor has received them in forms varying from the work of distinguished University Presses to that of amateur typists. The state in which each text was available will be seen from the note at the head of the chapter concerned.

This book has been compiled in the hope that it will perform two services to English-speaking Christians: that it will give Anglicans a comprehensive picture of what has been achieved so far in liturgical revision, and that it will help to draw together those who are concerned with Christian worship in the vernacular, whether they have or have not the tradition of the Book of Common Prayer behind them.

BERNARD WIGAN

Feast of the Nativity of our Lord, 1960

FOREWORD TO THE SECOND EDITION

THE only substantial change in this edition of the book is in Chapter XV, the Korean Liturgy. In Lent 1962 a bilingual edition of this rite was published in Seoul, whose English text is markedly different from that supplied to me in typescript in 1959. I am grateful to the Reverend Richard Rutt for drawing my attention to this discrepancy; and also for his patient assistance in presenting the official text, as well as in unravelling its history.

Since this book was first published, I have been informed of a few other Anglican liturgies. But, in view of the rapid changes now taking place, it did not seem right to enlarge and reshape the book at the present time, in order to include them.

B. J. W.

20 May 1963

CONTENTS

Acknowledgements — xiii

Abbreviations and Typographical Rules — xv

PART I

I. Common Forms — 3

II. The First English Liturgy (1549) — 10

III. The English Liturgy of 1662 and Related Rites — 26

IV. The Scottish Liturgy — 38

V. The American Liturgy — 52

VI. The Proposed English Revision (1928) — 62

VII. The South African Liturgy (with note on the Madagascar Liturgy) — 73

VIII. The Ceylon Liturgy — 82

IX. The Bombay Liturgy — 94

X. The Indian Liturgy, 1960 — 114

XI. The Japanese Liturgy — 127

XII. The Canadian Liturgy, 1959 — 136

XIII. The Liturgies of the Dioceses of Nyasaland and Northern Rhodesia — 145

XIV. The Swahili Mass — 162

XV. The Liturgy of the Church in Korea — 166

XVI. The Liturgy of the Church of the Province of the West Indies — 178

PART II

XVII. The Directory   189

XVIII. The Book of Common Order   192

XIX. A Congregationalist Liturgy   201

XX. The Liturgy of the Church of South India   209

PART III. APPENDIXES

A. Proper Prefaces   225

B. Offertory Sentences   239

C. Post-communion Collects   246

D. Introits and Graduals   251

E. Supplementary Consecration   252

ACKNOWLEDGEMENTS

EXTRACTS from the Book of Common Prayer of 1662 are Crown Copyright and are here reprinted by permission.

Thanks are also due to the following for permission to make use of copyright material in the chapters mentioned and also in the Appendixes:

Ch. IV	the Publications Committee of the Episcopal Church in Scotland, and the Cambridge University Press.
Ch. V	the Custodian of the Standard Book of Common Prayer, Washington.
Ch. VI	the Central Board of Finance of the Church Assembly.
Ch. VII	the Episcopal Synod of the Church of the Province of South Africa, and the Oxford University Press and S.P.C.K.
Chs. VIII, IX, and X	the Most Rev. the Metropolitan of the Church of India, Pakistan, Burma, and Ceylon, and the I.S.P.C.K.
Ch. XI	the Rt. Rev. Bishop Viall, S.S.J.E., acting on behalf of the Nippon Seikokai.
Ch. XII	the General Synod of the Anglican Church of Canada, and the Cambridge University Press.
Chs. XIII and XIV	the General Secretary of the Universities Mission to Central Africa.
Ch. XV	the Secretary of the Mission to Korea.
Ch. XVI	the provincial authorities of the West Indies, and the S.P.C.K.
Ch. XVIII	the Committee on Public Worship and Aids to Devotion of the General Assembly of the Church of Scotland, and the Oxford University Press.
Ch. XIX	the compilers of *A Book of Public Worship*, and the Oxford University Press.
Ch. XX	the Liturgical Committee of the Synod of the Church of South India, and the Oxford University Press.

I also wish to express my thanks to my friend Mr. Geoffrey Hunt, at whose suggestion this book was undertaken. I have greatly valued his assistance in dealing with several problems that have arisen concerning the arrangement and presentation of the texts here printed.

B. J. W.

ABBREVIATIONS AND TYPOGRAPHICAL RULES

1549	The liturgy of the first English Prayer Book.
1552	The liturgy of the second English Prayer Book.
1558	The liturgy of the Prayer Book of Queen Elizabeth I.
1662	The liturgy of the book annexed to the Act of Uniformity 1661/2.
1928	The alternative liturgy from the English Prayer Book with the additions and deviations proposed in 1928. [In Chapter V, however, '**1928**' refers to the current text of the American liturgy, dating from that year, as distinct from earlier forms.]
Afr	The liturgy of the South African Prayer Book (1954).
Amer	The liturgy of the American Prayer Book (1928).
BCO	*The Book of Common Order* of the Church of Scotland (1940).
Bom	The liturgy sanctioned for experimental use in the diocese of Bombay (1923).
BomR	'A Liturgy for India' in the Indian *Supplement* (1961).
Can	The liturgy of the Canadian Prayer Book (1918).
CanR	The liturgy of the Canadian Prayer Book, 1959 (including the Draft Book of 1955).
Cey	The Ceylon Liturgy (1938).
CF	'Common Form' with a number, referring to Chapter I. E.g. CF 4 = the Nicene Creed.
Cor	The Coronation Rite of Queen Elizabeth II (1953).
CSI	The liturgy of the Church of South India (1954).
Ind	The recension of **1662** printed in the Indian Prayer Book (1961), pp. 376–93. This abbreviation is also used to refer to material, such as Proper Prefaces, which is common to **Ind** and to **IndR**.
IndR	The Order of 1960 from the Indian Prayer Book (1961); (including the draft Books of 1952 and 1957).
Ire	The liturgy of the Irish Prayer Book.
Jap	An English translation of the Japanese Liturgy (1959).
Kor	An English translation of the liturgy of the Church in Korea (1962).
Nyas	The diocesan liturgy of Nyasaland.
rec	In Chapter III this signifies the agreement of the more 'recent' texts against **1552, 1558,** and **1662**. In practice it applies only to the italicization of 'Amen' and to a few corruptions of **1662** that have become universal.
Rhod	An English translation of the diocesan liturgy of Northern Rhodesia.

Abbreviations and typographical rules

Scot   The Scottish Liturgy from the Scottish Prayer Book (1929).
ScotE The version of **1662** printed in the Scottish Prayer Book.
WInd The liturgy of the Province of the West Indies.
Zan   An English translation of the Swahili Mass (Zanzibar).

Roman type in text and notes, and *italic* when used for responses, represent the liturgical text to be said or sung.

Italic type otherwise in text and notes represents rubric.

SMALL CAPITAL type is used to distinguish short editorial comment, usually abbreviated: e.g. OM[ITS], ADD[S], SUBST[ITUTES], PREF[IXES].

OMIT (the word printed in full) indicates that the book in question omits the whole section to which the group of notes refers.

SUBST is used only in cases where a book has a text entirely different from that on which the group of notes depends.

ADD (with no preceding text and bracket) indicates that what follows is added at the end of the text on which the group of notes depends.

⟦ ⟧ Longer editorial comment, whether in the text or in footnotes, is enclosed within double brackets. Footnotes which are not so enclosed are derived from the source in use.

[ ] and ( ) are used as in the sources. But a particular use is made of [ ] and ⟨ ⟩ in Chapter XIII, which is described in the introduction to that chapter.

/ in the notes indicates a division (such as a paragraph) in the original.

* in the Appendixes indicates optional texts.

The typographical variation '*Amen*' and '℟ Amen' is due to the circumstances explained in the Preface and is without significance.

PART I

CHAPTER I

COMMON FORMS

THESE forms are printed here once for all (in the text of the Book Annexed to the Act of Uniformity of 1662) in order to save space elsewhere. References to them in other parts of the book are given thus: 〚CF 10〛. In cases where another liturgy uses the 1662 text with only small variations, these are given in the notes in the appropriate place. The titles given below are editorial, and the same rules for printing the text have been followed as in Chapter III.

1   THE LORD'S PRAYER

Our Father which art in heaven,   Hallowed be thy Name. Thy kingdom come.   Thy will be done in earth as it is in heaven. Give us this day our daily bread.   And forgive us our trespasses, As we forgive them that trespass against us.   And lead us not into temptation,   But deliver us from evil.   For thine is the kingdom,   The power and the glory,   For ever and ever, Amen.

〚Variation in the use of 'who' for 'which' in the first clause, and in the use or disuse of the ascription ('For thine ... and ever') is indicated by the cues printed at each occurrence of the prayer〛

2   THE COLLECT FOR PURITY

Almighty God unto whom all hearts be open, all desires known, and from whom no secrets are hid: cleanse the thoughts of our hearts by the inspiration of thy holy Spirit, that we may perfectly love thee, and worthily magnify thy holy Name through Christ our Lord. Amen.

3   THE DECALOGUE

Minister. God spake these words and said, I am the Lord thy God, Thou shalt have none other gods but me.

People. Lord have mercy upon us, and incline our hearts to keep this Law.

Minister. Thou shalt not make to thyself any graven image, nor the likeness of any thing that is in heaven above; or in the earth beneath, or in the water under the earth. Thou shalt not bow down to them, nor worship them. For I the Lord thy God, am a jealous God, and visit the sins of the Fathers upon the children unto the third and fourth generation of them that hate me, and shew mercy unto thousands in them that love me, and keep my Commandments.

People. Lord have mercy upon us, and incline our hearts to keep this Law.

Minister. Thou shalt not take the name of the Lord thy God in vain, for the Lord will not hold him guiltless that taketh his Name in vain.

People. Lord have mercy upon us, and incline our hearts to keep this Law.

Minister. Remember that thou keep holy the Sabbath day. Six days shalt thou labour, and do all that thou hast to do, but the seventh day is the Sabbath of the Lord thy God. In it thou shalt do no manner of work, thou, and thy son, and thy daughter, thy man-servant, and thy maid-servant, thy Cattle, and the stranger that is within thy Gates. For in six days the Lord made heaven and earth, the sea, and all that in them is, and rested the seventh day: wherefore the Lord blessed the seventh day and hallowed it.

People. Lord have mercy upon us, and incline our hearts to keep this Law.

Minister. Honour thy father and thy mother, that thy days may be long in the land which the Lord thy God giveth thee.

People. Lord have mercy upon us, and incline our hearts to keep this Law.

Minister. Thou shalt do no murder.

People. Lord have mercy upon us, and incline our hearts to keep this Law.

Minister. Thou shalt not commit adultery.

People. Lord have mercy upon us, and incline our hearts to keep this Law.

Minister. Thou shalt not steal.

People. Lord have mercy upon us, and incline our hearts to keep this Law.

Minister. Thou shalt not bear false witness against thy neighbour.

People. Lord have mercy upon us, and incline our hearts to keep this Law.

Minister. Thou shalt not covet thy neighbour's house, thou shalt not covet thy neighbour's wife, nor his servant, nor his maid, nor his ox, nor his Ass, nor any thing that is his.

People. Lord have mercy upon us, and write all these thy Laws in our hearts, we beseech thee.

THE NICENE CREED

4

I believe in one God the Father Almighty, Maker of heaven and earth, and of all things visible, and invisible:

And in one Lord Jesus Christ, the only begotten Son of God, Begotten of his Father before all worlds, God of God, Light of Light, Very God of very God, Begotten not made, Being of one substance with the Father, By whom all things were made: Who for us men, and for our Salvation came down from heaven, And was incarnate by the holy Ghost of the Virgin Mary, And was made man, And was crucified also for us under Pontius Pilate. He suffered and was buried, And the third day he rose again according to the Scriptures, And ascended into heaven, And sitteth on the right hand of the Father. And he shall come again with glory to judge both the quick and the dead: Whose kingdom shall have no end.

And I believe in the holy Ghost, The Lord and giver of life, who proceedeth from the Father and the Son, who with the Father and the Son together is worshipped and glorified, who spake by the prophets. And I believe one Catholick and Apostolick Church. I acknowledge one Baptism for the remission of Sins. And I look for the Resurrection of the dead, And the life of the world to come. Amen.

THE LONG EXHORTATION

5

Dearly beloved in the Lord, ye that mind to come to the holy Communion of the Body and Blood of our Saviour Christ, must consider how Saint Paul exhorteth all persons diligently to try and examine themselves, before they presume to eat of that Bread, and drink of that Cup. For as the benefit is great, if with a true penitent heart, and lively faith we receive that holy Sacrament (for then we spiritually eat the flesh of Christ, and drink his Blood, then we dwell in Christ, and Christ in us, we are one with Christ, and Christ with us:) so is the danger great, if we receive the same unworthily, for then we are guilty of the body and blood of Christ our Saviour: we eat and drink our own damnation, not considering the Lord's Body: we kindle God's wrath against us: we provoke him to plague us with divers diseases, and sundry kinds of death. Judge therefore yourselves, brethren, that ye be not judged of the Lord. Repent you truly for your sins past: have a lively and stedfast faith in Christ our Saviour. Amend your lives, and be in perfect Charity with all men, so shall ye be meet partakers of those holy mysteries. And above all things ye must give most humble and hearty thanks to God the Father, the Son and the holy Ghost, for the redemption of the world by the death and passion of our Saviour Christ, both God and man, who did humble himself even to the death upon the Cross, for us miserable sinners; who lay in darkness and the shadow of death, that he might make us the children of God, and exalt us to everlasting life. And to the end that we should alway remember the exceeding great love of our Master, and only Saviour, Jesus Christ, thus dying for us, and the innumerable benefits which by his precious bloodshedding he hath obtained to us: he hath instituted and ordained holy mysteries as pledges of his love, and for a continual remembrance of his death, to our great and endless comfort. To him therefore with the Father and the holy Ghost, let us give, (as we are most bounden) continual thanks, submitting ourselves wholly to his holy Will and pleasure, and studying to serve him in true holiness and righteousness all the days of our life. Amen.

THE INVITATION

Ye that do truly and earnestly repent you of your Sins and are in love and charity with your neighbours, and intend to lead a new life, following the Commandments of God, and walking from henceforth in his holy ways, Draw near with faith, and take this holy Sacrament to your Comfort: and make your humble Confession to Almighty God, meekly kneeling upon your knees.

THE GENERAL CONFESSION

Almighty God, Father of our Lord Jesus Christ, Maker of all things, Judge of all men, We acknowledge and bewail Our manifold sins and wickedness, Which we from time to time Most grievously have committed, By thought, word and deed,

Against thy divine Majesty, Provoking most justly Thy wrath and indignation against us. We do earnestly repent, And are heartily sorry for these our misdoings, The remembrance of them is grievous unto us, The burden of them is intolerable. Have mercy upon us, Have mercy upon us most merciful Father; For thy Son our Lord Jesus Christ's sake, Forgive us all that is past, And grant that we may ever hereafter Serve and please thee In newness of life, To the honour and glory of thy name, Through Jesus Christ our Lord. Amen.

8   THE ABSOLUTION

Almighty God our heavenly Father, who of his great mercy hath promised forgiveness of sins to all them that with hearty repentance and true faith turn unto him: have mercy upon you, pardon and deliver you from all your sins, confirm and strengthen you in all goodness, and bring you to everlasting life, through Jesus Christ our Lord. Amen.

9   THE COMFORTABLE WORDS

Hear what comfortable words our Saviour Christ saith unto all that truly turn to him

Come unto me all that travail and are heavy laden, and I will refresh you.   St. Matt. 11. 28.

So God loved the world that he gave his only begotten Son, to the end that all that believe in him should not perish but have everlasting life.   St. John 3. 16.

Hear also what Saint Paul saith

This is a true saying, and worthy of all men to be received, that Jesus Christ came into the world to save sinners.   1 Tim. 1. 15.

Hear also what Saint John saith

If any man sin, we have an Advocate with the Father, Jesus Christ the righteous, and he is the propitiation for our sins.
                                        1 St. John 2. 1.

10   THE PRAYER OF HUMBLE ACCESS

We do not presume to come to this thy Table (O merciful Lord) trusting in our own righteousness, but in thy manifold, and great mercies. We are not worthy so much as to gather up the Crumbs under thy Table. But thou art the same Lord, whose property is always to have mercy: grant us therefore gracious Lord, so to eat the flesh of thy dear Son Jesus Christ, and to drink his blood, that our sinful bodies may be made clean by his body, and our souls washed through his most precious blood, and that we may evermore dwell in him, and he in us. Amen.

11   THE ADMINISTRATION OF THE SACRAMENT

(*a*) *And when he delivereth the bread to any one he shall say.*

The body of our Lord Jesus Christ, which was given for thee, preserve thy body and soul unto everlasting life: take and eat this in remembrance that Christ died for thee, and feed on him in thy heart by faith with thanksgiving.

(*b*) *And the Minister that delivereth the cup to any one, shall say.*

The blood of our Lord Jesus Christ, which was shed for thee, preserve thy body and soul unto everlasting life: drink this in remembrance that Christ's Blood was shed for thee, and be thankful.

12   THE PRAYER OF THANKSGIVING

Almighty and everliving God, We most heartily thank thee for that thou dost vouchsafe to feed us, who have duly received these holy mysteries, with the spiritual food of the most precious body and blood of thy Son our Saviour Jesus Christ, and dost assure us thereby of thy favour and goodness towards us, and that we are very members incorporate in the mystical body of thy Son which is the blessed company of all faithful people, and are also heirs through hope of thy everlasting kingdom, by the merits of the most precious death and passion of thy dear Son. And we most humbly beseech thee, O heavenly Father, so to assist us with thy grace, that we may continue in that holy fellowship, and do all such good works as thou hast prepared for us to walk in, through Jesus Christ our Lord to whom with thee and the holy Ghost be all honour and glory world without end. Amen.

GLORIA IN EXCELSIS

13

Glory be to God on high, and in Earth peace, good will towards men. We praise thee, we bless thee, we worship thee. We glorify thee, we give thanks to thee for thy great glory, O Lord God, heavenly King, God the Father Almighty:

O Lord the only begotten Son, Jesu Christ, O Lord God, Lamb of God, Son of the Father, that takest away the sins of the World, have mercy upon us. Thou that takest away the sins of the world, have mercy upon us. Thou that takest away the sins of the world, receive our prayers, Thou that sittest at the right hand of God the Father have mercy upon us.

For thou only art holy, thou only art the Lord, thou only, O Christ, with the holy Ghost, art most high in the Glory of God the Father. Amen.

THE BLESSING

14

The peace of God which passeth all understanding, keep your hearts and minds in the knowledge and love of God, and of his Son Jesus Christ our Lord: And the blessing of God Almighty, the Father, the Son, and the holy Ghost be amongst you, and remain with you always. Amen.

[Note that variations of capitals and punctuation between the above texts and the places that are referred to them later in the book are not normally noticed. It should also be said that in these respects the texts of the Lord's Prayer in the 'Book Annexed' are not consistent.]

CHAPTER II

THE FIRST ENGLISH LITURGY

THE text here reprinted is that of the 1549 Mass given in the 'Everyman'[1] edition of the Edwardine Prayer Books. The only modification of this text (apart from omissions and rearrangement in accordance with the general plan of this volume) is the expansion of the small number of contractions in the original, which are invariably the replacement of 'n' or 'm' by a line above the text. In view of the unique position of this liturgy, the 'Common Forms' have in this chapter been printed out in full.

1
THE
SUPPER OF THE LORDE
AND
THE HOLY COMMUNION,
COMMONLY CALLED THE MASSE

2 *Upon the daie and at the tyme appoincted for the ministracion of the holy Communion, the Priest that shal execute the holy ministery, shall put upon hym the vesture appoincted for that ministracion, that is to saye: a white Albe plain, with a vestement or Cope. And where there be many Priestes, or Decons, there so many shalbe ready to helpe the Priest, in the ministracion, as shalbee requisite: And shall haue upon them lykewise the vestures appointed for their ministery, that is to saye, Albes with tunacles. Then shall the Clerkes syng in Englishe for the office, or Introite, (as they call it,) a Psalme appointed for that daie.*

3 *The Priest standing humbly afore the middes of the Altar, shall saie the Lordes praier, with this Collect.*

Almightie God, unto whom all hartes bee open, and all desyres knowen, and from whom no secretes are hid: clense the thoughtes of our hartes, by the inspiracion of thy holy spirite: that we may perfectly loue thee, and worthely magnifie thy holy name: through Christ our Lorde. Amen.

[1] Last reprinted in 1949 with Introduction by E. C. S. G[ibson] and Bibliography by E. C. Ratcliff.

First English Liturgy, 1549

4 *Then shall he saie a Psalme appointed for the introite: whiche Psalme ended the Priest shall saye, or els the Clerkes shal syng,*

 iii. Lorde haue mercie upon us.
 iii. Christ haue mercie upon us.
 iii. Lorde haue mercie upon us.

5 *Then the Prieste standyng at Goddes borde shall begin,*
    Glory be to God on high.
The Clerkes. And in yearth peace, good will towardes men.

 We praise thee, we blesse thee, we worship thee, we glorifie thee, wee geue tankes to thee for thy greate glory, O Lorde GOD, heauenly kyng, God the father almightie.

 O Lorde the onely begotten sonne Jesu Christe, O Lorde GOD, Lambe of GOD, sonne of the father, that takest awaye the synnes of the worlde, haue mercie upon us: thou that takest awaye the synnes of the worlde, receiue our praier.

 Thou that sittest at the right hande of God the father, haue mercie upon us: For thou onely art holy, thou onely art the Lorde. Thou onely (O Christ) with the holy Ghoste, are moste high in the glory of God the father. Amen.

6 *Then the priest shall turne him to the people and saye,*
    The Lorde be with you.
The Aunswere. And with thy spirite.
The Priest. Let us praie.

7 *Then shall folowe the Collect of the daie, with one of these two Collectes folowynge, for the kyng.*

 Almightie God, whose kingdom is euerlasting, and power infinite, haue mercie upon the whole congregacion, and so rule the heart of thy chosen seruaunt Edward the sixt, our kyng and gouernour: that he (knowyng whose minister he is) maie aboue al thinges, seke thy honour and glory, and that we his subiectes (duely consydering whose auctoritie he hath) maye faithfully serue, honour, and humbly obeye him, in thee, and for thee, according to thy blessed word and ordinaunce: Through Jesus Christe oure Lorde, who with thee, and the holy ghoste, liueth and reigneth, euer one God, worlde without ende. Amen.

8 Almightie and euerlasting GOD, wee bee taught by thy holy worde, that the heartes of Kynges are in thy rule and

gouernaunce, and that thou doest dispose, and turne them as it semeth best to thy godly wisedom: We humbly besech thee, so to dispose and gouerne, the heart of Edward the sixt, thy seruaunt, our Kyng and gouernour, that in all his thoughtes, wordes, and workes, he maye euer seke thy honour and glory, and study to preserue thy people, committed to his charge, in wealth, peace, and Godlynes: Graunt this, O mercifull father, for thy dere sonnes sake, Jesus Christ our Lorde. Amen.

9 *The Collectes ended, the priest, or he that is appointed, shall reade the Epistle, in a place assigned for the purpose, saying,*

The Epistle of sainct Paule, written in the   Chapter of   to the

The Minister then shall reade thepistle. Immediatly after the Epistle ended, the priest, or one appointed to reade the Gospel, shall saie,

10 The holy Gospell, written in the   Chapter of

The Clearkes and people shall aunswere, Glory be to thee, O Lorde. *The priest or deacon then shall reade the Gospel: After the Gospell ended, the Priest shall begin,*

11 I beleue in one God.

The clerkes shall syng the rest.

The father almightie, maker of heauen and yearth, and of all thinges visible, and inuisible: And in one Lorde Jesu Christ, the onely begotten sonne of GOD, begotten of his father before all worldes, God of GOD, light of light, very God of very God, begotten, not made, beeyng of one substaunce with the father, by whom all things were made, who for us men, and for our saluacion, came doune from heauen, and was incarnate by the holy Ghoste, of the Virgin Mary, and was made manne, and was Crucified also for us under Poncius Pilate, he suffered and was buried, and the thirde daye he arose again according to the scriptures, and ascended into heauen, and sitteth at the right hande of the father: and he shall come again with glory, to iudge both the quicke and the dead.

And I beleue in the holy ghost, the Lorde and geuer of life, who procedeth from the father and the sonne, who with the father and the sonne together, is worshipped and glorified, who spake by the Prophetes. And I beleue one Catholike and Apostolike Churche. I acknowlege one Baptisme, for the remission of synnes. And I

First English Liturgy, 1549

loke for the resurreccion of the deade: and the lyfe of the worlde to come. Amen.

12 *After the Crede ended, shall folowe the Sermon or Homely, or some portion of one of the Homeleyes, as thei shalbe herafter deuided: wherein if the people bee not exhorted to the worthy receiuyng of the holy Sacrament of the bodye and bloude of our sauior Christ: then shal the Curate geue this exhortacion, to those yt be minded to receiue ye same.*

Derely beloued in the Lord, ye that mynde to come to the holy Communion of the bodye and bloude of our sauior Christe, must considre what S. Paule writeth to the Corinthians, how he exhorteth all persones diligently to trie and examine themselues, before they presume to eate of that breade, and drinke of that cup: for as the benefite is great, if with a truly penitent heart, and liuely faith, we receiue that holy Sacrament; (for then we spiritually eate the fleshe of Christ, and drinke his bloude, then we dwell in Christ and Christ in us, wee bee made one with Christ, and Christ with us;) so is the daunger great, yf wee receyue the same unworthely; for then wee become gyltie of the body and bloud of Christ our sauior, we eate and drinke our owne damnacion, not considering the Lordes bodye. We kyndle Gods wrathe ouer us, we prouoke him to plague us with diuerse dyseases, and sondery kyndes of death. Therefore if any here be a blasphemer, aduouterer, or bee in malyce, or enuie, or in any other greuous cryme (excepte he bee truly sory therefore, and earnestly mynded to leaue the same vices, and do trust himselfe to be reconciled to almightie God, and in Charitie with all the worlde), lette him bewayle his synnes, and not come to that holy table; lest after the taking of that most blessed breade, the deuyll enter into him, as he dyd into Judas, to fyll him full of all iniquitie, and brynge him to destruccion, bothe of body and soule.

13 Judge therfore yourselfes (brethren) that ye bee not iudged of the Lorde. Let your mynde be without desire to synne, repent you truely for your synnes past, haue an earnest and lyuely faith in Christ our sauior, be in perfect charitie with all men, so shall ye be mete partakers of those holy misteries. And aboue all thynges: ye must geue moste humble and hartie thankes to God the father, the sonne, and the holy ghost, for the redempcion of the worlde, by the death and passion of our sauior Christ, both God and man, who did humble himself euen to the death upon

the crosse, for us miserable synners, whiche laie in darknes and shadowe of death, that he myghte make us the children of God: and exalt us to euerlasting life. And to thende that wee should alwaye remember the excedyng loue of our master, and onely sauior Jesu Christe, thus diyng for us, and the innumerable benefites (whiche by his precious bloud-shedyng) he hath obteigned to us, he hath left in those holy Misteries, as a pledge of his loue, and a continuall remembraunce of the same his owne blessed body, and precious bloud, for us to fede upon spiritually, to our endles comfort and consolacion. To him therfore, with the father and the holy ghost, let us geue (as we are most bounden) continual thankes, submittyng ourselfes wholy to hys holy wil and pleasure, and studying to serue hym in true holines and righteousnes, al the daies of our life. Amen.

14 *In Cathedral churches or other places, where there is dailie Communion, it shall be sufficient to read this exhortacion aboue written, once in a moneth. And in parish churches, upon the weke daies it may be lefte unsayed.*

15 *And if upon the Sunday or holydaye the people be negligent to come to the Communion: Then shall the Priest earnestly exhorte his parishoners, to dispose themselfes to the receiuing of the holy communion more diligently, saiyng these or like wordes unto them.*

16 Dere frendes, and you especially upon whose soules I haue cure and charge, on   next, I do intende by Gods grace, to offre to all suche as shalbe godlye disposed, the moste comfortable Sacrament of the body and bloud of Christ, to be taken of them in the remembraunce of his moste fruitfull and glorious Passyon: by the whiche passion we have obteigned remission of our synnes, and be made partakers of the kyngdom of heauen, whereof wee bee assured and asserteigned, yf wee come to the sayde Sacrament, with hartie repentaunce for our offences, stedfast faithe in Goddes mercye, and earnest mynde to obeye Goddes will, and to offende no more. Wherefore our duetie is, to come to these holy misteries, with moste heartie thankes to bee geuen to almightie GOD, for his infinite mercie and benefites geuen and bestowed upon us his unworthye seruauntes, for whom he hath not onely geuen his body to death, and shed his bloude, but also doothe vouchesaue in a Sacrament and Mistery, to geue us his sayed bodye and bloud to feede upon spiritually. The whyche Sacrament beyng so Diuine

First English Liturgy, 1549

and holy a thyng, and so comfortable to them whiche receyue it worthilye, and so daungerous to them that wyll presume to take the same unworthely: My duetie is to exhorte you in the meane season, to consider the greatnes of the thing, and to serche and examine your owne consciences, and that not lyghtly nor after the maner of dissimulers with GOD: But as they whiche shoulde come to a moste Godly and heauenly Banket, not to come but in the mariage garment required of God in scripture, that you may (so muche as lieth in you) be founde worthie to come to suche a table. The waies and meanes thereto is,

17   First, that you be truly repentaunt of your former euill life, and that you confesse with an unfained hearte to almightie God, youre synnes and unkyndnes towardes his Maiestie committed, either by will, worde or dede, infirmitie or ignoraunce: and that with inwarde sorowe and teares you bewaile your offences, and require of almightie God mercie and pardon, promising to him (from the botome of your hartes) thamendment of your former lyfe. And emonges all others, I am commaunded of God, especially to moue and exhorte you to reconcile yourselfes to your neighbors, whom you haue offended, or who hath offended you, putting out of your heartes al hatred and malice against them, and to be in loue and charitie with all the worlde, and to forgeue other, as you woulde that god should forgeue you. And yf any man haue doen wrong to any other: let him make satisfaccion, and due restitucion of all landes and goodes, wronfully taken awaye or withholden, before he come to Goddes borde, or at the least be in ful minde and purpose so to do, as sone as he is able, or els let him not come to this holy table, thinking to deceyue God, who seeth all mennes hartes. For neither the absolucion of the priest, can any thing auayle them, nor the receiuyng of this holy sacrament doth any thing but increase their damnacion. And yf there bee any of you, whose conscience is troubled and greued in any thing, lackyng comforte or counsaill, let him come to me, or to some other dyscrete and learned priest, taught in the law of God, and confesse and open his synne and griefe secretly, that he may receiue suche ghostly counsaill, aduyse, and comfort, that his conscience maye be releued, and that of us (as of the ministers of GOD and of the churche) he may receiue comfort and absolucion, to the satisfaccion of his mynde, and auoyding of all scruple and doubtfulnes: requiryng suche as shalbe satisfied with a generall

confession, not to be offended with them that doe use, to their further satisfiyng, the auriculer and secret confession to the Priest: nor those also whiche thinke nedefull or conuenient, for the quietnes of their awne consciences, particuliarly to open their sinnes to the Priest: to bee offended with them that are satisfied, with their humble confession to GOD, and the generall confession to the churche. But in all thinges to folowe and kepe the rule of charitie, and euery man to be satisfied with his owne conscience, not iudgyng other mennes myndes or consciences; where as he hath no warrant of Goddes word to the same.

18 *Then shall folowe for the Offertory, one or mo, of these Sentences of holy scripture, to bee song whiles the people doo offer, or els one of theim to bee saied by the minister, immediatly afore the offeryng.*

[For Offertory Sentences, see Appendix B]

Where there be Clerkes, thei shall syng one, or many of the sentences aboue written, accordyng to the length and shortenesse of the tyme, that the people be offeryng.

19 *In the meane time, whyles the Clerkes do syng the Offertory, so many as are disposed, shall offer unto the poore mennes boxe euery one accordynge to his habilitie and charitable mynde. And at the offeryng daies appoynted, euery manne and woman shall paie to the Curate, the due and accustomed offerynges.*

20 *Then so manye as shalbe partakers of the holy Communion, shall tary still in the quire, or in some conuenient place nigh the quire, the men on the one side, and the women on the other syde. All other (that mynde not to receiue the said holy Communion) shall departe out of the quire, except the ministers and Clerkes.*

21 *Than shall the minister take so muche Bread and Wine, as shall suffice for the persons appoynted to receiue the holy Communion, laiyng the breade upon the corporas, or els in the paten, or in some other comely thyng, prepared for that purpose. And puttyng ye wyne into the Chalice, or els in some faire or conuenient cup, prepared for that use (if the Chalice will not serue), puttyng thereto a litle pure and cleane water: And settyng both the breade and wyne upon the Alter: then the Priest shall saye.*

22   The Lorde be with you.
Aunswere. And with thy spirite.
Priest. Lift up your heartes.

First English Liturgy, 1549

Aunswere. We lift them up unto the Lorde.
Priest. Let us geue thankes to our Lorde God.
Aunswere. It is mete and right so to do.
The Priest. It is very mete, righte, and our bounden dutie, that wee shoulde at all tymes, and in all places, geue thankes to thee, O Lorde holy father, almightie euerlastyng God.

23 *Here shall folowe the proper preface*[1] *accordyng to the tyme (if there bee any specially appoynted), or els immediatly shall folowe,*

Therefore with Angelles and Archangels, and with all the holy companye of heauen, we laude and magnify thy glorious name, euermore praisyng thee, and saying,

Holy, holy, holy, Lorde God of Hostes: heauen and earth are full of thy glory: Osanna in the highest. Blessed is he that commeth in the name of the Lorde: Glory be to thee, O lorde in the highest.

This the Clerkes shall also syng.

24 *When the Clerkes haue dooen syngyng, then shall the Priest, or Deacon, turne hym to the people, and saye,*

Let us praie for the whole state of Christes churche.

25 *Then the Priest, turnyng hym to the Altar, shall saye or syng, playnly and distinctly, this prayer folowyng:*

Almightie and euerliuyng GOD, whiche by thy holy Apostle haste taught us to make prayers and supplicacions, and to geue thankes for al menne: We humbly beseche thee moste mercyfully to receiue these our praiers, which we offre unto thy diuine Maiestie, beseching thee to inspire continually the uniuersal churche with the spirite of trueth, unitie, and concorde: And graunt that al they that do confesse thy holy name, maye agree in the trueth of thy holye worde, and liue in unitie and godly loue. Speciallye we beseche thee to saue and defende thy seruaunt Edwarde our Kyng, that under hym we maye be Godly and quietly gouerned. And graunt unto his whole counsaile, and to all that be put in auctoritie under hym, that they maye truely and indifferently minister iustice, to the punishemente of wickednesse and vice, and to the maintenaunce of Goddes true religion and vertue. Geue grace (O heauenly father) to all Bishoppes, Pastors, and Curates, that thei maie bothe by their life and doctrine set

---
[1] [[For Proper Prefaces, see Appendix A.]]

furthe thy true and liuely worde, and rightely and duely administer thy holy Sacramentes: and to al thy people geue thy heauenly grace, that with meke heart and due reuerence they may heare and receiue thy holy worde, truely seruyng thee in holynes and righteousnes all the dayes of their life: And we most humbly beseche thee of thy goodnes (O Lorde) to coumfort and succour all them, whyche in thys transytory life be in trouble, sorowe, nede, syckenes, or any other aduersitie. And especially we commend unto thy mercifull goodnes, this congregacion which is here assembled in thy name, to celebrate the commemoracion of the most glorious death of thy sonne: And here we do geue unto thee moste high praise, and heartie thankes, for the wonderfull grace and vertue, declared in all thy sainctes, from the begynning of the worlde: And chiefly in the glorious and moste blessed virgin Mary, mother of thy sonne Jesu Christe our Lorde and God, and in the holy Patriarches, Prophetes, Apostles and Martyrs, whose examples (o Lorde) and stedfastnes in thy fayth, and kepyng thy holy commaundementes, graunt us to folowe. We commend unto thy mercye (O Lorde) all other thy seruauntes, which are departed hence from us, with the signe of faith, and nowe do reste in the slepe of peace: Graunt unto them, we beseche thee, thy mercy, and euerlasting peace, and that, at the day of the generall resurreccion, we and all they which bee of the misticall body of thy sonne, may altogether be set on his right hand, and heare that his most ioyfull voyce: Come unto me, O ye that be blessed of my father, and possesse the kingdom, whiche is prepared for you from the begynning of the worlde: Graunt this, O father, for Jesus Christes sake, our onely mediatour and aduocate.

26 O God heauenly father, which of thy tender mercie diddest geue thine only sonne Jesu Christ to suffre death upon the crosse for our redempcion, who made there (by his one oblacion once offered) a full, perfect, and sufficient sacrifyce, oblacion, and satysfaccyon, for the sinnes of the whole worlde, and did institute, and in his holy Gospell commaund us, to celebrate a perpetuall memory of that his precious death, untyll his comming again: Heare us (o merciful father) we besech thee; and with thy holy spirite and worde, vouchsafe to bl✠esse and sanc✠tifie these thy gyftes, and creatures of bread and wyne, that they maie be unto us the bodye and bloude of thy moste derely beloued sonne Jesus Christe. Who in the same nyght that he was betrayed: tooke

First English Liturgy, 1549

breade, and when he had blessed, and geuen thankes: he brake it, and gaue it to his disciples, saiyng: Take, eate, this is my bodye which is geuen for you, do this in remembraunce of me. *Here the priest must take the bread into his handes.*

27 Likewyse after supper he toke the cuppe, and when he had geuen thankes, he gaue it to them, saiyng: drynk ye all of this, for this is my bloude of the newe Testament, whyche is shed for you and for many, for remission of synnes: do this as oft as you shall drinke it, in remembraunce of me. *Here the priest shall take the Cuppe into his handes.*

28 *These wordes before rehersed are to be saied, turning still to the Altar, without any eleuacion, or shewing the Sacrament to the people.*

29 Wherfore, O Lorde and heauenly father, accordyng to the Instytucyon of thy derely beloued sonne, our sauiour Jesu Christ, we thy humble seruauntes do celebrate, and make here before thy diuine Maiestie, with these thy holy giftes, the memoryall whyche thy sonne hath wylled us to make, hauyng in remembraunce his blessed passion, mightie resurreccyon, and gloryous ascencion, renderyng unto thee most hartie thankes, for the innumerable benefites procured unto us by the same, entierely desiryng thy fatherly goodnes, mercifully to accepte this our Sacrifice of praise and thankes geuing: most humbly beseching thee to graunt, that by the merites and death of thy sonne Jesus Christ, and through faith in his bloud, we and al thy whole church, may obteigne remission of our sinnes, and all other benefites of hys passyon. And here wee offre and present unto thee (O Lorde) oure selfe, oure soules, and bodies, to be a reasonable, holy, and liuely sacrifice unto thee: humbly besechyng thee, that whosoeuer shalbee partakers of thys holy Communion, maye worthely receiue the most precious body and bloude of thy sonne Jesus Christe: and bee fulfilled with thy grace and heauenly benediccion, and made one bodye with thy sonne Jesu Christe, that he maye dwell in them, and they in hym. And although we be unworthy (through our manyfolde synnes) to offre unto thee any Sacryfice: Yet we besech thee to accepte thys our bounden duetie and seruice, and commaunde these our prayers and supplicacions, by the Ministery of thy holy Angels, to be brought up into thy holy Tabernacle before the syght of thy dyuine maiestie; not waiyng our merites, but pardonyng our offences, through Christe our Lorde, by whome,

and with whome, in the unitie of the holy Ghost: all honour and glory, be unto thee, O father almightie, world without ende. Amen.

30   Let us praye.

As our sauiour Christe hath commaunded and taught us, we are bolde to saye. Our father, whyche art in heauen, halowed be thy name. Thy Kyngdome come. Thy wyll be doen in yearth, as it is in heauen. Geue us this daye our dayly breade. And forgeue us our trespaces, as wee forgeue them that trespasse agaynst us. And leade us not into temptacion.
The aunswere. But deliuer us from euill. Amen.

31 *Then shall the priest saye.*

             The peace of the Lorde be alwaye with you.
The Clerkes. And with thy spirite.

32 *The Priest.* Christ our Pascall lambe is offred up for us, once for al, when he bare our sinnes on hys body upon the crosse, for he is the very lambe of God, that taketh away the sinnes of the worlde: wherfore let us kepe a ioyfull and holy feast with the Lorde.

33 *Here the priest shall turne hym toward those that come to the holy Communion, and shall saye.*

You that do truly and earnestly repent you of your synnes to almightie God, and be in loue and charitie with your neighbors, and entende to lede a newe life, folowyng the commaundementes of God, and walkyng from hencefurth in his holy wayes: drawe nere and take this holy Sacrament to your comforte, make your humble confession to almightie God, and to his holy church here gathered together in hys name, mekely knelyng upon your knees.

34 *Then shall thys generall Confession bee made, in the name of al those that are minded to receiue the holy Communion, either by one of them, or els by one of the ministers, or by the prieste himselfe, all kneeling humbly upon their knees.*

Almyghtie GOD father of oure Lord Jesus Christ, maker of all thynges, iudge of all men, we knowlege and bewaile our manyfold synnes and wyckednes, which we from tyme to tyme, most greuously haue committed, by thought, word and dede, agaynst thy diuine maiestie, prouokyng moste iustely thy wrath and indignacion against us, we do earnestly repent and be hartely sory for these our misdoinges, the remembraunce of them is greuous unto us, the burthen of them is intollerable: haue mercye upon us, haue mercie upon us, moste mercyfull father, for thy sonne our Lorde Jesus Christes sake, forgeue us all that is past, and graunt that we may euer hereafter, serue and please thee in neunes of life, to the honor and glory of thy name: Through Jesus Christe our Lorde.

35 *Then shall the Prieste stande up, and turnyng himselfe to the people, say thus,*

Almightie GOD, our heauenly father, who of his great mercie hath promysed forgeuenesse of synnes to all them, whiche with hartye repentaunce and true fayth, turne unto him: haue mercy upon you, pardon and delyuer you from all youre sinnes, confirme and strengthen you in all goodnes, and bring you to euerlasting lyfe: through Jesus Christ our Lord. Amen.

36 *Then shall the Priest also say,*

Heare what coumfortable woordes our sauiour Christ sayeth, to all that truely turne to him.

Come unto me all that trauell, and bee heauy laden, and I shall refreshe you. So God loued the worlde that he gaue his onely begotten sonne, to the ende that al that beleue in hym, shoulde not perishe, but haue lyfe euerlasting.

Heare also what saint Paul sayeth.

This is a true saying, and woorthie of all men to bee receiued, that Jesus Christe came into thys worlde to saue sinners.

Heare also what saint John sayeth.

If any man sinne, we haue an aduocate with the father, Jesus Christ the righteous, and he is the propiciacion for our sinnes.

37 *Then shall the Priest turnyng him to gods boord, knele down, and say in the name of all them, that shall receyue the Communion, this prayer folowing.*

We do not presume to come to this thy table (o mercifull lord) trusting in our owne righteousnes, but in thy manifold and great mercies: we be not woorthie so much as to gather up the cromes under thy table: but thou art the same lorde whose propertie is alwayes to haue mercie: Graunt us therefore (gracious lorde) so to eate the fleshe of thy dere sonne Jesus Christ, and to drynke his bloud in these holy Misteries, that we may continuallye dwell in hym, and he in us, that our synfull bodyes may bee made cleane by his body, and our soules washed through hys most precious bloud. Amen.

38 *Then shall the Prieste firste receiue the Communion in both kindes himselfe, and next deliuer it to other Ministers, if any be there present, (that they may bee ready to helpe the chiefe Minister,) and after to the people.*

39 *And when he deliuereth the Sacramente of the body of Christe, he shall say to euery one these woordes.*

The body of our Lorde Jesus Christe whiche was geuen for thee, preserue thy bodye and soule unto euerlasting lyfe.

40 *And the Minister deliuering the Sacrament of the bloud, and geuing euery one to drinke once and no more, shall say,*

The bloud of our Lorde Jesus Christe which was shed for thee, preserue thy bodye and soule unto euerlastyng lyfe.

41 *If there be a Deacon or other Priest, then shal he folow with the Chalice: and as the Priest ministereth the Sacrament of the body, so shal he (for more expedition) minister the Sacrament of the bloud, in fourme before written.*

42 *In the Communion tyme the Clarkes shall syng,*

ii. O lambe of god, that takeste away the sinnes of the worlde: haue mercie upon us.

O lambe of god, that takeste away the synnes of the worlde: graunt us thy peace.

43 *Beginning so soone as the Prieste doeth receyue the holy Communion, and when the Communion is ended, then shall the Clarkes syng the post Communion.*

44 *Sentences of holy Scripture, to be sayd or song euery daye one, after the holy Communion, called the post Communion.*

If any man will folowe me, let him forsake hymselfe, and take up his crosse and folowe me. *Math.* xvi.

Whosoeuer shall indure unto thende, he shalbe saued. *Mar.* xiii.

Praysed be the Lorde god of Israell, for he hath visited and redemed hys people: therefore let us serue hym all the dayes of our lyfe, in holines and righteousnes accepted before hym. *Luc.* i.

Happie are those seruauntes, whome the Lord (when he cummeth) shall fynde waking. *Luc.* xii.

Be ye readye, for the sonne of manne will come at an hower when ye thinke not. *Luc.* xii.

The seruaunte that knoweth hys maisters will, and hath not prepared himself, neither hath doen according to his will, shalbe beaten with many stripes. *Luc.* xii.

The howre cummeth, and now it is, when true woorshippers shall wurship the father in spirite and trueth. *John* iiii.

Beholde, thou art made whole, sinne no more, lest any wurse thing happen unto thee. *John* v.

If ye shall continue in my woorde, then are ye my very disciples, and ye shall knowe the truth, and the truth shall make you free. *John* viii.

While ye haue lighte, beleue on the lyght, that ye may be the children of light. *John* xii.

He that hath my commaundementes, and kepeth them, the same is he that loueth me. *John* xiiii.

If any man loue me, he will kepe my woorde, and my father will loue hym, and wee will come unto hym, and dwell with hym. *John* xiiii.

If ye shall byde in me, and my woorde shall abyde in you, ye shall aske what ye will, and it shall bee doen to you. *John* xv.

Herein is my father gloryfyed, that ye beare much fruite, and become my disciples. *John* xv.

This is my commaundement, that you loue together as I haue loued you. *John* xv.

If God be on our syde, who can be agaynst us? which did not spare his owne sonne, but gaue him for us all. *Roma.* viii.

Who shall lay any thing to the charge of Goddes chosen? it is GOD that iustifyeth, who is he that can condemne? *Roma.* viii.

The nyght is passed and the day is at hande, let us therfore cast away the dedes of darkenes, and put on the armour of light. *Rom.* xiii.

Christe Jesus is made of GOD, unto us wisedome, and righteousnes, and sanctifying, and redempcion, that (according as it is written) he whiche reioyceth shoulde reioyce in the Lorde. 1 *Corin.* i.

Knowe ye not that ye are the temple of GOD, and that the spirite of GOD dwelleth in you? If any manne defile the temple of GOD, him shall God destroy. 1 *Corin.* iii.

Ye are derely bought, therfore glorifye God in your bodies, and in your spirites, for they belong to God. 1 *Cor.* vi.

Be you folowers of God as deare children, and walke in loue, euen as Christe loued us, and gaue himselfe for us an offeryng and a Sacrifyce of a sweete sauoure to God. *Ephes.* v.

45 *Then the Priest shall geue thankes to God, in the name of all them that haue communicated, turning him first to the people, and saying.*

The Lorde be with you.
The aunswere. And with thy spirite.

46 *The priest.* Let us pray.

Almightye and euerlyuyng GOD, we moste hartely thanke thee, for that thou hast vouchsafed to feede us in these holy Misteries, with the spirituall foode of the moste precious body and bloud of thy sonne, our sauiour Jesus Christ, and haste assured us (duely receiuing the same) of thy fauour and goodnes toward us, an that we be very membres incorporate in thy Misticall bodye, whiche is the blessed companye of all faythfull people, and heyres through hope of thy euerlasting kingdome, by the merites of the most precious death and passion, of thy deare sonne. We therfore most humbly beseche thee, O heauenly father, so to assist us with thy grace, that we may continue in that holy felowship, and doe all suche good woorkes, as thou hast prepared for us to walke in: through Jesus Christe our Lorde, to whome with thee and the holy gost, bee all honour and glory, world without ende.

47 *Then the Priest turning hym to the people, shall let them depart with this blessing:*

The peace of GOD (which passeth all understanding) kepe your hartes and mindes in the knowledge and loue of GOD, and of his sonne Jesus Christ our Lorde: And the blessing of God Almighty, the father, the sonne, and the holy Ghost, be amongst you and remain with you alwaye.

Then the people shall aunswere. Amen.

48 *Where there are no clerkes, there the Priest shall say al thinges appoynted here for them to sing.*

49 *When the holy Communion is celebrate on the workeday, or in priuate howses: Then may be omitted, the Gloria in excelsis, the Crede, the Homily, and the exhortacion, beginning.* Dearely beloued, &c.

First English Liturgy, 1549

50 *Upon wednesdaies and frydaies the English Letany shalbe said or song in all places, after suche forme as is appoynted by the kynges maiesties Iniunccions: Or as is or shal bee otherwyse appoynted by his highnes. And thoughe there be none to communicate with the Prieste, yet these dayes (after the Litany ended) the Priest shall put upon him a playn Albe or surplesse, with a cope, and say al thinges at the Altar (appoynted to be sayed at the celebracyon of the lordes supper), untill after the offertory. And then shall adde one or two of the Collectes aforewritten, as occasion shall serue by his discrecion. And then turning him to the people shall let them depart with the accustomed blessing. And the same order shall be used all other dayes whensoeuer the people be customably assembled to pray in the churche, and none disposed to communicate with the Priest.*

51 *For aduoyding of all matters and occasyon of dyscencyon, it is mete that the breade prepared for the Communion, bee made, through all thys realme, after one sort and fashion: that is to say, unleauened, and rounde, as it was afore, but without all maner of printe, and somethyng more larger and thicker than it was, so that it may be aptly deuided in diuers pieces: and euery one shall be deuided in two pieces, at the leaste, or more, by the discrecion of the minister, and so distributed. And menne muste not thynke lesse to be receyued in parte then in the whole, but in eache of them the whole body of our sauiour Jesu Christ.*

52 *And although it bee redde in aunciente writers, that the people many yeares past receiued at the priestes handes the Sacrament of the body of Christ in theyr owne handes, and no commaundement of Christ to the contrary: Yet forasmuche as they many tymes conueyghed the same secretelye awaye, kept it with them, and diuersly abused it to supersticion and wickednes: lest any suche thynge hereafter should be attempted, and that an uniformitie might be used, throughoute the whole Realme: it is thought conuenient the people commonly receiue the Sacrament of Christes body, in their mouthes, at the Priestes hande.*

CHAPTER III

THE ENGLISH LITURGY OF 1662 AND RELATED RITES

Copies of the Book of Common Prayer on sale today will be found to differ frequently in detail and occasionally in substance from the book annexed to the Act of Uniformity. Since none of these variations, so far as the eucharistic liturgy is concerned, has the authority of the law, the text printed in this chapter has been taken from the photo-lithographic facsimile of the Annexed Book which was published by the Queen's Printers in 1891. The spelling has been standardized; but the punctuation and the use of capital initial letters of the original have been retained. The printing of titles and of cross-headings can only be an approximation to the original. None is written in capitals, although there is a good deal of variation in size. They have therefore been rationalized into two sizes of capitals. On the other hand, no attempt has been made to record in the notes the points in which the other texts differ from the Annexed Book in the matter of capitals; and differences of punctuation have only been noted when they appeared to be of importance, for instance in the Creed and the Preface. Changes of wording have also been ignored where they have no liturgical or theological significance. For those who wish to make a minute comparison the texts are not hard to come by; and it would have reduced the usefulness of this book had the notes been made more complicated.

The notes to this chapter give the variations from the text of the Annexed Book of the following:

1552   The Second English Prayer Book, Parker Society, 1844.
1558   The Elizabethan Prayer Book, Parker Society, 1847.
Cor   The Communion Office as printed in *The Coronation Service of Queen Elizabeth II*, edited by E. C. Ratcliff, London, 1953.
Can   The Book of Common Prayer according to the Use of the Church of England in the Dominion of Canada (1918).
Ire   The Book of Common Prayer according to the Use of the Church of Ireland (1926).

ScotE The recension of **1662** printed in the *Scottish Book of Common Prayer* (1929).

Ind *The Book of Common Prayer according to the Use of the Church of India, Pakistan, Burma and Ceylon* (1960): the recension of **1662** printed on pp. 399–416. [Note: this recension reads 'Holy Spirit' for 'Holy Ghost' throughout.]

rec indicates agreement of the five recent and modern recensions against **1552, 1558,** and **1662.** It occurs only at the end of a paragraph of notes.

1

THE ORDER FOR THE ADMINISTRATION OF THE LORD'S SUPPER
OR HOLY COMMUNION

Cor. SUBST *THE INTROIT* [Ps. 84. 9, 10]   **Ind:** FOR] OF [no doubt following a corrupt text of 1662].COMMUNION] ADD THE ORDER OF 1662 [permits the use of the Introits of **IndR**]

2 *The Table at the Communion time having a fair white Linen cloth upon it, shall stand in the body of the Church, or in the Chancel, where Morning and Evening Prayer are appointed to be said. And the Priest standing at the north side of the Table shall say the Lord's Prayer with the Collect following, the people kneeling.*

1552, 1558: *the people kneeling*] OM **Cor:** SUBST *Then, the people kneeling, the Archbishop shall begin the Communion Service saying:* [4 infra] **Ire:** *where... said*] OM · *kneeling*] ADD *The Minister shall say the service following in a distinct and audible voice.* **ScotE:** *The Table*] *The Holy Table* · *upon it*] ADD *with other decent furniture meet for the High Mysteries there to be celebrated* · *in the body... to be said*] *at the uppermost part of the chancel or church* · *the north side of*] OM · *Table*] *Holy Table* · *the Lord's Prayer, with*] OM · *following*] ADD *for due preparation* **Ind:** *The Table... to be said. And*] OM [but see page 115, no. 9, first paragraph]

3 Our Father which art . . . [CF 1] . . . from evil. Amen.

1552, 1558, Cor, ScotE[1]: OMIT **Can, Ind:** which] who

4   THE COLLECT

Almighty God unto whom . . . [CF 2] . . . Lord. Amen.

1552, 1558, Cor, ScotE: OM TITLE **rec:** Amen] *Amen.*

5 *Then shall the Priest, turning to the people rehearse distinctly all the* TEN COMMANDMENTS: *And the People still kneeling, shall after every Commandment ask God mercy for their Transgression thereof for the time past, and grace to keep the same for the time to come, as followeth.*

[1] [Note that while **1552, 1558** do not print the text of the Lord's Prayer, they require its use. **Cor, ScotE** have removed this prayer from the rite.]

1552, 1558: *turning to the people*] OM · *still*] OM · *God*] *God's* · *thereof . . . followeth*] *of the same, after this sort*   **Cor**: OMIT   **Ire**: *followeth*] ADD *provided that the responses by the people as hereinafter set forth after each of the Commandments other than the fourth and tenth may be omitted, in which case the response after the fourth Commandment shall be,* Lord, have mercy upon us, and incline our hearts to keep these laws.   **ScotE**: *transgression*] ADD *of every duty therein, either according to the letter or according to the spiritual import* · *followeth*] ADD *The Ten Commandments may be rehearsed in the short form by stopping at the asterisks* [[*for this arrangement see the next section*]]   **Ind**: [[*has a rubric at the end permitting the use of the 'Shortened Commandments' or 'our Lord's Summary of the Law'. For the text of these see Chapter X*]]

6 Minister. God spake these words . . . [[CF 3]] . . . beseech thee.

1552, 1558: sins [[*in 2nd Comm.*]] sin   **Cor**: SUBST *Archbishop.* Lord have mercy upon us. *Answer.* Christ have mercy upon us. *Archbishop.* Lord have mercy upon us.[1]   **Can, Ire**: *beseech thee*] ADD *Or, he may rehearse instead of the Ten Commandments (which, however, shall be said at least once on the Lord's Day* [[*Sunday*, **Can**]], *and on the great festivals, when there is a celebration of Holy Communion)* [ADD *and that always at the chief Service of the day,* **Can**]] *our Blessed Lord's Summary of the Law, as followeth:* Hear what our Lord Jesus Christ saith: Thou shalt love the Lord thy God with all thy heart, and with all thy soul, and with all thy mind. This is the first and great Commandment, And the second is like unto it, Thou shalt love thy neighbour as thyself. On these two Commandments hang all the Law and the Prophets. *People.* Lord, have mercy upon us, and write [[both, **Can**]] these thy laws in our hearts, we beseech thee.   **ScotE**: [[*allows omissions from certain commandments as follows:* (2) 'For I the Lord . . . commandments', (3) 'For the Lord . . . in vain', (4) 'but the seventh . . . hallowed it', (5) 'that thy days . . . giveth thee', (10) 'thy neighbour's house . . . that is his']]   *beseech thee*] ADD *There may be substituted for the Ten Commandments (which, however, shall always be said at least once a month) the Summary of the Law:* Our Lord Jesus Christ said: Hear, O Israel, the Lord our God is one Lord: and thou shalt love the Lord thy God with all thy heart, and with all thy soul, and with all thy mind, and with all thy strength: This is the first commandment. And the second is like, namely this, Thou shalt love thy neighbour as thyself: there is none other commandment greater than these. On these two commandments hang all the Law and the Prophets. *People.* Lord have mercy upon us, and write these thy laws in our hearts, we beseech thee. *Or else, instead of, or in addition to, the Ten Commandments or the Summary of the Law, may be sung or said as followeth:* Lord, have mercy upon us. ℟ Christ, have mercy upon us. Lord have mercy upon us.   **Ind**: [[see note to no. 5 above]]

7 Then shall follow one of these two Collects for the King, the Priest standing as before, and saying.

Let us pray.[2]

Almighty God, whose kingdom is everlasting, and power infinite, have mercy upon the whole Church, and so rule the heart of thy chosen servant CHARLES, our King, and Governor, that he (knowing whose minister he is) may above all things seek thy

---

[1] [[It should be noticed that at the coronations of Edward VII, George V, and George VI the Decalogue was omitted and no other text inserted in its place.]]

[2] [[**Ire** prints 'Let us pray' before the rubric.]]

honour and glory; And that we and all his subjects (duly considering whose Authority he hath) may faithfully serve, honour, and humbly obey him in thee, and for thee according to thy blessed word, and ordinance, through Jesus Christ our Lord; who with thee and the holy Ghost, liveth and reigneth ever one God, world without end. Amen.

1552, 1558: *one of these . . . as before*] *the Collect of the day, with one of these two Collects following for the King: the Priest standing up* · Almighty God] PREF *Priest.* · church] congregation · and all] OM   **Cor, ScotE, Ind:** OMIT   **Ire:** *for the King*] ADD (*except when the King has been prayed for in any Service used along with this Office, or when the Prayer* For the whole state of Christ's Church *is said.*) **rec:** Amen] *Amen.*

Or

8 Almighty and everlasting God, we are taught by thy holy word, that the hearts of Kings are in thy Rule and governance, and that thou dost dispose and turn them as it seemeth best to thy godly wisdom; we humbly beseech thee so to dispose and govern the heart of CHARLES, thy servant, our King and Governor, that in all his thoughts, words and works, he may ever seek thy honour and glory, and study to preserve thy people committed to his charge, in wealth peace and godliness; Grant this O merciful Father for thy dear Son's sake, Jesus Christ our Lord. Amen.

1552, 1558: *Or*] OM   **Cor, ScotE, Ind:** OMIT   **Can, Ire:** Amen] *Amen.*

9 *Then shall be said the Collect of the day and immediately after the Collect, the Priest shall read the Epistle, saying,* The Epistle [*or* The portion of Scripture appointed for the Epistle] is written in the —— Chapter of —— beginning at the —— verse. *And the Epistle ended he shall say,* Here endeth the Epistle. *Then shall he read the Gospel (the People all standing up) saying,* The holy Gospel is written in the —— Chapter of —— beginning at the —— verse. *And the Gospel ended, shall be sung, or said the Creed following, the People still standing as before.*

1552, 1558: SUBST *Immediately after the Collects, the Priest shall read the Epistle, beginning thus.* The Epistle written in the —— Chapter of ——. *And the Epistle ended, he shall say the Gospel, beginning thus.* The Gospel, written in the —— Chapter of ——. *And the Epistle and Gospel being ended, shall be said the Creed.*   **Cor:** SUBST Let us pray [[+text of Collect]]. THE EPISTLE. *To be read by one of the Bishops.* [[text of Epistle]] THE GRADUAL. [[text of Gradual]] THE GOSPEL. *To be read by another Bishop, the Queen with the people standing.* [[text of Gospel]] *And the Gospel ended, shall be sung the Creed following, the Queen with the people standing as before.*   **Can:** Gospel . . . verse] ADD *Here shall be sung or said,* Glory be to thee, O Lord. · *Gospel ended*] ADD *the people shall in like manner sing or say,* Thanks be to thee, O Lord. Then   **Ire:** *the Priest . . . Epistle*] one of the Ministers shall read the Epistle · or The portion . . . Epistle] OM · he read the Gospel] one of the Ministers read the Gospel · Gospel . . . verse] ADD *Here may be said or sung,* Glory be to thee, O Lord. *And after the Gospel ended,* Thanks be to thee, O Lord, *or* Hallelujah.   **ScotE:** *the Priest*] ADD, *turning to the people*. · *Then shall he*] Then, turning to the people, he shall · verse] ADD *When the Minister announceth the Gospel of the Day, the people standing up may devoutly sing or say,* Glory be to thee, O Lord. *And after the Gospel the people may in like manner sing or say,* Thanks be to thee, O Lord, for this thy glorious Gospel.

10 I believe in one God . . . ⟦CF 4⟧ . . . world to come. Amen.

1552: God of God] God of goddes   **Can, Ire:** Father, By whom] Father; By whom · The Lord and giver] The Lord, and Giver   **ScotE:** The Lord and giver] The Lord, The Giver · one Catholick] one Holy Catholic   **Ind:** Ghost] Spirit

11 *Then the Curate shall declare unto the People what holy-Days, or fasting-days are in the week following to be observed. And then also (if occasion be) shall notice be given of the Communion: and the Banns of Matrimony published, and Briefs, Citations and excommunications read. And nothing shall be proclaimed or published in the Church during the time of divine service, but by the Minister: nor by him anything but what is prescribed in the Rules of this Book, or enjoined by the King or by the Ordinary of the place.*

1552, 1558, Cor: OMIT ⟦for 1552, 1558 see no. 12 below⟧   **Can:** *Briefs, Citations and*] OM · *excommunications*] ADD *and other ecclesiastical notices*   **Ire:** *and the Banns . . . read*] Banns of Matrimony shall be published, and such other matters as may be directed by the Ordinary, · *by the King*] by the General Synod of the Church of Ireland · *or by the Ordinary*] or permitted by the Ordinary   **ScotE:** *Curate*] Priest · *Matrimony*] ADD *may be* · *or enjoined . . . place*] or enjoined or allowed by the Bishop.   **Ind:** *Matrimony*] ADD *may be* · *by the King, or*] OM ⟦**Ind** permits the use of OT lesson and canticle from **IndR**⟧

12 *Then shall follow the Sermon or one of the Homilies already set forth, or hereafter to be set forth by Authority.*

Then shall the Priest return to the Lord's Table and begin the Offertory saying one or more of these sentences[1] *following, as he thinketh most convenient in his discretion.*

1552, 1558: SUBST *After the Creed, if there be no sermon, shall follow one of the homelies already set forth, or hereafter to be set forth by common authority. After such sermon, homily, or exhortation, the Curate shall declare unto the people whether there be any holy days or fasting days the week following: and earnestly exhort them to remember the poor, saying one or more of these Sentences following, as he thinketh most convenient by his discretion.*   **Cor:** SUBST *Then shall the organ play and the people shall with one voice sing this hymn:* ⟦text of hymn⟧   **Ire:** *Then shall . . . Authority*] Here followeth the Sermon   **ScotE:** *Then shall . . . Authority*] Then may follow the Sermon ⟦and then add⟧ *Upon such days as the Minister giveth warning for the celebration of the Holy Communion he may read to the people at such times as he shall think convenient one of*

[1] ⟦For Offertory Sentences, see Appendix B.⟧

the two Exhortations[1] appended on pages —. The Bishop may enjoin the use of one of them on such occasions as he shall see fit.

13 Whilst these sentences are in reading, the Deacons, Church-wardens, or other fit person appointed for that purpose, shall receive the Alms for the Poor, and other devotions of the People, in a decent Bason to be provided by the parish for that purpose; and reverently bring it to the Priest, who shall humbly present, and place it upon the holy Table.

And when there is a Communion, the Priest shall then place upon the Table so much bread and Wine as he shall think sufficient. After which done the Priest shall say.

1552, 1558: *Whilst these . . . sufficient*] Then shall the Churchwardens, or some other by them appointed, gather the devotion of the people, and put the same into the poor men's box: and upon the offering days appointed, every man and woman shall pay to the Curate the due and accustomed offerings: **Cor**: SUBST *The hymn ended and the people kneeling, first the Queen shall offer Bread and Wine for the Communion, which being brought out of Saint Edward's Chapel, and delivered into her hands . . . shall be received from the Queen by the Archbishop, and reverently placed upon the Altar, and decently covered with a fair linen cloth, the Archbishop first saying this prayer:* Bless, O Lord, we beseech thee, these thy gifts, and sanctify them unto this holy use, that by them we may be made partakers of the Body and Blood of thine only-begotten Son Jesus Christ, and fed unto everlasting life of soul and body: And that thy servant Queen Elizabeth may be enabled to the discharge of her weighty office, whereunto of thy great goodness thou hast called and appointed her. Grant this, O Lord, for Jesus Christ's sake, our only Mediator and Advocate. ℟. Amen. *Then the Queen kneeling, as before, shall make her Oblation, offering a Pall or Altar-cloth . . . and an Ingot or Wedge of Gold of a pound weight, . . . and the Archbishop coming to her, shall receive and place them upon the Altar. . . . Then the Archbishop, returning to the Altar, shall say:*   **Ire**: *reading*] ADD, *or whilst, in addition to the Sentences, an Anthem or Hymn is sung* · *person*] *persons* · *in a decent . . . purpose*] OM · *bring it*] bring them · *place it*] *place them* · *Table*] ADD *But, subject to the control of the Ordinary, alms may be collected at other times during Divine Service, with or without the use of the Offertory Sentences; provided that when the Holy Communion is celebrated, a collection shall be made as here directed.* · *sufficient*] ADD *if this have not already been done.* · *After which . . . say*] *The Priest shall then say.*   **ScotE**: *Deacons . . . appointed*] *persons appointed* · *devotions*] *offerings* · *for the poor*] OM · *in a decent . . . purpose*] OM · *it*] [passim] *them* · *sufficient*] ADD *After offering the elements, the Priest may say,* Thine, O Lord is the greatness . . . given thee. [1 Chron. 29. 11, 14] *The Priest may here bid special prayers and thanksgivings.*

14 Let us pray for the whole state of Christ's Church militant here in earth.

Almighty and everliving God, who by thy holy Apostle hast taught us to make prayers and supplications, and to give thanks for all men: We humbly beseech thee most mercifully (to accept our

---

[1] [The Exhortations are the two provided in the 1662 Prayer Book. A rubric is added to the former concerning auricular confession.]

Alms and Oblations and) to receive these our prayers, which we offer unto thy divine Majesty, beseeching thee to inspire continually the universal Church with the spirit of truth, unity and concord: and grant that all they that do confess thy holy Name may agree in the truth of thy holy word, and live in unity and godly love. *If there be no Alms or Oblations, then shall the words [of accepting our Alms and oblations] be left out unsaid.* We beseech thee also to save and defend all christian Kings, Princes and Governors, and specially thy servant CHARLES our King, that under him we may be Godly and quietly governed: and grant unto his whole Council, and to all that are put in Authority under him that they may truly and indifferently minister Justice, to the punishment of wickedness, and vice, and to the maintenance of thy true religion and Virtue. Give grace (O heavenly Father) to all Bishops, and Curates, that they may both by their life and doctrine set forth thy true and lively word, and rightly and duly administer thy holy Sacraments: And to all thy people give thy heavenly grace, and specially to this Congregation here present that with meek heart and due reverence they may hear and receive thy holy word, truly serving thee in holiness and righteousness all the days of their life. And we most humbly beseech thee of thy goodness (O Lord) to comfort and succour all them who in this transitory life are in trouble, sorrow, need, sickness, or any other Adversity. And we also bless thy holy name, for all thy servants departed this life in thy faith and fear, beseeching thee to give us grace so to follow their good examples, that with them we may be partakers of thy heavenly kingdom. Grant this, O Father, for Jesus Christ's sake our only Mediator and Advocate. Amen.

1552, 1558: and Oblations] OM · *or Oblations] given unto the poor* · and oblations [in rubric]] OM · thy true religion] God's true religion · Bishops] ADD Pastors · And we also bless . . . kingdom] OM   **Cor:** our Alms and Oblations] these oblations [rubric omitted]]   **Can:** indifferently] impartially · lively] living   **Ind:** We beseech thee . . . religion and virtue] We beseech thee also to lead all nations in the way of righteousness and peace; and so to direct all kings and rulers, that under them thy people may be godly and quietly governed. [The forms of the Prayer for the Church prescribed in **IndR** (Chapter X) may be used in the 1662 rite]]   **rec:** Amen] *Amen.*

[Here follow the Exhortations giving warning for the Communion.]]

15 *At the time of the Celebration of the Communion, the Communicants being conveniently placed for the receiving of the holy Sacrament, the Priest shall say this exhortation.*

1662 and Related Rites

1552, 1558: *At the time... shall]* Then shall the Priest   **Cor:** OMIT   **Can:** shall] may   **Ire:** Communion] ADD *(those who do not intend to communicate having had opportunity to withdraw)* · shall] may · exhortation] ADD Note, that if this Exhortation be not read at the time of the celebration of the Communion, it shall, nevertheless, be read to the people by the Curate at such times as he shall think fit, and at least three times in the year.   **ScotE, Ind:** OMIT

16 Dearly beloved in the Lord... 〚CF 5〛... days of our life. Amen.

1552, 1558: how Saint Paul] what Saint Paul writeth to the Corinthians, how he · kinds of death] ADD Therefore, if any of you be a blasphemer of God, an hinderer or slanderer of his word, an adulterer, or be in malice or envy, or in any other grievous crime, bewail your sins, and come not to this holy Table, lest after the taking of that holy Sacrament, the devil enter into you, as he entered into Judas, and fill you full of all iniquities, and bring you to destruction, both of body and soul. · and for a continual] and continual   **Cor:** OMIT   **Can:** damnation] condemnation · considering] discerning · we kindle... death] OM   **Ire:** try and examine] prove and examine · our own damnation] judgement to ourselves · we kindle... death] OM   **ScotE, Ind:** OMIT[1]   **rec:** Amen] *Amen*.

17 *Then shall the Priest say to them that come to receive the holy Communion.*

Ye that do truly... 〚CF 6〛... your knees.

1552, 1558: with faith] OM · Almighty God] ADD before this congregation here gathered together in his holy name   **Cor:** Then... Communion] THE INVITATION

18 *Then shall this general Confession be made in the Name of all those that are minded to receive the holy Communion, by one of the ministers, both he and all the people kneeling humbly upon their knees and saying.*

Almighty God, Father of our Lord Jesus Christ... 〚CF 7〛... our Lord. Amen.

1552, 1558: *Communion]* ADD *either by one of them, or else* · both... people] or by the Priest himself, all · and saying] OM · Amen] OM 〚1552 only〛   **Cor:** Then shall... saying] THE GENERAL CONFESSION.   **rec:** Amen] *Amen*.

19 *Then shall the Priest (or the Bishop being present) stand up, and turning himself to the people, pronounce this Absolution.*

Almighty God, our heavenly Father... 〚CF 8〛... our Lord. Amen.

1552, 1558: *pronounce this Absolution]* say thus   **Cor:** Then shall... Absolution] THE ABSOLUTION.   **rec:** Amen] *Amen*.

[1] 〚But both print the text elsewhere.〛

20 *Then shall the Priest say.* Hear what comfortable ... ⟦CF 9⟧ ... our sins.

 1552, 1558 *say*] *also say* **rec**: Jesus Christ ⟦1 Tim. 1. 15⟧] Christ Jesus.

21 *After which the Priest shall proceed, saying.*
   Lift up your hearts.
Answer. We lift them up unto the Lord.
Priest. Let us give thanks unto our Lord God.
Answer. It is meet and right so to do.

Then shall the Priest turn to the Lord's Table, and say,

It is very meet, right, and our bounden duty, that we should at all times and in all places, give thanks unto thee, O Lord, Holy Father, Almighty everlasting God. *These words,* HOLY FATHER, *must be omitted on Trinity Sunday.*

 ⟦The rubric directing the omission of 'Holy Father' occurs only in **1662**, **Can**, and **Ind**. The other texts (except, of course, **Cor**) deal with the problem by revising the Trinity Preface or by printing the whole text of the Preface of Trinity Sunday among the Propers. See Appendix A⟧

 1552: *Then shall the Priest ... say*] OM 1558: *Then shall the Priest ... say*] *Priest.*
⟦Note that neither **1552** nor **1558** has a comma after 'Lord'. **Ire**, **Can**, **ScotE**, **Ind** add a further comma after 'Almighty', as do some modern copies of **1662**. **Cor** preserves the original punctuation of **1662** except that it adds a comma after 'times', as do **1552**, **Can**, **ScotE**, **Ind**⟧

22 *Here shall follow the proper Preface, according to the time, if there be any specially appointed: or else immediately shall follow,*

Therefore with Angels and Archangels, and with all the company of heaven, we laud and magnify thy glorious Name, evermore praising thee, and saying, Holy, holy, holy, Lord God of Hosts, Heaven and Earth are full of thy Glory, Glory be to thee, O Lord most high. Amen.

 1552, 1558: Amen] OM ⟦**rec** print the Sanctus as a separate paragraph⟧ ⟦Here follow the proper Prefaces: see Appendix A. **ScotE** allows the use of those of the Scottish Liturgy and **Ind** those of **IndR**⟧

23 *Then shall the Priest kneeling down at the Lord's Table, say in the Name of all them that shall receive the Communion, this prayer following.*
We do not presume ... ⟦CF 10⟧ ... he in us. Amen.

 1552, 1558: *the Lord's Table*] *God's board* **Cor**: *Then shall ... following*] THE PRAYER OF HUMBLE ACCESS **rec**: Amen] *Amen.*

24 *When the Priest, standing before the Table, hath so ordered the bread and Wine, that he may with the more readiness and decency break the*

1662 and Related Rites

Bread before the people, and take the Cup into his hands; he shall say the Prayer of Consecration as followeth.

1552, 1558: SUBST *Then the Priest standing up shall say, as followeth.*   **Cor:** SUBST THE PRAYER OF CONSECRATION   **Ire:** *he shall*] ADD , *standing at the north side of the Table,*

25 Almighty God, our heavenly Father, who of thy tender mercy didst give thine only Son Jesus Christ to suffer death upon the Cross for our redemption, who made there (by his one oblation of himself once offered) a full, perfect, and sufficient Sacrifice, oblation and satisfaction for the sins of the whole World, and did institute and in his holy Gospel command us to continue a perpetual memory of that his precious death, until his coming again: Hear us, (O merciful Father, we most humbly beseech thee, and grant that we receiving these thy Creatures of Bread and Wine, according to thy Son our Saviour Jesus Christ's holy Institution, in remembrance of his death and passion, may be partakers of his most blessed body and blood: who in the same night that he was betrayed ᵃTOOK BREAD, and when he had given thanks, ᵇHE BRAKE IT, and gave it to his disciples, saying, take, eat, ᶜTHIS IS MY BODY which is given for you, do this in remembrance of me. Likewise after supper ᵈHE TOOK THE CUP, and, when he had given thanks, he gave it to them, saying, Drink ye all of this, for this ᵉIS MY BLOOD of the new testament, which is shed for you and for many for the remission of Sins: Do this as oft as ye shall drink it in remembrance of me. Amen.

ᵃ *Here the Priest is to take the Paten into his hands.*
ᵇ *And here to break the bread.*
ᶜ *And here to lay his hand upon all the bread.*
ᵈ *Here he is to take the Cup into his hands.*
ᵉ *And here to lay his hand upon every Vessel (be it Chalice or Flagon) in which there is any Wine to be consecrated.*

1552, 1558: *most humbly*] OM · 〚*no rubrics*〛 · *Amen*] OM   **rec:** *Amen*] *Amen.*

26 *Then shall the Minister first receive the Communion in both kinds himself, and then proceed to deliver the same to the Bishops, Priests, and Deacons in like manner (if any be present) and after that to the people also in order, into their hands, all meekly kneeling.*

1552, 1558: *and then ... manner*] *and next deliver it to other ministers · present*] ADD 〚*within parentheses*〛 *that they may help the chief minister · after that to ... kneeling*] *after to the people in their hands kneeling*   **Cor:** SUBST *When the Archbishops and the Dean of Westminster, with the Bishops Assistant ... have communicated in both kinds, the Queen with the Duke of Edinburgh shall advance to the steps of the Altar and both kneeling down, the Archbishop shall administer the Bread, and the Dean of Westminster* *the Cup, to them, and in the meantime the choir shall sing:* ⟦text of Communion Anthem⟧

27 *And when he delivereth . . .* ⟦CF 11 (a)⟧ *. . . with thanksgiving.*

    1552: *to any one*] OM   The body . . . life] OM   **1558:** *to any one*] OM   life] ADD and   **Cor:** *And when he . . . say*] *At the delivery of the Bread shall be said:*

28 *And the Minister . . .* ⟦CF 11 (b)⟧ *. . . thankful.*

    1552: *to any one*] OM · The blood . . . life] OM   **1558:** *to any one*] OM · life] ADD and   **Cor:** *And the Minister . . . say*] *At the delivery of the Cup*   **ScotE:** thankful] ADD / *The Priest at his discretion may use the first half of each Form alone.*

29 *When all have communicated, the Minister shall return to the Lord's Table, and reverently place upon it what remaineth of the consecrated Elements, covering the same with a fair Linen cloth.*

    1552, 1558, Cor: OMIT.

30 *Then shall the Priest say the Lord's Prayer, the People repeating after him every petition.*

    Our Father which art . . . ⟦CF 1⟧ . . . For ever and ever, Amen.

    1552, 1558: Our Father . . . ever. Amen.] OM   **Cor:** Then shall . . . petition] *After which the Queen and the Duke of Edinburgh shall return to their faldstools; and the Archbishop shall go on to the Post-Communion, he and the people saying:*   **Can, Ind:** which art] who art

31 *After shall be said as followeth.*

O Lord and heavenly Father, We thy humble servants entirely desire thy fatherly goodness mercifully to accept this our Sacrifice of praise and thanksgiving, most humbly beseeching thee to grant that by the merits and death of thy son Jesus Christ, and through faith in his blood, we and all thy whole Church may obtain Remission of our Sins, and all other benefits of his passion. And here we offer and present unto thee, O Lord, ourselves, our souls and Bodies to be a reasonable holy and lively sacrifice unto thee, humbly beseeching thee, that all we who are partakers of this holy Communion, may be fulfilled with thy Grace, and heavenly Benediction. And although we be unworthy through our manifold sins to offer unto thee any sacrifice, yet we beseech thee to accept this our bounden duty and service; not weighing our merits, but pardoning our offences, through Jesus Christ our Lord; by whom, and with whom, in the unity of the holy Ghost, all honour and glory be unto thee, O Father Almighty, World without end. Amen.

1662 and Related Rites 37

Ire: *After ... followeth*] *After shall be said either or both of the following prayers.*
Ind: Ghost] Spirit **rec:** Amen] *Amen.*

32 *Or this.*
Almighty and everliving God . . . ⟦CF 12⟧ . . . without end. Amen.

1552, 1558: the mystical body of thy son] thy mystical body · And we] We now **Cor:** OMIT **Can:** without end. *Amen*] ADD *Note, That at the discretion of the Minister both the foregoing prayers may be used.* **Ire:** *Or this.*] OM **ScotE:** without end. Amen] ADD *Both the prayers* O Lord and heavenly Father *and* Almighty and everliving God *may be said in succession at the same Service.* **Ind:** Ghost] Spirit **rec:** Amen] *Amen.*

33 *Then shall be said or sung.* Glory be to God on high . . . ⟦CF 13⟧ . . . the Father. Amen.

Cor: *said or*] OM **Ire:** *Then*] ADD, *all standing up,* **Ind:** Ghost] Spirit
⟦**ScotE** provides for Post-communion Collects at this point. See Appendix C⟧

34 *Then the Priest (or Bishop if he be present) shall let them depart with this blessing.*
The peace of God . . . ⟦CF 14⟧ . . . with you always. Amen.

Cor: *Then the Priest . . . blessing*] *Then, the people kneeling, the Archbishop shall say:* Prevent us, O Lord, in all our doings, with thy most gracious favour and further us with thy continual help; that in all our works begun, continued, and ended in thee, we may glorify thy holy Name, and finally by thy mercy obtain everlasting life; through Jesus Christ our Lord. Amen. **Ind:** Ghost] Spirit **rec:** Amen] *Amen.*

35 *And if any of the Bread and wine remain unconsecrated, the Curate shall have it to his own use: but if any remain of that which was consecrated, it shall not be carried out of the Church, but the Priest, and such other of the communicants as he shall then call unto him, shall, immediately after the blessing, reverently eat and drink the same.*

1552, 1558: *unconsecrated*] OM · *but if any . . . the same*] OM **Cor:** OMIT **Ind:** OMIT ⟦But see Chapter X, no. 47⟧ **Ire:** *of the Bread . . . remain of that*] remain of the Bread and Wine

CHAPTER IV

THE SCOTTISH LITURGY

THE text printed in this chapter is that which is to be found in the Scottish Book of Common Prayer of 1929. The Scottish liturgy has a history long enough to make its development interesting. The notes of this chapter, therefore, give the variations between the current text of the rite and those of 1637 and 1764. They do not amount to a full and detailed *apparatus criticus*, since the Scottish Prayer Book for long lacked an official text and there were in use editions differing considerably in detail, none of which could easily establish a claim to be the official and authorized text. Two authoritative sources have therefore been drawn upon in the present edition: the text of 1637 printed in G. Donaldson, *The Making of the Scottish Prayer Book of 1637* (Edinburgh, 1954), and the text of the Liturgy edited in J. Dowden, *The Scottish Communion Office of 1764* (2nd edition, Oxford, 1922). It should be noted that Dr. Dowden had to reconstruct the parts of the Liturgy numbered 1 to 14 in this chapter since they were not printed with the remainder of the rite.

Two points may be noted here once for all, to the simplification and shortening of the notes:
(1) Variations in the use of roman and italic type for 'Amen' are here ignored. It appears that in 1637 it was always in roman, while 1764 agreed with the 1929 text.
(2) In referring to 'Common Forms' no attention is drawn to the fact that the Scottish Liturgy in all its recensions has 'Presbyter' where 1662 has 'Priest' or 'Minister'.

1

THE SCOTTISH LITURGY
FOR THE CELEBRATION OF THE HOLY EUCHARIST
AND ADMINISTRATION OF HOLY COMMUNION

commonly called

THE SCOTTISH COMMUNION OFFICE

1637: The Order of the Administration of the Lord's Supper, or Holy Communion   **1764**: The Communion Office for the use of the Church of Scotland, as far as concerneth the Ministration of that Holy Sacrament

The Scottish Liturgy 39

THE INTRODUCTION

2   1637, 1764: OMIT

3   *The Holy Table, having at the Communion time a fair white linen cloth upon it, with other decent furniture meet for the High Mysteries there to be celebrated, shall stand at the uppermost part of the chancel or church. And the Presbyter, standing at the Holy Table, shall say the Collect following for due preparation, the people kneeling.*

1637: *Communion time*] ADD *a carpet and* · *And the Presbyter*] *where the Presbyter* · *standing . . . Table*] *standing at the north side or end thereof* · *shall say*] ADD *the Lord's Prayer with* · *the Collect*] *this Collect* · *the people kneeling*] OM   **1764**: OMIT

⟦**1637, 1764** add the text of the Lord's Prayer, **1764** reading 'who art in heaven'⟧

4   Almighty God, unto whom . . . ⟦CF 2⟧ . . . our Lord. *Amen*.

5   *Then shall the Presbyter, turning to the people, rehearse distinctly all the Ten Commandments: the people all the while kneeling, and asking God mercy for the transgression of every duty therein, according to the letter or to the spiritual import of each Commandment, and grace to keep the same for the time to come. The Ten Commandments may be rehearsed in the short form by stopping at the asterisks.*

1637, 1764: *God mercy*] *God's mercy* · *therein*] ADD *either* · *spiritual . . . each*] *mystical importance of the said* · *and grace . . . asterisks*] OM

6   God spake these words . . . ⟦CF 3⟧ . . . beseech thee.

⟦The text of the Commandments in **1637** and **1764** differs in minor particulars from that printed in CF 3, being that of the Authorized Version of the Bible⟧

⟦The asterisks of **1929** allow the following omissions from the text of certain commandments: (2) 'For I the Lord . . . commandments', (3) 'For the Lord . . . vain', (4) 'but the seventh . . . hallowed it', (5) 'that thy days . . . thee', (10) 'thy neighbour's house . . . is his'⟧

7   *Or he may rehearse, instead of the Ten Commandments, the Summary of the Law as followeth:*

Our Lord Jesus Christ said: Hear, O Israel, the Lord our God is one Lord: and thou shalt love the Lord thy God with all thy heart, and with all thy soul, and with all thy mind, and with all thy strength: This is the first commandment. And the second is like, namely this, Thou shalt love thy neighbour as thyself: there is none other commandment greater than these.

On these two commandments hang all the Law and the Prophets.

People. Lord, have mercy upon us, and write these thy laws in our hearts, we beseech thee.

1637: OMIT   **1764**: *he may rehearse*] OM · *as followeth*] OM · *Our Lord*] OM · *Christ*] OM · *Hear . . . Lord: and*] OM · *and with all thy strength*] OM · *the first*] ADD *and great* · *like*] ADD *unto it* · *namely this*] OM · *there is . . . these*] OM

8 *Or else, instead of, or in addition to, the Ten Commandments or the Summary of the Law, may be sung or said as followeth:*

Lord, have mercy upon us.
> Christ, have mercy upon us.

Lord, have mercy upon us.

1637, 1764: OMIT

9 *Then shall the Presbyter say,*
> The Lord be with you;

Answer. And with thy spirit.

Then shall be said the Collect or Collects, the Presbyter standing as before and first saying, Let us pray.

1637: SUBST *Then shall follow one of these two Collects for the King, and the Collect of the day; the Presbyter standing up, and saying,* Let us pray. [[The text of the second Collect is identical with that printed in Chapter III, no. 8. The text of the first Collect varies from Chapter III, no. 7 as follows: the whole Church and] thy holy Catholic Church: and in this particular Church in which we live · we and all his subjects] we his subjects]]   **1764**: SUBST *Then shall follow one of these Collects and the Collect for the day, the Presbyter standing up and saying,* Let us pray [[**1764** places the Collect 'O Almighty Lord... direct, sanctify, and govern...' before the Collects for the Sovereign, thus allowing three alternatives. The text of the Collects agrees with **1637**, except that 'we his subjects' is replaced by 'we and all his subjects', as in Chapter III, no. 7]]

10   THE MINISTRY OF THE WORD

Then the Presbyter, or some other Presbyter or Deacon, turning to the people, shall read the Epistle or Lesson, saying, The Epistle [or The Lesson] is written in the —— chapter of —— beginning at the —— verse. *And, the Epistle or Lesson ended, he shall say,* Here endeth the Epistle [or Lesson]. *Then shall the Presbyter, or some other Presbyter or Deacon, turning to the people, read the Gospel, saying,* The Holy Gospel is written in the —— chapter of the Gospel according to ——, beginning at the —— verse; *and the people, all standing up, shall devoutly sing or say,*

Glory be to thee, O Lord.

And, the Gospel ended, the people shall in like manner sing or say,

Thanks be to thee, O Lord, for this thy glorious Gospel.

1637: THE... WORD] OM · *Then*] *Immediately after the Collects,* · *or Deacon... people*] OM · *or Lesson*] OM [[and so throughout]] · is written] written · beginning] OM · *Then shall... saying*] *And the Epistle ended the Gospel shall be read, the Presbyter saying* · the Gospel according to] OM · *devoutly sing or*] OM · *And the Gospel ended*] *At the end of the Gospel the Presbyter shall say:* So endeth the holy Gospel · *the people*

The Scottish Liturgy 41

... *or say*] *And the People shall answer* · for this ... Gospel] OM 1764 THE ... WORD] OM · Then] *Immediately after the Collects,* · *or some* ... *people*] OM · or Lesson] OM [[*and so throughout*]] · *is written*] written · beginning] OM · *Then shall* ... *saying*] = 1637 · the Gospel according to] OM · beginning] OM · Glory ... Lord] Glory be to thee, O God · *And the Gospel* ... *people shall*] At the end of the Gospel the Presbyter shall say: Thus endeth the holy Gospel, *and the People may*

11 Then shall be sung or said this Creed¹ following, the people still reverently standing.

I believe in one God ... [[CF 4]] ... to come. Amen.

[[**1929** reads 'The Lord, The Giver' and 'one Holy Catholic']]

12 Then the Presbyter shall declare unto the people what Holy-days or Fasting-days are to be observed in the week. And also (*if occasion be*) notice shall be given of the Holy Communion; Banns of Matrimony may be published; and, subject to the authority of the Bishop, other notices may be read.

1637, 1764: OMIT

13 If there be a Sermon, it followeth here.

1637: SUBST *After the Creed, if there be no Sermon, shall follow one of the Homilies which shall hereafter be set forth by common authority. After such Sermon, Homily, or Exhortation, the Presbyter or Curate shall declare unto the People whether there be any Holy-days, or Fasting-days the week following, and earnestly exhort them to remember the poor, saying (for the Offertory) one or more of these Sentences following, as he thinketh most convenient by his discretion, according to the length or shortness of the time that the people are offering.* [[For Sentences, see Appendix B]] **1764**: SUBST *A Sermon.*

14 When the Presbyter giveth warning of the Holy Communion he may, at his discretion, use the first or second of the Exhortations appended on page ——²

1637, 1764: OMIT

15 The Exhortation³ appended on page —— may be used at the discretion of the Presbyter before the Offertory, the people standing.

The Presbyter may here bid special prayers and thanksgivings.

1637: OMIT [[But see note under no. 19]] **1764**: SUBST *The Exhortation. Dearly beloved* ... [[CF 5]] ... *life. Amen.*

16 THE OFFERTORY

Then, the people standing until after the Sanctus, the Presbyter, or Deacon, shall say, Let us present our offerings to the Lord with reverence and godly fear.

1637: OMIT **1764**: THE OFFERTORY] OM · *the people* ... Sanctus] OM

¹ [[may be omitted on weekdays except on Red Letter Days. See no. 50, below]]
² Viz. the Exhortations beginning 'Dearly beloved, on —— I purpose' and 'Dearly beloved, on —— I intend'. These texts do not appear in **1764**.]]
³ [[Viz. CF 5 with minor variants.]]

17 *Then the Presbyter shall begin the Offertory, saying one or more of these Sentences following, as he thinketh most convenient.*

1637: [[See no. 13 above]]   **1764**: *convenient*] ADD *by his discretion, according to the length or shortness of the time that the people are offering.*
[[For Offertory Sentences, see Appendix B]]

18(a) *While the Presbyter distinctly pronounceth one or more of these Sentences for the Offertory, the Deacon, or (if no such be present) some other fit person, shall receive the devotions of the people there present, in a bason provided for that purpose. And when all have offered, he shall reverently bring the said bason, with the offerings therein, and deliver it to the Presbyter; who shall humbly present it before the Lord, and set it upon the Holy Table.*

(b) *And the Presbyter shall then offer up, and place the bread and wine prepared for the Sacrament upon the Lord's Table; and shall say,*

1637: *one or more*] *some or all* · *some . . . person*] *one of the Churchwardens* · *offerings*] *oblations*   **1764**: *one or more*] *some or all* · *offerings*] *oblations* · *Holy Table*] ADD *saying* [[and no. 19 below. '*And the Presbyter . . . shall say*' follows no. 19 and introduces no. 20]]

19 Blessed be thou, O Lord God, for ever and ever. Thine, O Lord, is the greatness, and the glory, and the victory, and the majesty: for all that is in the heaven and in the earth is thine: thine is the kingdom, O Lord, and thou art exalted as head above all: both riches and honour come of thee, and of thine own do we give unto thee. *Amen.*

1637: SUBST [[Prayer for the Church, Exhortations, Invitation, Confession, Absolution and Comfortable Words. See nos. 31, 38–41 below. The Exhortations are those of **1552**]]

20   THE CONSECRATION
Then shall the Presbyter say,
            The Lord be with you;
Answer. And with thy spirit.
Presbyter. Lift up your hearts;
Answer. We lift them up unto the Lord.
Presbyter. Let us give thanks unto our Lord God;
Answer. It is meet and right so to do.

1637: THE CONSECRATION] OM · *Then . . . say*] *After which the Presbyter shall proceed, saying,* · The Lord . . . spirit] OM   **1764**: THE CONSECRATION] OM · *Then . . . say*] [[SUBST 18(b) above]]

21 *Presbyter.*
It is very meet, right, and our bounden duty, that we should

The Scottish Liturgy

at all times, and in all places, give thanks unto thee, O Lord, Holy Father, Almighty, Everlasting God.

Here shall follow the Proper Preface,[1] *according to the time, if there be any especially appointed; or else immediately shall follow,*

Therefore with Angels and Archangels, and with all the company of heaven, we laud and magnify thy glorious Name; evermore praising thee and saying:

Holy, holy, holy, Lord God of hosts, heaven and earth are full of thy glory. Glory be to thee, O Lord most high. Amen. *Presbyter and People.*

1637: *Presbyter and People*] OM · Amen] OM · 〚In **1637, 1764** the second half of the Preface and the Sanctus are one paragraph〛   **1764**: Holy Father] ADD *These words* (holy Father) *must be omitted on Trinity Sunday* · *Presbyter and People*] OM

22 *Here may be sung or said:*

Blessed is he that cometh in the Name of the Lord. Hosanna in the highest.

When this is sung or said, Amen *shall be omitted after the Sanctus.*

1637, 1764: OMIT

23 *Then the Presbyter, standing at such a part of the Holy Table as he may with the most ease and decency use both his hands, shall say the Prayer of Consecration, as followeth:*

1637: at such ... hands] up · followeth] ADD *But then, during the time of Consecration, he shall stand at such a part of the holy Table, where he may with the more ease and decency use both his hands.*

24 All glory and thanksgiving be to thee, Almighty God, our heavenly Father, for that thou of thy tender mercy didst give thine only Son Jesus Christ to suffer death upon the cross for our redemption; who, by his own oblation of himself once offered, made a full, perfect, and sufficient sacrifice, oblation, and satisfaction, for the sins of the whole world; and did institute, and in his holy Gospel command us to continue, a perpetual memorial of that his precious death and sacrifice until his coming again.

1637: All glory ... to thee] OM · for that thou] which · by his ... made] made there (by his one oblation of himself once offered) · memorial] memory · again] ADD *Hear us, O merciful Father, we most humbly beseech thee, and of thy Almighty goodness vouchsafe so to bless and sanctify with thy word and Holy Spirit these thy gifts and creatures of bread and wine, that they may be unto us the body and blood of thy most dearly beloved Son; so that we, receiving them*

---

[1] 〚For Proper Prefaces, see Appendix A.〛

according to thy Son our Saviour Jesus Christ's holy institution, in remembrance of his death and passion, may be partakers of the same his most precious body and blood   1764: and thanksgiving] OM

25   For, in the night that he was betrayed, ªhe took bread; and when he had given thanks, ᵇhe brake it, and gave it to his disciples, saying, Take, eat, ᶜthis is my Body, which is given for you: Do this in remembrance of me. Likewise after supper ᵈhe took the cup; and when he had given thanks, he gave it to them, saying, Drink ye all of this, for ᵉthis is my Blood of the new testament, which is shed for you and for many for the remission of sins: Do this as oft as ye shall drink it in remembrance of me.

ª *Here the Presbyter is to take the paten in his hands:*

ᵇ *And here to break the bread:*

ᶜ *And here to lay his hands upon all the bread.*

ᵈ *Here he is to take the cup into his hand:*

ᵉ *And here to lay his hand upon every vessel (be it chalice or flagon) in which there is any wine to be consecrated.*

1637: For] Who · he took] took · [[Rubrics (b) and (c) are omitted; (d) and (e) are combined at (d)]]

1637: ADD *Immediately after shall be said this Memorial or Prayer of Oblation, as followeth.*

26   Wherefore, O Lord, and heavenly Father, according to the institution of thy dearly beloved Son our Saviour Jesus Christ, we thy humble servants do celebrate and make here before thy Divine Majesty, with these thy holy gifts, which we now offer unto thee, the memorial thy Son hath commanded us to make; having in remembrance his blessed passion, and precious death, his mighty resurrection, and glorious ascension; rendering unto thee most hearty thanks for the innumerable benefits procured unto us by the same, and looking for his coming again with power and great glory.

The Oblation.

1637: *The Oblation*] OM · which we ... thee] OM · memorial] ADD which · commanded] willed · and precious death] OM · and looking ... glory] OM.   1764: and looking ... glory] OM

27   And we thine unworthy servants beseech thee, most merciful Father, to hear us, and to send thy Holy Spirit upon us and upon these thy gifts and creatures of bread and wine, that, being blessed and hallowed by his life-giving power, they may become the Body and Blood of thy most dearly beloved Son, to the end that all who shall receive the same may be sanctified both in body and soul, and preserved unto everlasting life.

The Invocation.

The Scottish Liturgy 45

1637: OMIT   **1764**: thine unworthy servants] most humbly · most merciful] O merciful · and to send ... power] and of thy almighty goodness vouchsafe to bless and sanctify, with thy word and Holy Spirit, these thy gifts and creatures of bread and wine, that · to the end ... life] OM   [[cf. no. 24 (**1637**)]]

28   And we earnestly desire thy fatherly goodness, mercifully to accept this our sacrifice of praise and thanksgiving, most humbly beseeching thee to grant, that by the merits and death of thy Son Jesus Christ, and through faith in his blood, we and all thy whole Church may obtain remission of our sins, and all other benefits of his passion.

1637: earnestly] entirely

29   And here we humbly offer and present unto thee, O Lord, ourselves, our souls and bodies, to be a reasonable, holy, and living sacrifice unto thee, beseeching thee that all we who shall be partakers of this Holy Communion may worthily receive the most precious Body and Blood of thy Son Jesus Christ, and be fulfilled with thy grace and heavenly benediction, and made one body with him, that he may dwell in us and we in him.

1637: humbly] OM · living] lively · sacrifice unto thee] ADD humbly · all we who] whosoever · in us and we in him] in them and they in him   **1764**: living] lively · all we] whosoever · in us and we in him] in them and they in him.

30   And although we be unworthy, through our manifold sins, to offer unto thee any sacrifice; yet we beseech thee to accept this our bounden duty and service, not weighing our merits, but pardoning our offences, through Jesus Christ our Lord: by whom, and with whom, in the unity of the Holy Ghost, all honour and glory be unto thee, O Father Almighty, world without end. Amen.

31   *Then shall the Presbyter or Deacon say,*

Let us pray for the whole state of Christ's Church.

The Presbyter.

Almighty and Everliving God, who by thy holy Apostle hast taught us to make intercessions and to give thanks for all men: We humbly pray thee most mercifully to receive these our supplications which we offer unto thy Divine Majesty; beseeching thee to inspire continually the universal Church with the spirit of truth, unity, and concord; and grant that all they that do confess thy holy Name may agree in the truth of thy holy word, and live in unity and godly love.

1637: ⟦This prayer occurs earlier in **1637**. See note before no. 20⟧ *Then shall . . . say*] *And then he* ⟦sc. the Presbyter⟧ *shall say,* · *Church*] ADD *here in earth.* · *The Presbyter*] OM · *who by*] *which by* · *intercessions*] *prayers and supplications* · *mercifully*] ADD (*to accept our alms, and*) · *our supplications*] *our prayers* ⟦and the rubric *If there be no alms given to the poor, then shall the words* (*of accepting our alms*) *be left out unsaid.*⟧ **1764**: *Then shall . . . say*] OM · *The Presbyter*] OM · *intercessions*] *prayers and supplications* · *mercifully*] ADD *to accept our alms and oblations and* · *supplications*] *prayers*

32   We beseech thee also to save and defend all Kings, Princes, and Governors, and especially thy servant *George* our King, and all who are put in authority under him, that we may be godly and quietly governed.

1637: *defend all*] ADD *Christian* · *and all . . . governed*] *that under him we may be godly and quietly governed: and grant unto his whole Council, and to all that be put in authority under him, that they may truly and indifferently minister justice, to the punishment of wickedness and vice and to the maintenance of God's* ⟦*thy*, **1764**⟧ *true religion and virtue.* **1764**: *defend all*] ADD *Christian* · ⟦OM name of sovereign⟧ · *and all . . . governed*] = **1637**

33   Give grace, O heavenly Father, to all Bishops, Priests, and Deacons, [and especially to thy servant *N.* our Bishop,] that they may both by their life and doctrine set forth thy true and living word, and rightly and duly administer thy holy Sacraments: and to all thy people give thy heavenly grace, and especially to this Congregation here present, that they may hear and receive thy holy word, truly serving thee in holiness and righteousness all the days of their life.

We most humbly beseech thee of thy goodness, O Lord, to comfort and succour all those who in this transitory life are in trouble, sorrow, need, sickness, or any other adversity.

1637: *Priests, and Deacons*] *Presbyters, and Curates* · *and especially . . . Bishop*] OM · *living*] *lively* · *and especially . . . present*] OM · *that they may hear*] *that with meek heart and due reverence they may hear* · *their life*] ADD [*And we commend especially unto thy merciful goodness, the congregation which is here assembled in thy Name, to celebrate the commemoration of the most precious death and sacrifice of thy Son and our Saviour Jesus Christ*] ⟦*to be omitted when there is no Communion.*⟧ · *We most humbly*] *And we most humbly* · *those who*] *them which* · *are in*] *be in.*   **1764**: *and especially . . . Bishop*] OM · *living*] *lively* · *and especially . . . present*] OM · *that they may hear*] *that with meek heart and due reverence they may hear* · *their life*] ADD *And we commend . . .* ⟦= **1637**; but with no rubric allowing omission⟧ · *We most*] *And we most*

34   We commend to thy gracious keeping, O Lord, all thy servants departed this life in thy faith and fear, beseeching thee to grant them everlasting light and peace.

1637: SUBST *And we also bless thy holy Name for all those thy servants, who,*

having finished their course in faith, do now rest from their labours.   **1764:**
SUBST And we also bless thy holy name for all thy servants, who, having finished
their course in faith, do now rest from their labours.

35   And we yield unto thee most high praise and hearty thanks, for the wonderful grace and virtue declared in all thy Saints, who have been the choice vessels of thy grace, and the lights of the world in their several generations[1]: beseeching thee to give us grace to follow the example of their stedfastness in thy faith, and obedience to thy holy commandments, that at the day of the general resurrection, we, and all they who are of the mystical body of thy Son, may be set on his right hand, and hear his most joyful voice, Come ye blessed of my Father, inherit the kingdom prepared for you from the foundation of the world.

Grant this, O Father, for Jesus Christ's sake, our only Mediator and Advocate. *Amen.*

1637: beseeching . . . grace] most humbly beseeching thee that we may have grace · they who are] they which are · his most joyful] that his most joyful
1764: beseeching] most humbly beseeching · his most joyful] that his most joyful

36   *Then shall the Presbyter say,*

As our Saviour Christ hath commanded and taught us, we are bold to say,
Our Father . . . 〚CF 1〛 . . . ever. Amen.

1764: which art] who art   〚**1929** has inset rubric '*Presbyter and People*'〛

37   *Here the Presbyter shall break the consecrated Bread; and silence may be kept for a brief space.*

Then shall the Presbyter say:

The peace of the Lord be with you all;
Answer. And with thy spirit.
Presbyter. Brethren, let us love one another, for love is of God.
1637, 1764: OMIT

COMMUNION

38   *Then the Presbyter or Deacon shall say this invitation to them that come to receive the Holy Communion,*

---

[1] *On feasts of the Blessed Virgin and the Saints for which a Proper Preface is provided, this commemoration may be inserted with the Bishop's consent:* and chiefly in the Blessed Virgin Mary, Mother of thy Son Jesus Christ our Lord and God, and in the Holy Patriarchs, Prophets, Apostles, and Martyrs, beseeching thee to give us grace, &c. 〚This addition does not occur in **1637** or **1764**.〛

[1]Ye that do truly . . . ⟦CF 6⟧ . . . knees.

1637: ⟦Occurs earlier: see note to no. 19⟧ COMMUNION] OM · *or Deacon*] OM · with faith] OM · Almighty God] ADD before this congregation here gathered together in his holy Name   **1764**: COMMUNION] OM · *or Deacon*] OM · with faith] OM · meekly . . . knees] OM

39 *Then shall this general Confession be made by the people, along with the Presbyter; he first kneeling down,*

Almighty God, Father . . . ⟦CF 7⟧ . . . our Lord. Amen.

1637: ⟦see note under no. 19⟧ *by the people . . . down*] *in the name of all those that are minded to receive the holy Communion, by the Presbyter himself, or the Deacon; both he and all the people kneeling humbly upon their knees.*

40 *Then shall the Presbyter, or the Bishop if he be present, stand up, and, turning himself to the people, pronounce the Absolution as followeth:*

Almighty God, our heavenly . . . ⟦CF 8⟧ . . . Lord. Amen.

1637: ⟦see note under no. 19⟧

41 *Then shall the Presbyter also say,*

[1]Hear what comfortable . . . ⟦CF 9⟧ . . . our sins.

1637: ⟦See note under no. 19⟧ ⟦**1637, 1764,** and **1929** all follow the A.V.⟧

42 *Then shall the Presbyter, turning him to the Altar, kneel down, and say, in the name of all them that shall communicate, this Collect of humble access to the Holy Communion, as followeth:*

We do not presume . . . ⟦CF 10⟧ . . . in us. Amen.

1637: *turning . . . Altar*] OM · *kneel down and*] *kneeling down at God's board*   ⟦**1764** and **1929** read 'this thy Holy Table' and 'made clean by his most sacred Body'⟧

43 *Here may be sung or said:*

O Lamb of God, that takest away the sins of the world: have mercy upon us.

O Lamb of God, that takest away the sins of the world: have mercy upon us.

O Lamb of God, that takest away the sins of the world: grant us thy peace.

1637, 1764: OMIT

44 *Then shall he that celebrateth first receive the Communion in both kinds himself, and next deliver the same to the Bishops, Presbyters, and*

---

[1] ⟦May be omitted on weekdays except on Red Letter Days. See no. 50 below.⟧

The Scottish Liturgy

Deacons (if there be any present), and after to the people in due order, into their hands, all humbly kneeling. And when he receiveth himself or delivereth the Sacrament of the Body of Christ to any other, he shall say,

The Body of our Lord Jesus Christ, which was given for thee, preserve thy body and soul unto everlasting life.

Here the person receiving shall say, Amen.

And the Presbyter that receiveth the Cup himself, as likewise the Presbyter or Deacon that delivereth it to any other, shall say,

The Blood of our Lord Jesus Christ, which was shed for thee, preserve thy body and soul unto everlasting life.

Here the person receiving shall say, Amen.

1637: he that celebrateth] the Bishop, if he be present, or else the Presbyter that celebrateth · the same] it · the Bishops] other Bishops · present] ADD that they may help him that celebrateth · into their hands] OM · the Sacrament . . . other] the bread to others · shall say] ADD this benediction · person] party · And the Presbyter] ADD or Minister · as likewise . . . delivereth] or delivereth · to any other] to others · shall say] ADD this benediction · person] party   1764 〖= 1637, except that it reads 'the sacrament of the body of Christ'; 'soul and body' (twice); 'person' (twice)〗

45 *When all have communicated, he that celebrateth shall go to the Lord's Table, and cover with a fair linen cloth that which remaineth of the consecrated Elements.*

1637: cloth] ADD or corporal · Elements] ADD and then say this Collect of thanksgiving, as followeth 〖no. 47〗   1764: Elements] ADD , and then say〗

46   THANKSGIVING AFTER COMMUNION

Then the Presbyter or Deacon, turning to the people, shall say,

Having now received the precious Body and Blood of Christ, let us give thanks to our Lord God, who hath graciously vouchsafed to admit us to the participation of his Holy Mysteries; and let us beg of him grace to perform our vows, and to persevere in our good resolutions; and that being made holy, we may obtain everlasting life, through the merits of the all-sufficient sacrifice of our Lord and Saviour Jesus Christ.

This Exhortation may be omitted except on Sundays and the Great Festivals.

1637: OMIT   1764: THANKSGIVING . . . COMMUNION] OM 〖for rubric see No. 45〗 · This Exhortation . . . Festivals]OM

47 *Then the Presbyter shall say this Collect of thanksgiving as followeth:*

Almighty and Everliving God, we most heartily thank thee, for that thou dost vouchsafe to feed us, who have duly received these Holy Mysteries, with the spiritual food of the most precious Body and Blood of thy Son our Saviour Jesus Christ; and dost assure us thereby of thy favour and goodness towards us, and that we are very members incorporate in the mystical Body of thy Son, which is the blessed company of all faithful people; and are also heirs through hope of thy everlasting kingdom, by the merits of his most precious death and passion. We now most humbly beseech thee, O heavenly Father, so to assist us with thy Holy Spirit, that we may continue in that holy communion and fellowship, and do all such good works as thou hast prepared for us to walk in; through Jesus Christ our Lord, to whom, with thee and the Holy Ghost, be all honour and glory, world without end. *Amen.*

1637: [[For rubric see no. 45]] the mystical . . . Son] thy mystical body · his most . . . passion] the most precious death and passion of thy dear Son · thy Holy Spirit] thy grace · communion and] OM   **1764:** thy Holy Spirit] thy grace and Holy Spirit · prepared for] commanded · with thee] with the Father

48 *Then shall be sung or said* ¹Gloria in excelsis, *by the Presbyter and people, as followeth:*

Glory be to God in the highest, and in earth peace, good will towards men. We praise thee, we bless thee, we worship thee, we glorify thee, we give thanks to thee for thy great glory, O Lord God, heavenly King, God the Father Almighty; and to thee, O God, the only-begotten Son Jesu Christ; and to thee, O God, the Holy Ghost.

O Lord, the only-begotten Son, Jesu Christ; O Lord God, Lamb of God, Son of the Father, who takest away the sins of the world, have mercy upon us. Thou that takest away the sins of the world, receive our prayer. Thou that sittest at the right hand of God the Father, have mercy upon us.

For thou only art holy, thou only art the Lord, thou only, O Christ, with the Holy Ghost, art most high in the glory of God the Father. *Amen.*

1637: by . . . people] *in English* [[text as in CF 13]]   **1764:** by . . . people] OM [[Post-communion Collects may be said here upon certain days and at certain seasons, **1929**]]

¹ [[May be omitted on weekdays. See no. 50 on next page.]]

49 Then the Presbyter, or the Bishop if he be present, shall let them depart with this Blessing.

The peace . . . ⟦CF 14⟧ . . . always. *Amen.*

50 *The Creed, the Exhortation* Ye that do truly, *the* Comfortable Words *and the* Gloria in excelsis *may be omitted on Weekdays except on Red Letter Days.*

1637, 1764: OMIT

CHAPTER V

THE AMERICAN LITURGY

THE American Liturgy descends from the 1764 recension of the Scottish Liturgy. The text here printed is that of *The Book of Common Prayer according to the use of the Protestant Episcopal Church in the United States of America*, 1928. The notes signify the substantial variations between this text and the earlier recensions of 1790 and 1892, taken from W. McGarvey, *Liturgiae Americanae*, Philadelphia, 1895.

1   THE ORDER FOR THE
ADMINISTRATION OF THE LORD'S SUPPER
OR
HOLY COMMUNION

2 *At the Communion-time the Holy Table shall have upon it a fair white linen cloth. And the Priest, standing reverently before the Holy Table, shall say the Lord's Prayer and the Collect following, the People kneeling; but the Lord's Prayer may be omitted at the discretion of the Priest.*

   1790, 1892: At the . . . before the Holy Table] The Table at the Communion-time having a fair white linen cloth upon it, shall stand in the body of the Church, or in the Chancel; and the Minister standing at the north [[right 1892]] side of the Table, or where Morning and Evening Prayer are appointed to be said . at the discretion . . . Priest] if Morning Prayer hath been said immediately before.

3 Our Father, who art . . . [[CF 1]] . . . from evil. Amen.

   [[The American rite has always read 'on earth' for 'in earth' and 'those who' for 'them that']]
   [[**1790**: adds ascription, reading 'and the power']]

4   *The Collect*
Almighty God, unto whom . . . [[CF 2]] . . . Lord. *Amen.*

5 *Then shall the Priest, turning to the People, rehearse distinctly The Ten Commandments; and the People, still kneeling, shall, after every Commandment, ask God mercy for their transgressions for the time past, and grace to keep the law for the time to come.*

The American Liturgy

And NOTE, *That in rehearsing The Ten Commandments, the Priest may omit that part of the Commandment which is inset.*

The Decalogue *may be omitted, provided it be said at least one Sunday in each month.* But NOTE, *That whenever it is omitted, the Priest shall say the Summary of the Law, beginning,* Hear what our Lord Jesus Christ saith.

1790: *Priest*] Minister · time to come] ADD , as followeth · And NOTE . . . Christ saith] OM   1892: *Priest*] Minister [[twice]] · time to come] ADD as followeth · And NOTE . . . inset] OM · at least one . . . month] once on each Sunday [[following the decision of the General Convention of 1883]]

6 The Decalogue

God spake these words . . . [[CF 3]] . . . beseech thee.

[[1790, 1892 follow CF exactly but omit the title. 1928 has the following passages inset (see second paragraph of no. 5 above): (2) 'for I . . . commandments', (3) 'for the Lord . . . vain', (4) 'Six days . . . hallowed it', (5) 'that thy days . . . giveth thee', (10) 'thy neighbour's house . . . that is his'.]]

7 *Then may the Priest say,*

Hear what our Lord Jesus Christ saith.

Thou shalt love the Lord thy God with all thy heart, and with all thy soul, and with all thy mind. This is the first and great commandment. And the second is like unto it; Thou shalt love thy neighbour as thyself. On these two commandments hang all the Law and the Prophets.

1790, 1892: *Priest*] Minister · Hear what] Hear also what

8 *Here, if the* Decalogue *hath been omitted, shall be said,*

Lord, have mercy upon us.
   Christ, have mercy upon us.
Lord, have mercy upon us.

1790: OMIT

9 *Then the Priest may say,*

O Almighty Lord, and everlasting God, vouchsafe, we beseech thee, to direct, sanctify, and govern, both our hearts and bodies, in the ways of thy laws, and in the works of thy commandments; that, through thy most mighty protection, both here and ever, we may be preserved in body and soul; through our Lord and Saviour Jesus Christ. Amen.

1790, 1892: *Then . . . say*] Let us pray

10 *Here shall be said,*

>   The Lord be with you.
> *Answer.* And with thy spirit.
> *Minister.* Let us pray.

1790, 1892: OMIT

11 *Then shall the Priest say the Collect of the Day. And after the Collect the Minister appointed shall read the Epistle, first saying,* The Epistle is written in the —— Chapter of ——, beginning at the —— Verse. *The Epistle ended, he shall say,* Here endeth the Epistle.

1790, 1892: *the Priest say*] *be said · appointed*] OM · *saying,* The Epistle] ADD [*or,* The Portion of Scripture appointed for the Epistle]

12 *Here may be sung a Hymn or an Anthem.*

1790, 1892: OMIT

13 *Then, all the People standing, the Minister appointed shall read the Gospel, first saying,* The Holy Gospel is written in the —— Chapter of ——, beginning at the —— Verse.

1790, 1892: *the Minister appointed*] *he*

14 *Here shall be said,* Glory be to thee, O Lord.

1790: *Here . . . said*] Here the people shall say   1892: *said*] ADD *or sung*

15 *And after the Gospel may be said,* Praise be to thee, O Christ.

1790, 1892: OMIT

16 *Then shall be said the Creed commonly called the Nicene, or else the Apostles' Creed; but the Creed may be omitted, if it hath been said immediately before in Morning Prayer; Provided, that the Nicene Creed shall be said on Christmas Day, Easter Day, Ascension Day, Whitsunday, and Trinity Sunday.*

1790: SUBST *Then shall be read the Apostles', or Nicene Creed: unless one of them hath been read immediately before, in the Morning Service.*

17 I believe in one God . . . [[CF 4]] . . . world to come. Amen.

1790: [[omits text of Creed]]   1892, 1928: [[have considerable variants from the CF punctuation including 'of one substance with the Father;' and 'the Lord, and Giver of Life'.]]

18 *Then shall be declared unto the People what Holy Days, or Fasting Days, are in the week following to be observed; and (if occasion be) shall Notice be given of the Communion, and of the Banns of Matrimony, and of other matters to be published.*

The American Liturgy 55

19 *Here, or immediately after the Creed, may be said the Bidding Prayer, or other authorized prayers and intercessions.*

1790, 1892: OMIT

20 *Then followeth the Sermon. After which, the Priest, when there is a Communion, shall return to the Holy Table, and begin the Offertory, saying one or more of these Sentences following, as he thinketh most convenient.*

1790, 1892: *Priest*] Minister · *Holy Table*] Lord's Table
〚For Offertory Sentences, see Appendix B〛

21 *And* NOTE, *that these Sentences may be used on any other occasion of Public Worship when the Offerings of the People are to be received.*

1790: OMIT   1892: 〚places this rubric before the text of the sentences〛

22 *The Deacons, Church-wardens, or other fit persons appointed for that purpose, shall receive the Alms for the Poor, and other Offerings of the People, in a decent Basin to be provided by the Parish; and reverently bring it to the Priest, who shall humbly present and place it upon the Holy Table.*

1790, 1892: *The Deacons*] PREF *While these Sentences are in Reading* · *Offerings*] Devotions

23 *And the Priest shall then offer, and shall place upon the Holy Table, the Bread and the Wine.*

And when the Alms and Oblations are being received and presented, there may be sung a Hymn, or an Offertory Anthem in the words of Holy Scripture or of the Book of Common Prayer, under the direction of the Priest.

Here the Priest may ask the secret intercessions of the Congregation for any who have desired the prayers of the Church.

1790: *And the Priest . . . Wine*] And the Priest shall then place upon the Table so much Bread and Wine as he shall think sufficient. · *And when the Alms . . . of the Church*] OM
1892: *And the Priest . . . Wine*] = 1790 · *being received and presented*] presented · *of the Priest*] of the Minister. · *Here the Priest . . . Church*] OM

24 *Then shall the Priest say,*

Let us pray for the whole state of Christ's Church.

Almighty and everliving God, who by thy holy Apostle hast taught us to make prayers, and supplications, and to give thanks for all men; We humbly beseech thee most mercifully to accept our [alms and] oblations, and to receive these our prayers, which we offer unto thy Divine Majesty; beseeching thee to inspire continually the Universal Church with the spirit of truth, unity, and concord: And grant that all those who do confess thy holy Name may agree in the truth of thy holy Word, and live in unity and godly love.

We beseech thee also, so to direct and dispose the hearts of all Christian Rulers, that they may truly and impartially administer justice, to the punishment of wickedness and vice, and to the maintenance of thy true religion, and virtue.

Give grace, O heavenly Father, to all Bishops and other Ministers, that they may, both by their life and doctrine, set forth thy true and lively Word, and rightly and duly administer thy holy Sacraments.

And to all thy People give thy heavenly grace; and especially to this congregation here present; that, with meek heart and due reverence, they may hear, and receive thy holy Word; truly serving thee in holiness and righteousness all the days of their life.

And we most humbly beseech thee, of thy goodness, O Lord, to comfort and succour all those who, in this transitory life, are in trouble, sorrow, need, sickness, or any other adversity.

And we also bless thy holy Name for all thy servants departed this life in thy faith and fear; beseeching thee to grant them continual growth in thy love and service, and to give us grace so to follow their good examples, that with them we may be partakers of thy heavenly kingdom. Grant this, O Father, for Jesus Christ's sake, our only Mediator and Advocate. *Amen.*

1790, 1892: Christ's Church] ADD militant · to accept our [alms and] oblations and] [to accept our alms and oblations, and] [[with this rubric inset: '*If there be no alms or oblations, then shall the words* (to accept our alms and oblations) *be left unsaid*']] · to grant them continual . . . service, and] OM

[[In 1790 and 1892 here follows a version of CF 5.   1928 prints the Exhortation at the end of the rite, permitting its use upon any occasion, and ordering it upon Advent I, Lent I, and Trinity Sunday]]

25 Then shall the Priest say to those who come to receive the Holy Communion,

Ye who do truly . . . [[CF 6]] . . . devoutly kneeling.

[[All read 'devoutly kneeling' for 'meekly . . . knees']]

The American Liturgy

26 *Then shall this General Confession be made, by the Priest and all those who are minded to receive the Holy Communion, humbly kneeling.*

Almighty God, Father of our Lord Jesus Christ . . . 〚CF 7〛 . . . our Lord. Amen.

27 *Then shall the Priest (the Bishop if he be present) stand up, and turning to the People, say,*

Almighty God, our heavenly Father . . . 〚CF 8〛 . . . our Lord. Amen.

〚The American rite has always read 'those who' for 'them that'〛

28 *Then shall the Priest say,*

Hear what comfortable words . . . 〚CF 9〛 . . . our sins.

〚All read 'who truly turn' and 'Christ Jesus' (1 Tim. 1. 15). **1928** reads 'all that travail'〛

29 *After which the Priest shall proceed, saying,*

      Lift up your hearts.
Answer. We lift them up unto the Lord.
Priest. Let us give thanks unto our Lord God.
Answer. It is meet and right so to do.

Then shall the Priest turn to the Holy Table, and say,

It is very meet, right, and our bounden duty, that we should at all times, and in all places, give thanks unto thee, O Lord, Holy Father, Almighty, Everlasting God.

Here shall follow the Proper Preface,[1] according to the time, if there be any specially appointed; or else immediately shall be said or sung by the Priest,

Therefore with Angels and Archangels, and with all the company of heaven, we laud and magnify thy glorious Name; evermore praising thee, and saying,

Holy, Holy, Holy, Lord God of hosts, Heaven and earth are full of thy glory: Glory be to thee, O Lord Most High. Amen.   *Priest and People.*

1790: *Holy Table*] *Lord's Table* · *Holy Father*] 〚ADD this rubric inset: *These words* [Holy Father] *must be omitted on Trinity Sunday.*〛 · *sung by the Priest*] *sung by the Priest and People* · *Priest and People* 〚inset〛] OM   **1892**: 〚= **1790** down to 'Almighty, Everlasting God'; thereafter = **1928**〛

〚Here **1790** and **1892** have the *Prayer of Humble Access* (no. 36 below)〛

[1] 〚For Proper Prefaces, see Appendix A.〛

30 *When the Priest, standing before the Holy Table, hath so ordered the Bread and Wine, that he may with the more readiness and decency break the Bread before the People, and take the Cup into his hands, he shall say the Prayer of Consecration, as followeth.*

1790, 1892: Holy Table] Table

31 All glory be to thee, Almighty God, our heavenly Father, for that thou, of thy tender mercy, didst give thine only Son Jesus Christ to suffer death upon the Cross for our redemption; who made there (by his one oblation of himself once offered) a full, perfect, and sufficient sacrifice, oblation, and satisfaction, for the sins of the whole world; and did institute, and in his holy Gospel command us to continue, a perpetual memory of that his precious death and sacrifice, until his coming again: For in the night in which he was betrayed, (*a*) he took Bread; and when he had given thanks, (*b*) he brake it, and gave it to his disciples, saying, Take, eat, (*c*) this is my Body, which is given for you; Do this in remembrance of me. Likewise, after supper, (*d*) he took the Cup; and when he had given thanks, he gave it to them, saying, Drink ye all of this; for (*e*) this is my Blood of the New Testament, which is shed for you, and for many, for the remission of sins; Do this, as oft as ye shall drink it, in remembrance of me.

(*a*) *Here the Priest is to take the Paten into his hands.*
(*b*) *And here to break the Bread.*
(*c*) *And here to lay his hand upon all the Bread.*
(*d*) *Here he is to take the Cup into his hands.*
(*e*) *And here he is to lay his hand upon every vessel in which there is any Wine to be consecrated.*

32 Wherefore, O Lord and heavenly Father, according to the institution of thy dearly beloved Son our Saviour Jesus Christ, we, thy humble servants, do celebrate and make here before thy Divine Majesty, with these thy holy gifts, which we now offer unto thee, the memorial thy Son hath commanded us to make; having in remembrance his blessed passion and precious death, his mighty resurrection and glorious ascension; rendering unto thee most hearty thanks for the innumerable benefits procured unto us by the same. *The Oblation*

33 And we most humbly beseech thee, O merciful Father, to hear us; and, of thy almighty goodness, vouchsafe to bless and sanctify, with thy Word and Holy Spirit, these thy gifts and creatures of bread and wine; that we, receiving them according to thy Son our Saviour Jesus Christ's holy institution, *The Invocation*

The American Liturgy

in remembrance of his death and passion, may be partakers of his most blessed Body and Blood.

34 And we earnestly desire thy fatherly goodness, mercifully to accept this our sacrifice of praise and thanksgiving; most humbly beseeching thee to grant that, by the merits and death of thy Son Jesus Christ, and through faith in his blood, we, and all thy whole Church, may obtain remission of our sins, and all other benefits of his passion. And here we offer and present unto thee, O Lord, ourselves, our souls and bodies, to be a reasonable, holy, and living sacrifice unto thee; humbly beseeching thee, that we, and all others who shall be partakers of this Holy Communion, may worthily receive the most precious Body and Blood of thy Son Jesus Christ, be filled with thy grace and heavenly benediction, and made one body with him, that he may dwell in us, and we in him. And although we are unworthy, through our manifold sins, to offer unto thee any sacrifice; yet we beseech thee to accept this our bounden duty and service; not weighing our merits, but pardoning our offences, through Jesus Christ our Lord; by whom, and with whom, in the unity of the Holy Ghost, all honour and glory be unto thee, O Father Almighty, world without end. *Amen.*

    1790: [[has 33 and 34 in one paragraph]]   dwell in us and we] dwell in them, and they

35 And now, as our Saviour Christ hath taught us, we are bold to say, Our Father, who art in heaven . . . [[CF 1]] . . . ever and ever. Amen.

    [reading 'on earth', as before]   **1790, 1892**: OMIT   [But see no. 41 below]

36 *Then shall the Priest, kneeling down at the Lord's Table, say, in the name of all those who shall receive the Communion, this Prayer following.*
We do not presume . . . [[CF 10]] . . . he in us. *Amen.*

    [[**1790, 1892** place this prayer between nos. 29 and 30 above]]

37 *Here may be sung a Hymn.*

    1790: *may*] *shall* · Hymn] ADD *or part of a Hymn, from the Selection for the Feasts and Fasts,*[1] *etc.*

38 *Then shall the Priest first receive the Holy Communion in both kinds*

---

[1] [[American eighteenth-century Prayer Books commonly contained such a Selection.]]

himself, and proceed to deliver the same to the Bishops, Priests, and Deacons, in like manner, (if any be present,) and, after that, to the People also in order, into their hands, all devoutly kneeling. And sufficient opportunity shall be given to those present to communicate.

1790: *And sufficient . . . communicate*] OM

39 *And when he delivereth the Bread, he shall say,*
The Body . . . [[CF 11]] . . . thanksgiving.

40 *And the Minister who delivereth the Cup shall say,*
The Blood . . . [[CF 11]] . . . thankful.

41 *When all have communicated, the Priest shall return to the Lord's Table, and reverently place upon it what remaineth of the consecrated Elements, covering the same with a fair linen cloth.*

1790, 1892: *Priest*] Minister [[1790, 1892 add here: 'Then shall the Minister say the Lord's Prayer, the People repeating after him every petition. Our Father . . . (CF 1) . . . ever. Amen.' Text as at no. 3]]

42 *Then shall the Priest say,*
Let us pray.
Almighty and everliving God, we most heartily thank thee . . . [[CF 12]] . . . without end. *Amen.*

1790, 1892: *Then shall . . . pray*] After shall be said as followeth · 1928: *the most . . . dear Son*] his most precious death and passion

43 *Then shall be said the* Gloria in excelsis, *all standing, or some proper Hymn.*

1790, 1892: *said*] ADD or sung · *Hymn*] ADD from the Selection.

44 Glory be to God on high . . . [[CF 13]] . . . the Father. Amen.

[[1892, 1928 read 'on earth peace' 1928 omits 'Thou that takest . . . upon us']]

45 *Then, the People kneeling, the Priest* (*the Bishop if he be present*) *shall let them depart with this Blessing.*
The Peace of God . . . [[CF 14]] . . . remain with you always. *Amen.*

1790, 1892: *the People kneeling*] OM

46 GENERAL RUBRICS

In the absence of a Priest, a Deacon may say all that is before appointed unto the end of the Gospel.

Upon the Sundays and other Holy Days, (though there be no Sermon or Communion,) may be said all that is appointed at the Communion, unto the end of the Gospel, concluding with the Blessing.

And if any of the consecrated Bread and Wine remain after the Communion, it shall not be carried out of the Church; but the Minister and other Communicants shall, immediately after the Blessing, reverently eat and drink the same.

1790, 1892: *In the absence . . . Gospel*] OM · *may be said*] *shall be said*

CHAPTER VI

THE PROPOSED ENGLISH REVISION (1928)

THE revision of the Book of Common Prayer submitted to Parliament in 1927–8 contained two liturgies. That of 1662 was reproduced intact, and a considerably revised rite was added. It is this that is printed here. In spite of its double failure to be accepted by Parliament, several features of the revised liturgy have been and are widely used (the CONSECRATION, however, is a notable exception to this statement); and the hierarchy is accustomed to treat any prayer or practice contained in the Deposited Book as having 'lawful authority'. That the 1928 liturgy has been influential in various parts of the Church is plain from the liturgies contained in this book; but similarity is in some cases to be explained by the same influences bearing upon 1928 and other rites, rather than by the influence of 1928 itself.

1   A DEVOTION

which may be said by the Priest and people immediately before the celebration of the Holy Communion.

The whole shall be said throughout in a distinct and audible voice.

2 *The Priest, standing at God's Board, shall say with the Ministers and the people, all kneeling, as follows.*

Priest. In the name of the Father, and of the Son, and of the Holy Ghost. Amen.

3 *Anthem.* I will go unto the altar of God: even unto the God of my joy and gladness.

〚Psalm 43, with *Gloria* and repetition of Anthem

4 *Priest.*   Our help standeth in the name of the Lord;
Answer. Who hath made heaven and earth.
Priest.   Wilt thou not turn again and quicken us;
Answer. That thy people may rejoice in thee?
Priest.   O Lord, shew thy mercy upon us;
Answer. And grant us thy salvation.

Priest. O Lord, hear our prayer;
Answer. And let our cry come unto thee.
Priest. The Lord be with you;
Answer. And with thy spirit.
Priest. Let us pray.

Then shall the Priest proceed with the celebration of the Holy Communion.

5   AN ALTERNATIVE ORDER FOR THE
       ADMINISTRATION OF THE LORD'S SUPPER
                        OR
                HOLY COMMUNION

The Priest standing at God's Board shall say the Lord's Prayer with the Collect following, the people kneeling.

6   THE INTRODUCTION

Our Father, which art . . . ⟦CF 1⟧ . . . evil. Amen.
                The Collect
Almighty God, unto whom . . . ⟦CF 2⟧ . . . our Lord. *Amen.*

Then shall the Priest, turning to the people, rehearse distinctly all the TEN COMMANDMENTS; and the people, still kneeling, shall after every commandment ask God mercy for their transgression of every duty therein (either according to the letter or according to the spiritual import thereof) for the time past, and grace to keep the same for the time to come, as followeth.

Priest. God spake these words and said: . . . ⟦CF 3⟧ . . . we beseech thee.

⟦With the following omissions: (2) 'For I the Lord . . . commandments', (3) 'for the Lord . . . vain', (4) 'In it thou . . . hallowed it', (5) 'that thy days . . . thee', (9) 'against thy neighbour', (10) 'thy neighbour's house . . . is his'⟧

7 *The Ten Commandments may be omitted, provided that they be rehearsed at least once on a Sunday in each month: and when they are so omitted, then shall be said in place thereof our Lord's Summary of the Law.*

Priest. Our Lord Jesus Christ said: Hear O Israel, The Lord our God is one Lord; and thou shalt love the Lord thy God with all thy heart, and with all thy soul, and with all thy mind, and with all thy strength. This is the first commandment. And the second is

like, namely this: Thou shalt love thy neighbour as thyself. There is none other commandment greater than these. On these two commandments hang all the Law and the Prophets.
Answer. Lord, have mercy upon us, and incline our hearts to keep this law.

8 *Or else the following may be sung or said.*

Lord, have mercy.		Kyrie, eleison.
Christ, have mercy.	or,	Christe, eleison.
Lord, have mercy.		Kyrie, eleison.

The Ten Commandments or else the Summary shall be said on Sundays. At other times, instead thereof, the following may be sung or said:

Lord, have mercy.		Kyrie, eleison.
Christ, have mercy.	or,	Christe, eleison.
Lord, have mercy.		Kyrie, eleison.

9 *Then the Priest standing as before, shall say,*

> The Lord be with you;

Answer. And with thy spirit.
> Let us pray.

And turning to the Holy Table he shall say the Collect of the Day. Other Collects contained in this Book or authorized by the Bishop may follow.

10   THE MINISTRY OF THE WORD

Immediately thereafter he that readeth the Epistle shall say, The Epistle [*or* The Lesson] is written in the —— chapter of —— beginning at the —— verse. *And the reading ended, he shall say,* Here endeth the Epistle [*or* the Lesson].

11 *Then the Deacon or Priest that readeth the Gospel (the people all standing up) shall say,* The Holy Gospel is written in the —— chapter of the Gospel according to Saint ——, beginning at the —— verse.

Answer. Glory be to thee, O Lord.

And the Gospel shall be read.

He that readeth the Epistle or the Gospel shall so stand and turn himself as he may best be heard of the people.

The Gospel ended, there may be said, Praise be to thee, O Christ.

Proposed Liturgy of 1928

12 *Then shall be sung or said the Creed following, the people still standing as before: except that at the discretion of the Minister it may be omitted on any day not being a Sunday or a Holy-day.*

I believe in one God . . . ⟦CF 4⟧ . . . to come. Amen.

⟦But reading 'The Lord, The giver' and 'One Holy Catholick'⟧

13 *Then the Curate shall declare unto the people what Holy-days or Fasting Days are in the week following to be observed. And then also, if occasion be, shall notice be given of the Holy Communion, or of other Services; Banns of matrimony may be published, and Briefs, Citations, and Excommunications shall be read, and Bidding of Prayers may be made. And nothing shall be proclaimed or published in the church during the time of Service, but by the Minister: nor by him any thing but what is prescribed in the rules of this Book, or enjoined by the King, or enjoined or permitted by the Bishop.*

14 *Then may follow the Sermon, or one of the Homilies already set forth, or hereafter to be set forth, by authority.*

When the Minister giveth warning for the celebration of the Holy Communion, he may read to the people, at such times as he shall think convenient, one of the two Exhortations placed at the end of this Order.

15   THE OFFERTORY

Then shall the Priest, standing at the Lord's Table, begin the Offertory, saying one or more of these Sentences following, as he thinketh most convenient in his discretion, or the Priests and Clerks shall sing the same.

⟦For Offertory Sentences, see Appendix B⟧

While these Sentences are said or sung, the Deacons, Churchwardens, or other fit persons appointed for that purpose, shall receive the alms for the poor, or other devotions of the people, and reverently bring them to the Priest, who shall humbly present and place them upon the Holy Table in a decent bason to be provided for that purpose.

And when there is a Communion, the Priest shall place upon the Holy Table so much Bread and Wine, as he shall think sufficient.

It is an ancient tradition of the Church to mingle a little water with the wine.

The Priest may here bid special prayers and thanksgivings.

Then he shall begin the Intercession.

16 THE INTERCESSION

Let us pray for the whole state of Christ's Church.

Almighty and everliving God, who by thy holy Apostle hast taught us to make prayers, and supplications, and to give thanks, for all men: We humbly beseech thee most mercifully [*to accept our alms and oblations, and] to receive these our prayers, which we offer unto thy Divine Majesty; beseeching thee to inspire continually the universal Church with the spirit of truth, unity, and concord: And grant, that all they that do confess thy holy name may agree in the truth of thy holy Word, and live in unity, and godly love.

* If there be no alms or oblations, then shall the words [of accepting our alms and oblations] be left out unsaid.

We beseech thee also to lead all nations in the way of righteousness and peace; and so to direct all kings and rulers, that under them thy people may be godly and quietly governed. And grant unto thy servant GEORGE our King, and to all that are put in authority under him, that they may truly and impartially minister justice, to the punishment of wickedness and vice, and to the maintenance of thy true religion, and virtue.

Give grace, O heavenly Father, to all Bishops, Priests, and Deacons, especially to thy servant N. our bishop, that they may both by their life and doctrine set forth thy true and living Word and rightly and duly administer thy Holy Sacraments.

Guide and prosper, we pray thee, those who are labouring for the spread of thy Gospel among the nations, and enlighten with thy Spirit all places of education and learning; that the whole world may be filled with the knowledge of thy truth.

And to all thy people give thy heavenly grace; and specially to this congregation here present; that, with meek heart and due reverence, they may hear, and receive thy holy Word; truly serving thee in holiness and righteousness all the days of their life.

And we most humbly beseech thee of thy goodness, O Lord, to comfort and succour all them, who in this transitory life are in trouble, sorrow, need, sickness, or any other adversity.

And we commend to thy gracious keeping, O Lord, all thy servants departed this life in thy faith and fear, beseeching thee to grant them everlasting light and peace.

And here we give thee most high praise and hearty thanks for all thy Saints, who have been the chosen vessels of thy grace, and lights of the world in their several generations; and we pray, that rejoicing in their fellowship, and following their good examples, we may be partakers with them of thy heavenly kingdom.

Grant this, O Father, for Jesus Christ's sake, our only Mediator and Advocate; who liveth and reigneth with thee in the unity of the Holy Ghost, one God, world without end. *Amen.*

17   THE PREPARATION

At the time of the celebration of the Holy Communion, the communicants being conveniently placed for the receiving of the Holy Sacrament, the Priest may say this Exhortation. And if this Exhortation be not read at the time of the celebration of the Holy Communion, it shall nevertheless be read to the people by the Curate at such times as he think fit, and at the least on either the fourth or fifth Sunday in Lent.

Dearly beloved in the Lord . . . ⟦CF 5⟧ . . . days of our life.

⟦Divided into five paragraphs and omitting 'we eat and drink . . . kinds of death'⟧

18 *Then shall the Minister say to them that come to receive the Holy Communion.*

Ye that do truly . . . ⟦CF 6⟧ . . . your knees.

19 *Then shall this general Confession be begun, in the name of all those that are minded to receive the Holy Communion, by the Priest or one of the Ministers; both he and all the people kneeling humbly upon their knees, and saying,*

Almighty God, Father . . . ⟦CF 7⟧ . . . our Lord. Amen.

20 *Then shall the Priest (or the Bishop, being present) stand up, and turning himself to the people, pronounce this Absolution.*

Almighty God, our heavenly . . . ⟦CF 8⟧ . . . our Lord. *Amen.*

21 *The foregoing form of Invitation, Confession, and Absolution shall be said on Sundays: but otherwise the following forms may be said at the discretion of the Priest.*

Draw near with faith, and take this Holy Sacrament to your comfort; and make your humble confession to Almighty God, meekly kneeling upon your knees.

22 *Then shall be said by the Minister and people together, kneeling;*

We confess to God Almighty, the Father, the Son, and the Holy

Ghost, that we have sinned in thought, word, and deed, through our own grievous fault. Wherefore we pray God to have mercy upon us.

23 *And the Priest (or the Bishop, being present) standing up and turning himself to the people shall say:*

Almighty God have mercy upon you, forgive you all your sins, and deliver you from all evil, confirm and strengthen you in all goodness, and bring you to life everlasting; through Jesus Christ our Lord. Amen.

24 *Then shall the Priest say,*

Hear what comfortable . . . ⟦CF 9⟧ . . . our sins.

⟦But reading 'Christ Jesus' in 1 Tim. 1. 15⟧

25 *Then shall the Priest, kneeling down at the Lord's Table, say in the name of all them that shall receive the Holy Communion,*

Let us pray.

We do not presume . . . ⟦CF 10⟧ . . . in us. Amen.

When the Priest, standing before the Holy Table, hath so ordered the Bread and Wine, that he may with the more readiness and decency break the Bread before the people, and take the Cup into his hands, he shall begin the Consecration, as followeth.

26 THE CONSECRATION

Turning himself to the people he shall say,

 The Lord be with you;
Answer. And with thy spirit.

Priest. Lift up your hearts;
Answer. We lift them up unto the Lord.

Priest. Let us give thanks unto our Lord God;
Answer. It is meet and right so to do.

Then shall the Priest turn to the Lord's Table, and say,

It is very meet, right, and our bounden duty, that we should at all times, and in all places, give thanks unto thee, O Lord, Holy Father, Almighty, Everlasting God.

Here shall follow the Proper Preface,[1] *according to the time, if there be any specially appointed, or else immediately shall follow,*

[1] ⟦For Proper Prefaces, see Appendix A.⟧

Proposed Liturgy of 1928

Therefore with angels and archangels and with all the company of heaven, we laud and magnify thy glorious name; evermore praising thee, and saying,

Holy, holy, holy, Lord God of hosts, heaven and earth are full of thy glory. Glory be to thee, O Lord most High. Amen.

27 *Then shall the Priest continue thus.*

All glory be to thee, Almighty God, our heavenly Father, for that thou of thy tender mercy didst give thine only Son Jesus Christ to suffer death upon the Cross for our redemption; who made there (by his one oblation of himself once offered) a full, perfect, and sufficient sacrifice, oblation, and satisfaction for the sins of the whole world; and did institute, and in his Holy Gospel command us to continue, a perpetual memory of that his precious death until his coming again;

28 Who, in the same night that he was betrayed, ^atook Bread; and when he had given thanks, ^bhe brake it, and gave it to his disciples, saying, Take, eat, ^cthis is my Body which is given for you; Do this in remembrance of me. Likewise after supper he ^dtook the Cup; and when he had given thanks, he gave it to them, saying, Drink ye all of this; for this ^eis my Blood of the New Covenant, which is shed for you and for many for the remission of sins; Do this, as oft as ye shall drink it, in remembrance of me.

a Here the Priest is to take the Paten into his hands:
b And here to break the Bread:
c And here to lay his hand upon all the Bread.
d Here he is to take the Cup into his hand:
e And here to lay his hand upon every vessel (be it Chalice or Flagon) in which there is any Wine to be consecrated.

29 Wherefore, O Lord and heavenly Father, we thy humble servants, having in remembrance the precious death and passion of thy dear Son, his mighty resurrection and glorious ascension, according to his holy institution, do celebrate, and set forth before thy Divine Majesty with these thy holy gifts, the memorial which he hath willed us to make, rendering unto thee most hearty thanks for the innumerable benefits which he hath procured unto us.

30 Hear us, O merciful Father, we most humbly beseech thee, and with thy Holy and Life-giving Spirit vouchsafe to bless and sanctify both us and these thy gifts of Bread and Wine, that they may be unto us the Body and Blood of thy Son, our Saviour, Jesus Christ, to the end that we, receiving the same, may be strengthened and refreshed both in body and soul.

31   And we entirely desire thy fatherly goodness mercifully to accept this our sacrifice of praise and thanksgiving; most humbly beseeching thee to grant, that by the merits and death of thy Son Jesus Christ, and through faith in his blood, we and all thy whole Church may obtain remission of our sins, and all other benefits of his passion.

32   And here we offer and present unto thee, O Lord, ourselves, our souls and bodies, to be a reasonable, holy, and living sacrifice unto thee: humbly beseeching thee, that all we, who are partakers of this Holy Communion, may be fulfilled with thy grace and heavenly benediction.

33   And although we be unworthy, through our manifold sins, to offer unto thee any sacrifice, yet we beseech thee to accept this our bounden duty and service; not weighing our merits, but pardoning our offences;

34   Through Jesus Christ our Lord, by whom, and with whom, in the unity of the Holy Ghost, all honour and glory be unto thee, O Father Almighty, world without end.

And all the people shall answer Amen.

35 *Here shall the people join with the Priest in the Lord's Prayer, the Priest first saying,*

As our Saviour Christ hath commanded and taught us, we are bold to say,
Our Father . . . [[CF 1]] . . . and ever. Amen.

36 *Then may the priest say:*

   The peace of God be alway with you;
Answer. And with thy spirit.

37   THE COMMUNION OF THE PRIEST
                    AND PEOPLE

Then shall the Priest first receive the Communion in both kinds himself, and then proceed to deliver the same to the Bishops, Priests, and Deacons, in like manner, (if any be present,) and after that to the people also in order, into their hands, all meekly kneeling. And, when he delivereth the Bread to any one, he shall say,

The Body . . . [[CF 11]] . . . thankful.

38 *When occasion requires, the Minister may, instead of saying all the above Words of Administration to each communicant, say first in an*

audible voice to the whole number of them that come to receive the Holy Communion,

Draw near and receive the Body of our Lord Jesus Christ which was given for you, and his Blood which was shed for you. Take this in remembrance that Christ died for you, and feed on him in your hearts by faith with thanksgiving.

And then in delivering the Bread to each communicant he shall say, either, The Body of our Lord Jesus Christ, which was given for thee, preserve thy body and soul unto everlasting life, *or,* Take and eat this in remembrance that Christ died for thee, and feed on him in thy heart by faith with thanksgiving. *And in delivering the Cup to each communicant he shall say, either,* The Blood of our Lord Jesus Christ, which was shed for thee, preserve thy body and soul unto everlasting life, *or,* Drink this in remembrance that Christ's Blood was shed for thee, and be thankful.

Or else, when occasion requires, the Minister may say the whole form of words once to each row of communicants, or to a convenient number within each row, instead of saying them to each communicant severally.

When all have communicated, the Priest shall return to the Lord's Table, and reverently place upon it what remaineth of the consecrated Elements, covering the same with a fair linen cloth.

39 THE THANKSGIVING

Then shall the Priest give thanks to God in the name of all them that have communicated, turning him first to the people, and saying,

Having now by faith received the precious Body and Blood of Christ, let us give thanks unto our Lord God.

Almighty and everliving . . . ⟦CF 12⟧ . . . without end. *Amen.*

40 *Then shall the Priest with the people say or sing,*

Glory be to God . . . ⟦CF 13⟧ . . . the Father. Amen.

At the discretion of the Minister, this Hymn may be omitted on any day not being a Sunday or a Holy-day.

41 *Then the Priest (or the Bishop if he be present), turning to the people, shall let them depart with this Blessing.*

The peace . . . ⟦CF 14⟧ . . . always. *Amen.*

42 *If any of the consecrated Bread and Wine remain, apart from that which may be reserved for the Communion of the sick, as is provided in the Alternative Order for the Communion of the Sick, it shall not be carried out of the church; but the Priest, and such other of the communicants as he shall call unto him, shall, immediately after the Blessing, reverently eat and drink the same.*

CHAPTER VII

THE SOUTH AFRICAN LITURGY

THE South African Prayer Book was first published in its entirety in 1954. But it had been compiled piecemeal over a long period. The Liturgy in its final form, with the eucharistic propers, was published in 1929, 'set forth by authority for use in the Province of South Africa where allowed by the Bishop'. In 1954 the requirement that its use be 'allowed by the Bishop' was done away; but a preface was added in which the forms of the new Prayer Book were described as 'set forth by the Provincial Synod of the Church of the Province of South Africa, as being adaptations, abridgements and additions to the Book of Common Prayer (1662) required by the circumstances of the Province and consistent with the spirit and teaching of that Book'. The South African Liturgy and that of 1662 are alternatives; but they may not be mingled the one with the other.

1 THE ORDER FOR THE ADMINISTRATION OF
THE LORD'S SUPPER OR
HOLY COMMUNION

The Table at the Communion-time shall have a fair white linen cloth upon it. And the Priest, standing at the Table, shall say in a distinct and audible voice, the people devoutly kneeling,

INTRODUCTION

2 Our Father, who art . . . ⟦CF 1⟧ . . . evil. Amen.

The Collect

3 Almighty God, unto whom . . . ⟦CF 2⟧ . . . our Lord. *Amen.*

4 *Then shall the Priest, turning to the people, rehearse distinctly all the* TEN COMMANDMENTS; *and the people still kneeling shall, after every Commandment, ask God mercy for their transgression of every duty therein (either according to the letter or to the spiritual import thereof) for the time past, and grace to keep the same for the time to come, as followeth.*

Minister. God spake . . . ⟦CF 3⟧ . . . hearts, we beseech thee.

⟦Omit as follows: (2) 'For I the Lord . . . commandments', (3) 'for the Lord . . .

in vain', (4) 'In it thou shalt ... hallowed it', (5) 'that thy days ... giveth thee', (9) 'against thy neighbour', (10) 'thy neighbour's house ... that is his']]

5 *Provided that the* Ten Commandments *be rehearsed at least once on each Lord's Day in Advent and Lent, they may be omitted at other times. When they are so omitted, then shall follow:*

Jesus said: Thou shalt love the Lord thy God with all thy heart, and with all thy soul, and with all thy mind: This is the first and great commandment. And the second is like unto it, Thou shalt love thy neighbour as thyself. On these two commandments hang all the law and the prophets.

People. Lord, have mercy upon us, and write these thy laws in our hearts, we beseech thee.

6 *After this summary, or instead of it, may be said:*

Lord, have mercy upon us.
   Christ, have mercy upon us.
Lord, have mercy upon us.

7 *Then shall be said:*

Priest. The Lord be with you;
People. And with thy spirit.

Let us pray.

Then shall be said the Collect of the Day. Other Collects, as appointed or authorised, may follow, and the last of these shall have the full ending.

8 INSTRUCTION

And immediately after the Collect the Priest shall read the Epistle, saying, The Epistle [*or,* The Lesson] is written in the —— Chapter of —— beginning at the —— Verse. *Which ended, he shall say,* Here endeth the Epistle [*or,* the Lesson]. *Then shall he read the Gospel (the people all standing up), saying,* The Holy Gospel is written in the —— Chapter of —— beginning at the —— Verse.

People. Glory be to thee, O Lord.

And after the Gospel the people shall say, Thanks be to thee, O Lord.

And he that readeth the Epistle or Gospel shall so turn to the people that all may hear.

9 *If unbaptised or penitents be present the Sermon may here follow, after which they shall be dismissed with prayer and blessing. And then shall be said the Creed following, the people all standing.*

The South African Liturgy

¹I believe in one God . . . 〚CF 4〛 . . . to come. Amen.

〚But reading 'The Lord, the Giver of Life' and 'One, Holy, Catholick'〛

10 *Then the Curate shall declare unto the people what Feasts, or Fasting-days, are in the Week following to be observed. And then also (if occasion be) shall notice be given of the Communion, and Banns of Matrimony published; and Briefs, Citations and Excommunications read. And nothing shall be proclaimed or published in the Church, during the time of Divine Service, but by the Minister: nor by him any thing, but what is prescribed in the Rules of this Book, or enjoined by the Bishop.*

11 *Then may follow the Sermon, unless it shall have been already preached before the Creed.*

12 OFFERTORY

Then shall the Priest return to the Lord's Table, and begin the Offertory, saying one or more of these Sentences following, as he thinketh most convenient in his discretion.

〚For Offertory Sentences, see Appendix B〛

13 *Whilst these Sentences are in reading, the Deacons, Churchwardens, or other fit person appointed for that purpose, shall receive the Alms and other offerings of the people, in a decent bason to be provided by the Parish for that purpose; and reverently bring it to the Priest, who shall humbly present and place it upon the holy Table.*

And the Priest shall place upon the Table so much Bread and Wine, as he shall think sufficient, saying:

Bless, O Lord, we beseech thee, these thy gifts and sanctify them unto this holy use, that by them we may be fed unto everlasting life of soul and body; through Jesus Christ our Lord. Amen.

14 *When Intercession or Thanksgiving is to be offered for any special object, it shall be provided for by a Form of Bidding either here or before the Offertory.*

15 *After which done, the Priest shall say,*

Let us pray for the whole state of Christ's Church.

Almighty and everliving God, who by thy holy Apostle hast

---

¹ 〚May be omitted on 'working days, not being Feasts' by permission of the Bishop.〛

taught us to make prayers, and supplications, and to give thanks, for all men: We humbly beseech thee most mercifully to accept our [alms and] oblations and to receive these our prayers, which we offer unto thy Divine Majesty; beseeching thee to inspire continually the universal Church with the spirit of truth, unity, and concord: And grant, that all they that do confess thy holy Name may agree in the truth of thy holy Word, and live in unity, and godly love.

We beseech thee also to lead all nations into the way of righteousness and peace, and to direct all Kings, Presidents and Rulers that under them the world may be godly and quietly governed. And grant unto thy Servant *ELIZABETH* our Queen, her ministers and parliaments, and all that are set in authority throughout her Dominions, that they may truly and impartially minister justice to the removing of wickedness and vice, and to the maintenance of order and right living.

Give grace, O heavenly Father, to all Bishops, Priests and Deacons, and especially to thy Servant *N.* our Bishop, that they may both by their life and doctrine set forth thy true and living Word, and rightly and duly administer thy holy Sacraments: And to all thy people give thy heavenly grace; and specially to this congregation here present; that, with meek heart and due reverence, they may hear, and receive thy holy Word; truly serving thee in holiness and righteousness all the days of their life. [Guide and prosper, we pray thee, all those who are labouring for the spread of thy Gospel among the nations.]

[And to all Schools and Universities grant the light of thy Spirit, that the world may be filled with the knowledge of thy Truth.] [And grant to all men in their several callings that they may seek the common welfare, and promote good will and brotherhood on earth.]

And we most humbly beseech thee of thy goodness, O Lord, to comfort and succour all them, who in this transitory life are in trouble, sorrow, need, sickness, or any other adversity.

And we commend to thy gracious keeping, O Lord, all thy servants departed this life in thy faith and fear, beseeching thee to grant them mercy, light and peace both now and at the day of resurrection.

And here we do give unto thee, O Lord, most high praise and hearty thanks for the wonderful grace and virtue declared in all

The South African Liturgy

thy Saints, and chiefly in the Blessed Virgin Mary, Mother of thy Son Jesus Christ our Lord and God, and in the holy Patriarchs, Prophets, Apostles and Martyrs; beseeching thee to give us grace that we, rejoicing in the Communion of the Saints, and following the good examples of those who have served thee here, may be partakers with them of thy heavenly kingdom:

    Grant this, O Father, for Jesus Christ's sake, our only Mediator and Advocate. *Amen.*

16   PREPARATION

Then shall the Priest say to them that come to receive the Holy Communion,

Ye that do truly ... [[CF 6]] ... your knees.

17

[a]

Then shall this general Confession be made, in the name of all those that are minded to receive the Holy Communion, by one of the Ministers; both he and all the people kneeling humbly upon their knees, and saying,

Almighty God, Father of our Lord ... [[CF 7]] ... our Lord. Amen.

[b]

On working days, not being Feasts, with the permission of the Bishop, the following may be used:

We confess to God Almighty, the Father, the Son, and the Holy Ghost, that we have sinned in thought, word, and deed through our own grievous fault. Wherefore we pray God to have mercy upon us.

18

[a]

Then shall the Priest (or the Bishop, being present,) stand up, and turning himself to the people, pronounce this Absolution.

Almighty God, our heavenly Father ... [[CF 8]] ... our Lord. Amen.

[b]

THE ABSOLUTION

Almighty God have mercy upon you; forgive you all your sins and deliver you from all evil; confirm and strengthen you in all goodness; and bring you to everlasting life. *Amen.*

19 *Then shall the Priest say,*

Hear what comfortable ... [[CF 9]] ... our sins.

[[But reading 'Christ Jesus' in 1 Tim. 1. 15]]

20 CONSECRATION

When the Priest, standing before the Table, hath so ordered the Bread and Wine, that he may with the more readiness and decency break the Bread before the people, and take the Cup into his hands, he shall say the Prayer of Consecration, as followeth:

Priest. The Lord be with you;
℟. And with thy spirit.
℣. Lift up your hearts;
℟. We lift them up unto the Lord.
℣. Let us give thanks unto our Lord God;
℟. It is meet and right so to do.

Then shall the Priest turn to the Lord's Table, and say,
It is very meet, right, and our bounden duty, that we should at all times, and in all places, give thanks unto thee, O Lord, Holy Father, Almighty, Everlasting God.

Here shall follow the Proper Preface[1] according to the time, if there be any specially appointed.

On other days shall follow immediately:

Therefore with Angels and Archangels and with all the company of heaven, we laud and magnify thy glorious Name; evermore praising thee, and saying:
Holy, holy, holy, Lord God of hosts, heaven and earth are full of thy glory: Glory be to thee, O Lord most High. Amen.

21 All Glory and Thanksgiving be to thee, Almighty God our heavenly Father, for that thou of thy tender mercy didst give thine only Son Jesus Christ to take our nature upon him, and to suffer death upon the Cross for our redemption; who (by his one oblation of himself once offered) made a full, perfect, and sufficient sacrifice, oblation, and satisfaction, for the sins of the whole world; and did institute, and in his holy Gospel command us to continue, a perpetual memory of that his precious death, until his coming again.

22   Hear us, O merciful Father, we most humbly beseech thee; and grant that we, receiving these thy creatures of bread and wine, according to thy Son our Saviour Jesus Christ's holy institution, in remembrance of his death and passion, may be partakers of his

[1] [[For Proper Prefaces, see Appendix A.]]

The South African Liturgy

most blessed Body and Blood: who, in the same night that he was betrayed, ᵃtook bread; and, when he had given thanks, ᵇhe brake it, and gave it to his disciples, saying, Take, eat, ᶜthis is my Body which is given for you: Do this in remembrance of me. Likewise after supper he ᵈtook the Cup; and, when he had given thanks, he gave it to them, saying, Drink ye all of this; for this ᵉis my Blood of the New Testament, which is shed for you and for many for the remission of sins: Do this, as oft as ye shall drink it, in remembrance of me.

^a *Here the Priest is to take the Paten into his hands;*

^b *And here to break the Bread;*

^c *And here to lay his hand upon all the Bread;*

^d *Here he is to take the Cup into his hand;*

^e *And here to lay his hand upon every vessel (be it Chalice or Flagon) in which there is any Wine to be consecrated.*

23 Wherefore, O Lord and heavenly Father, according to the institution of thy dearly beloved Son, our Saviour Jesus Christ, we thy humble servants, having in remembrance his blessed passion and precious death, his mighty resurrection and glorious ascension, do render unto thee most hearty thanks for the innumerable benefits procured unto us by the same; and, looking for his coming again with power and great glory, we offer here unto thy divine majesty this holy Bread of eternal life and this Cup of everlasting salvation; and we humbly beseech thee to pour thy Holy Spirit upon us and upon these thy gifts, that all we who are partakers of this holy Communion may worthily receive the most precious Body and Blood of thy Son, and be fulfilled with thy grace and heavenly benediction.

24 And we entirely desire thy fatherly goodness mercifully to accept this our sacrifice of praise and thanksgiving; most humbly beseeching thee to grant, that by the merits and death of thy Son Jesus Christ, and through faith in his blood, we and all thy whole Church may obtain remission of our sins, and all other benefits of his passion.

25 And here we offer and present unto thee, O Lord, ourselves, our souls and bodies, to be a reasonable, holy, and living sacrifice unto thee.

26 And although we be unworthy, through our manifold sins, to offer unto thee any sacrifice, yet we beseech thee to accept this our bounden duty and service; not weighing our merits, but pardoning our offences, through Jesus Christ our Lord; by whom, and with whom, in the unity of the Holy Ghost, all honour and glory be unto thee, O Father Almighty, world without end.

Here let all the people say, Amen.

27 As our Saviour Jesus Christ hath commanded and taught us, we are bold to say:

Then shall the Priest and People say together the Lord's Prayer.

Our Father who art . . . ⟦CF 1⟧ . . . ever. Amen.

28   COMMUNION

Then shall silence be kept for a space, after which shall follow this prayer, said by the Priest, kneeling, in the name of all them that shall receive the Communion,

We do not presume . . . ⟦CF 10⟧ . . . in us. Amen.

29 *Then shall the Priest break the Bread, and first receive the Communion in both kinds himself, and then proceed to deliver the same to the Bishops, Priests and Deacons, in like manner, (if any be present,) and after that to the people also in order, into their hands, all meekly kneeling. And, when he delivereth the Bread to any one, he shall say,*

The Body of our Lord . . . ⟦CF 11⟧ . . . be thankful.

Or else the Priest shall, before he delivereth the Bread to the people, say to the whole Congregation,

Draw near and receive the Body and Blood of our Lord Jesus Christ, which were given for you, and feed on him in your hearts by faith with thanksgiving.

And if he have so said, when he delivereth the Bread to any one, he shall say,

The Body of our Lord Jesus Christ preserve thy body and soul unto everlasting life.

And the Minister that delivereth the Cup to any one shall say,

The Blood of our Lord Jesus Christ preserve thy body and soul unto everlasting life.

When all have communicated, the Priest shall return to the Lord's Table, and reverently place upon it what remaineth of the consecrated Elements, covering the same with a fair linen cloth; or else, at his discretion, reverently consume the same.

THANKSGIVING

30 *Then shall he say this Thanksgiving for Communion.*
Priest. O give thanks unto the Lord, for he is gracious;
℞. And his mercy endureth for ever.
Almighty and everliving God... ⟦CF 12⟧... without end. *Amen.*

31 *Then shall be said,*
¹Glory be to God... ⟦CF 13⟧... the Father. Amen.

32 *Then the Priest (or the Bishop, if he be present) shall let them depart with this Blessing.*
The peace of God... ⟦CF 14⟧... always. *Amen.*

33 *And if any remain of the Bread and Wine which was consecrated, it shall not be carried out of the Church, but the Priest and such other of the Communicants as he shall then call unto him shall, immediately after the Blessing, reverently eat and drink the same: except so far as is otherwise provided in the Order for the Communion of the Sick.*

¹ ⟦May be omitted on 'working days, not being Feasts' with permission of the Bishop.⟧

NOTE

THE MADAGASCAR LITURGY

THE Madagascar Liturgy is printed only in Malagasy and has not, at least in its present form, been translated into English at all. It is believed to derive from the South African Liturgy, but to depart less radically from the English Liturgy of 1662.

CHAPTER VIII

THE CEYLON LITURGY

THE Ceylon Liturgy has not previously been published in England except in *Anglican Liturgies* (see preface to this book). It was first printed as a pamphlet in Colombo in 1933, and a second edition appeared in 1935. The text printed below has been taken from *Anglican Liturgies*.

The Ceylon Liturgy was at first sanctioned by the Episcopal Synod of the diocese of Colombo for limited experimental use. In 1938 the Synod of the Church of India, Burma, and Ceylon authorized it for general use in the diocese of Colombo. It has been widely used, and has a Sinhalese version and musical setting. Moreover, it remains in use, and has not been superseded by the 1960 liturgy of C.I.P.B.C.

1   A DEVOTION

which may be said by the Priest with the ministers present either in the sacristy or at the foot of the Altar immediately before the Introduction.

When it is said at the foot of the Altar, the Priest may say it either with the ministers present or with the ministers and with the people.

Priest. In the name of the Father, and of the Son, and of the Holy Ghost. Amen.

2 *Anthem.* I will go unto the altar of God: even unto the God of my joy and gladness.

⟦Here follows Psalm 43 with *Gloria Patri*⟧

Anthem. I will go unto the altar of God: even unto the God of my joy and gladness.

3 *Priest.* Our help standeth in the name of the Lord;
Answer. Who hath made heaven and earth.

When this Devotion is said in the sacristy, the Priest may add a suitable prayer here.

The Ceylon Liturgy

AN ORDER FOR THE ADMINISTRATION OF
THE HOLY COMMUNION

THE INTRODUCTION

4 *During the entry of the Priest and his attendants a Psalm or Hymn may be sung.*

When there is an Introit, the Devotion, if it is to be said by the Priest and people, will immediately follow the Introit.

The Priest standing at the foot of the Altar shall say:

5   Let us pray.

Almighty God, unto whom ... [[CF 2]] ... our Lord. *Amen.*

Then shall the following Confession be said by the Priest and people together, all kneeling, the Deacon first saying:

6 Let us make humble confession of our sins to God.

We confess to God Almighty, the Father, the Son, and the Holy Ghost, that we have sinned in thought, word, and deed, through our own grievous fault. Wherefore we pray God to have mercy upon us.

7 Almighty God, have mercy upon us, forgive us all our sins and deliver us from all evil, confirm and strengthen us in all goodness, and bring us to life everlasting; through Jesus Christ our Lord. *Amen.*

8 *And the Priest (or the Bishop being present) standing up and turning to the people shall say:*

May the Almighty and merciful Lord grant unto you pardon and remission of all your sins, time for amendment of life, and the grace and comfort of the Holy Spirit. *Amen.*

9 *The following shall then be sung or said, the Priest standing at the Altar:*

    Lord, have mercy.
       Lord, have mercy.
    Lord, have mercy.
    Christ, have mercy.
       Christ, have mercy.   [[The Greek text may be used]]
    Christ, have mercy.
    Lord, have mercy.
       Lord, have mercy.
    Lord, have mercy.

10 *On Sundays (except in Advent, and on the Sundays from Septuagesima to Palm Sunday inclusive) and other Greater Feasts throughout the year the* Gloria in Excelsis *may be said or sung here.*

When it is omitted in this place, it is to be said or sung before the Blessing on Sundays (except in Advent, and on the Sundays from Septuagesima to Palm Sunday inclusive) and other Greater Feasts throughout the year.

11 *Then shall the Priest say:*

    The Lord be with you.
Answer. And with thy spirit.
Priest.   Let us pray.

Then shall be said the Collect of the Day.

Other Collects, as appointed or authorized, may follow, and the last of these shall have the full ending.

12   THE MINISTRY OF THE WORD

Immediately thereafter he that readeth the Epistle (the people being seated) shall say: The Epistle [*or* The Lesson] is written in the —— chapter of ——, beginning at the —— verse. *And the reading ended, he shall say:* Here endeth the Epistle [*or* the Lesson].

13 *A Psalm or a portion of a Psalm or a Hymn may be sung here.*

14 *Then the Deacon or Priest that readeth the Gospel (the people all standing up) shall say:*

    The Lord be with you.
Answer. And with thy spirit.

Deacon or Priest. The Holy Gospel is written in the —— chapter of the Gospel according to Saint ——, beginning at the —— verse.
Answer. Glory be to thee, O Lord.
The Gospel ended, there may be said:
Praise be to thee, O Christ.

Alleluia *may be added to the responses before and after the Gospel from Easter Day until Trinity Sunday inclusive.*

15 *On Sundays and other Greater Feasts shall then be sung or said the Creed following, the people all standing and the Deacon first saying:*

The Ceylon Liturgy

Let us make profession of our Christian belief.
I believe in one God ... [[CF 4]] ... world to come. Amen.
[[But reading 'The Lord, The Giver of life' and 'One Holy Catholic']]

16 *Notices may be given out here.*

Biddings for special thanksgiving and prayer may be made here by the Deacon. In making the biddings to thanksgiving and prayer, the Deacon may stand on the chancel step facing the people, the people all standing.

17 *A Sermon or Instruction may follow here.*

18   THE OFFERTORY

Then the Priest, turning to the people, shall say:
Beloved, let us love one another: for love is of God.

And turning again to the Altar, the Priest shall begin the Offertory saying one or more of the Sentences following, or the Priest and Clerks shall sing the same.
[[For Offertory Sentences, see Appendix B]]

The Priest shall then place upon the Holy Table so much Bread and Wine mingled with a little pure water, as he shall think sufficient, whilst the alms and other devotions of the people are received.

During this a Psalm or Hymn may be sung.

When the alms and other devotions of the people have been presented before God by the Priest, he shall say the prayer that followeth, first saying:
[[For the alternative see page 91]]

               Let us pray.

19 We humbly beseech thee, O Father, most mercifully to accept these our (alms and) oblations which we offer unto thy Divine Majesty; through Jesus Christ our Lord. Amen.

Then shall the Deacon standing begin the Litany following, which may be sung or said:
Almighty God, who hast taught us to make prayers, supplications, and intercessions for all men; hear us when we pray:
   That it may please thee to inspire continually the universal Church with the spirit of truth, unity, and concord;
     Hear us, we beseech thee.

That it may please thee to grant that all they that do confess thy holy name may agree in the truth of thy holy Word, and live in unity and godly love;
Hear us, we beseech thee.

That it may please thee to lead all nations in the paths of righteousness and peace;
Hear us, we beseech thee.

That it may please thee to direct all kings and rulers, especially thy servant *George*, our King, that under them the world may be godly and quietly governed;
Hear us, we beseech thee.

That it may please thee to give grace to all Bishops, Priests, and Deacons, especially to thy servants *N.*, our Metropolitan, and *N.*, our Bishop, that by their life and doctrine they may set forth thy true and living Word, and rightly and duly administer thy Holy Sacraments;
Hear us, we beseech thee.

That it may please thee to guide and prosper all those who are labouring for the spread of thy Gospel among the nations, and to enlighten with thy Spirit all places of education and learning;
Hear us, we beseech thee.

That it may please thee that through thy heavenly benediction we may be saved from dearth and famine, and may with thankful hearts enjoy the fruits of the earth in their season;
Hear us, we beseech thee.

That it may please thee to give to all thy people thy heavenly grace; and specially to this congregation here present; that, with meek heart and due reverence, they may hear, and receive thy holy Word; truly serving thee in holiness and righteousness all the days of their life;
Hear us, we beseech thee.

That it may please thee of thy goodness, O Lord, to comfort and succour all them, who in this transitory life are in trouble, sorrow, need, sickness, or any other adversity;
Hear us, we beseech thee.

That it may please thee to grant to all thy servants departed this life in thy faith and fear, mercy, everlasting light, and peace;
Hear us, we beseech thee.

That it may please thee to give us grace that we may be partakers of thy heavenly kingdom with all thy Saints, holy Patriarchs, Prophets, Apostles, and Martyrs;
>Hear us, we beseech thee.

The Litany ended, the Priest shall say:

20   Let us pray.

Almighty God, the fountain of all wisdom, who knowest our necessities before we ask, and our ignorance in asking; We beseech thee to have compassion upon our infirmities; and those things, which for our unworthiness we dare not, and for our blindness we cannot ask, vouchsafe to give us, for the worthiness of thy Son Jesus Christ our Lord. Amen.

21   THE CONSECRATION

Then the Priest, turning to the people, shall say:
>The Lord be with you;

Answer. And with thy spirit.
Priest. Lift up your hearts;
Answer. We lift them up unto the Lord.
Priest. Let us give thanks unto our Lord God;
Answer. It is meet and right so to do.

And turning again to the Altar, the Priest shall proceed saying:
It is very meet, right, and our bounden duty, that we should at all times, and in all places, give thanks unto thee, O Lord, Holy Father, Almighty, Everlasting God.

Here shall follow the Proper Preface, according to the time,[1] if there be any specially appointed; or else immediately shall follow:
Therefore with angels and archangels and with all the company of heaven, we laud and magnify thy glorious name; evermore praising thee, and saying,

Holy, holy, holy, Lord God of hosts, heaven and earth are full of thy glory. Glory be to thee, O Lord most High.

Then shall the Priest proceed saying:

22 Holy in truth art thou, Father Almighty, Eternal King, and in thine every gift and work thou dost reveal thy holiness unto men. Holy is thine only-begotten Son, our Saviour Jesus Christ,

---

[1] 〖For Proper Prefaces, see Appendix A.〗

through whom thou didst frame the worlds; and holy is thine ever-blessed Spirit, who searcheth out all things, yea, the deep things of thee, O God.

23 Even as thou thyself art holy, so also didst thou create man in thine own image that he might dwell in holiness before thee; and when he transgressed thy commandments, thou didst not abandon him, but didst chasten him as a merciful Father; thou spakest unto him through the law and by the prophets, and, when the fulness of time was come, thou spakest by thine only-begotten Son, whom thou didst send forth into the world to take our nature upon him, that he might renew thine image within us;

24 Who, suffering death upon the Cross for our redemption, made there (by his one oblation of himself once offered) a full, perfect, and sufficient sacrifice, oblation, and reconciliation, for the sins of the whole world; and did institute, and in his Holy Gospel command us to continue, a perpetual memorial of that his precious death until his coming again.

25 For, in the same night that he was betrayed, he [a]took Bread; and when he had given thanks to thee, O Father Almighty, he blessed it and [b]brake it, and gave it to his disciples, saying, Take, eat, [c]this is my Body which is given for you; Do this in remembrance of me.

[a] Here the Priest is to take the Bread into his hands:
[b] And here to break the Bread:
[c] And here to lay his hand upon all the Bread.

26 Likewise after supper he [d]took the Cup; and when he had given thanks to thee, he blessed it and gave it to them, saying, Drink ye all of this; for [e]this is my Blood of the New Covenant, which is shed for you and for many for the remission of sins; Do this, as oft as ye shall drink it, in remembrance of me.

[d] Here he is to take the Cup into his hand:
[e] And here to lay his hand upon every vessel in which there is any Wine to be consecrated.

27 Wherefore, O heavenly Father, we thy humble servants, having in remembrance the precious death and passion of thy dear Son, his mighty resurrection, his ascension into heaven, and his session in glory, and looking for his coming again; according to his holy institution, do celebrate, and set forth before thy Divine Majesty with these thy gifts, the memorial which he hath commanded us to make, rendering unto thee most hearty thanks for the innumerable benefits which he hath procured unto us.

28 And we beseech thee most merciful Father, to hear us, and to send thy Holy Spirit upon us and upon these thy gifts, that they,

The Ceylon Liturgy

being blessed and hallowed by his life-giving power, may be unto us the Body and Blood of thy most dearly beloved Son, to the end that we, receiving the same, may be sanctified both in body and soul, and preserved unto life everlasting.

29 And we entirely desire thy fatherly goodness mercifully to accept this our sacrifice of praise and thanksgiving; most humbly beseeching thee to grant, that by the merits and death of thy Son Jesus Christ, and through faith in his blood, we and all thy whole Church may obtain remission of our sins, and all other benefits of his passion.

30 And here we offer and present unto thee, O Lord, ourselves, our souls and bodies, to be a reasonable, holy, and living sacrifice unto thee: humbly beseeching thee, that all we, who are partakers of this Holy Communion, may be fulfilled with thy grace and heavenly benediction.

31 And although we be unworthy, through our manifold sins, to offer unto thee any sacrifice, yet we beseech thee to accept this our bounden duty and service; not weighing our merits, but pardoning our offences;

32 Through Jesus Christ our Lord, by whom, and with whom, in the unity of the Holy Ghost, all honour and glory be unto thee, O Father Almighty, world without end. *Amen.*

33 Let us pray.

As our Saviour Christ hath commanded and taught us, we are bold to say:
Our Father, which art . . . [[CF 1]] . . . for ever and ever. Amen.

34 *Then shall the Priest say:*
The peace of the Lord be alway with you.
Answer. And with thy spirit.

35 *Here the Priest and people shall say or sing:*
Hosanna in the highest. Blessed is he that cometh in the name of the Lord: Hosanna in the highest.
Then shall silence be kept for a space.

36 THE COMMUNION

Then shall the Priest, kneeling down at the Lord's Table, say in the name of all them that shall receive the Holy Communion:

The Liturgy in English

Let us pray.

We do not presume . . . [[CF 10]] . . . in us. *Amen.*

37 *Here shall follow this Anthem (which may be said or sung) the Priest standing; immediately after which or during which the Priest shall make his Communion.*

O Lamb of God that takest away the sins of the world,
Have mercy upon us (*or, at Requiems and funerals*, Grant them rest).
   O Lamb of God that takest away the sins of the world,
Have mercy upon us (*or, at Requiems and funerals*, Grant them rest).
   O Lamb of God that takest away the sins of the world,
Grant us thy peace (*or, at Requiems and funerals*, Grant them rest eternal).

38 *The Priest shall receive the Communion in both kinds, saying*[1] *when he partaketh of the consecrated Bread:* THE BODY OF CHRIST, THE BREAD OF LIFE; *and, when he partaketh of the Cup:* THE BLOOD OF CHRIST, THE CHALICE OF LIFE; *and to whomsoever the Communion be administered, these same words shall be used therewith.*

The Priest, after he has himself received the Communion, turning to the people shall say to them that come to receive the Holy Communion:

Draw near with faith, and take this Holy Sacrament to your comfort.

During Communion time Anthems and Hymns may be sung.

And when all have communicated, the Priest shall return to the Altar and shall reverently consume what remaineth of the consecrated Elements, and thereafter he shall cleanse the sacred vessels after the usual manner, and again cover them with a veil.

During this a Psalm or Hymn may be sung.

39   THE THANKSGIVING

Then shall the Priest say:

    The Lord be with you.
Answer. And with thy spirit.

[1] [[The **1662** or **1928** form may be used.]]

The Ceylon Liturgy

Then shall the Priest give thanks to God in the name of all them that have communicated, the Deacon first saying:

Let us give thanks unto God who hath refreshed us with food from his heavenly Table.
Almighty and everliving God . . . ⟦CF 12⟧ . . . world without end. Amen.

Other prayers may be said here.

40 *Here shall be said or sung the* Gloria in Excelsis *on Sundays (except in Advent and on the Sundays from Septuagesima to Palm Sunday inclusive) and other Greater Feasts throughout the year, if it has not already been said or sung in the Introduction.*

If the Gloria in Excelsis *has already been said or sung, a Psalm or Hymn may be sung instead.*

Glory be to God on high . . . ⟦CF 13⟧ . . . the Father. Amen.
⟦For alternative form, see no. 44 below⟧

41 *Then the Priest (or the Bishop if he be present) shall let them depart with this Blessing.*

The peace of God, which passeth all understanding, keep your hearts and minds in the knowledge and love of God, and of his Son Jesus Christ our Lord: and the blessing of God Almighty, the Father, the Son, and the Holy Ghost, be amongst you and remain with you always. *Amen.*

42 *And, the people being thus dismissed, the Priest and those with him in the sanctuary shall forthwith return to the sacristy.*

⟦ALTERNATIVE FORMS⟧

43 *In place of the Prayer and the Litany on page* ⟦85⟧, *the following Offertory Prayer may be used, the Priest first saying:*

Let us pray.

Almighty and everliving God, who by thy holy Apostle hast taught us to make prayers, and supplications, and to give thanks, for all men: We humbly beseech thee most mercifully to accept our [alms and] oblations, and to receive these our prayers, which we offer unto thy Divine Majesty; beseeching thee to inspire continually the universal Church with the spirit of truth, unity, and concord. And grant, that all they that do confess thy holy name may agree in the truth of thy holy Word, and live in unity, and godly love.

We beseech thee also to lead all nations in the paths of righteousness and peace; and so to direct all kings and rulers, especially thy servant *George*, our King, that under them the world may be godly and quietly governed.

Give grace, O heavenly Father, to all Bishops, Priests, and Deacons, especially to thy servants *N.*, our Metropolitan, and *N.*, our Bishop, that by their life and doctrine they may set forth thy true and living Word, and rightly and duly administer thy holy Sacraments.

Guide and prosper, we pray thee, all those who are labouring for the spread of thy Gospel among the nations, and enlighten with thy Spirit all places of education and learning; that the whole world may be filled with the knowledge of thy truth.

We entreat thee also, O Lord, that through thy heavenly benediction we may be saved from dearth and famine, and may with thankful hearts enjoy the fruits of the earth in their season.

And to all thy people give thy heavenly grace; and specially to this congregation here present; that, with meek heart and due reverence, they may hear, and receive thy holy Word; truly serving thee in holiness and righteousness all the days of their life.

And we most humbly beseech thee of thy goodness, O Lord, to comfort and succour all them, who in this transitory life are in trouble, sorrow, need, sickness, or any other adversity.

We commend to thy fatherly goodness, O Lord, all thy servants departed this life in thy faith and fear, [1]beseeching thee to grant them mercy, everlasting light, and peace.

And here we give thee most high praise and hearty thanks for all thy Saints, who have been the chosen vessels of thy grace, and lights of the world in their several generations; and we pray, that rejoicing in their fellowship, and following their good examples, we may be partakers with them of thy heavenly kingdom.

Grant this, O Father, for Jesus Christ's sake, our Advocate and only Mediator; who liveth and reigneth with thee in the unity of the Holy Ghost, ever one God, world without end. *Amen.*

44 *The* Gloria in Excelsis *may be said or sung in the following form:*
Glory be to God on high, and in earth peace, good will towards

---

[1] ⟦The words 'beseeching ... and peace' may be omitted.⟧

men. We praise thee, we bless thee, we worship thee, we glorify thee; We give thanks to thee for thy great glory, O Lord God, heavenly King, God the Father Almighty, and to thee, O God, the only-begotten Son Jesu Christ, and to thee, O God, the Holy Ghost.

O Lord, the only-begotten Son Jesu Christ; O Lord God, Lamb of God, Son of the Father, that takest away the sins of the world, have mercy upon us. Thou that takest away the sins of the world, receive our prayer. Thou that sittest on the right hand of God the Father, have mercy upon us.

For thou only art holy, thou only art the Lord; thou only, O Christ, art most high in the glory of God the Father. Amen.

CHAPTER IX

THE BOMBAY LITURGY

THIS liturgy was first printed in 1920, in *The Eucharist in India, A Plea for a Distinctive Liturgy for the Indian Church*, by J. C. Winslow, E. C. Ratcliff, and others, with the approval of the Bishop of Bombay (E. J. Palmer). Slightly modified, the liturgy was authorized for experimental use in the diocese of Bombay in 1923, and in the whole province in 1933. A revised and abridged edition appeared in 1943; a further revision of 1948 was incorporated in *A Proposed Prayer Book* (1951) as 'A Liturgy for India'. It appears under the same title in *The Supplement to the Book of Common Prayer* (1961). The notes indicate differences of the edition of 1923 from that of 1948–61. It should be noted that this liturgy has its own table of lessons and gradual psalms.

1   THE PRAYERS BEFORE THE SERVICE

Before the service there shall be set in readiness upon the altar so much bread upon the Paten, and so much wine, mixed with a little pure water, in the Chalice, as shall be sufficient; and the Priest shall bless them, saying the prayer following:

there shall be] the Deacon shall · upon the altar] OM

2 O Lord our God, who didst send forth thy heavenly Bread, the food of the whole world, even Jesus Christ thine only Son, to save us and to redeem us, to bless us and to sanctify us: Vouchsafe now to ✠ bless this our oblation, and to accept it on thine altar in Heaven. Do thou remember, O Lover of Man, both them that offer it and them for whom it is offered; and do thou preserve us thy servants uncondemned in the ministration of the divine mysteries: for hallowed and blessed is thy glorious name, O Father, Son, and Holy Spirit, now and ever, and world without end. Amen.

The blessing of the bread and wine may be performed in a side-chapel or in the vestry, and the elements may be brought to the altar during the singing of a Hymn before the Prayers of the Faithful. [[no. 26 below]]

without end. Amen] ADD / Then shall the Deacon set the sacred vessels upon the altar, covering them with a decent veil. · The blessing . . . Faithful] OMIT.

The Bombay Liturgy

3 *And at the time appointed, being duly vested, the Priest and all those who are to share in the service of the sanctuary, shall say the prayers following:*
Priest. Peace be with you;
Answer. And with thy spirit.
Priest. Glory be to the Father, and to the Son: and to the Holy Ghost;
Answer. As it was in the beginning, is now, and ever shall be: world without end. Amen.
sanctuary] ADD *standing in the vestry*

4 *Priest.* Let us pray.
Almighty and all-holy Father, we thine unworthy servants humbly entreat thy Majesty so to prepare us for this sacred service, that entering with a pure heart into thy sanctuary, we may offer to thee the sacrifice of this Holy Eucharist for thy honour and glory; in remembrance of thy manifold mercies vouchsafed to us in our Saviour Jesus Christ; for the well-being of thy whole Church; and to the remission of our own manifold sins and offences. Vouchsafe, O Fountain of Mercy, to accept this our pure sacrifice through the merits of Jesus Christ our Saviour; who liveth and reigneth with thee and the Holy Spirit, ever one God, world without end. *Amen.*
Amen] Amen

5   THE PRAYERS OF THE CATECHUMENS
[*While a hymn is sung, the Priest, having set on incense and blessed it, shall solemnly cense the altar and sanctuary therewith, after which he shall cense the other ministers and persons in the sanctuary, as also the choir, congregation, and the whole church, the people standing.*

6 *And at the time when he censes the altar the Priest shall say:*
May the incense of the merits of Christ our Saviour which we plead before thee, O Lord our God, avail unto us for the remission of our sins and for the reward of eternal life; and do thou, O life-giving Son, who by thy Cross hast saved us, set us on thy right hand in the day when thy mercy dawneth; who livest and reignest God for ever and ever. Amen.]*

7 *Priest.* The Word was made flesh, and dwelt among us, and we beheld his glory.

 * *Where incense is not used, the portions within brackets may be omitted.*

[[In 1923 nos. 5 and 6 were placed after *Gloria in Excelsis* with these variants of the text printed above: 5 *While . . . sung*] The Introit ended · he shall cense the] the Deacon, taking the censer from him, shall cense the celebrant and   6 Amen] *And the people shall answer here, and after all other prayers which the Priest says with a loud voice,* Amen   7 OMIT]]

8 *People.* Glory be to God on high, and in earth peace, good will towards men. We praise thee, we bless thee, we worship thee, we glorify thee, we give thanks to thee for thy great glory, O Lord God, heavenly King, God the Father Almighty.

O Lord, the only-begotten Son Jesu Christ; O Lord God, Lamb of God, Son of the Father, that takest away the sins of the world, have mercy upon us. Thou that takest away the sins of the world, have mercy upon us. Thou that takest away the sins of the world, receive our prayer. Thou that sittest at the right hand of God the Father, have mercy upon us.

For thou only art holy; thou only art the Lord; thou only, O Christ, with the Holy Ghost, art most high in the glory of God the Father. Amen.

People] *During the entry of the Priest and his attendants into the church, shall be sung the Introit, which at Christmas, Easter, and other Great Festivals shall be as follows:* · on high] in the highest · in earth] upon earth · good will towards] good hope unto · we glorify] the fulness of glory do we offer · O Lord God] O Lord our Maker · O Lord] PREF and to thee · Jesu Christ] ADD with the Holy Ghost · Son] ADD and Word · takest away] bearest now as once thou didst bear · sins] sin · Thou that takest . . . upon us] OM · takest . . . prayer] bearest now, as once thou didst bear, the sin of the world, incline thine ear and hear our prayer · sittest] ADD in glory · God the Father] the Father shew thy pity and · thou only, O Christ] O Jesu Christ · art most high] OM.

9 *Priest.* Holy God,
   People. Holy and mighty,
      Holy and immortal,
      Have mercy upon us.

Priest. Holy God,
People. Holy and mighty,
      Holy and immortal,
      Have mercy upon us.

Priest. Holy God,
People. Holy and mighty,
      Holy and immortal,
      Have mercy upon us.

The Bombay Liturgy

SUBST *Then shall the Deacon say the Litany, which shall always include at least these biddings here following: and if there be any other matters, concerning which thanksgiving or prayer is to be offered, they shall be inserted after that bidding with which they shall appear most consonant. / After each several bidding to thanksgiving the people shall answer:* Thanks be to God; *and after each bidding to prayer:* Lord have mercy. / Let us thank God for his manifold mercies vouchsafed to us. / Let us pray for Christian people, specially for those in this diocese. / Let us pray for the healing of the divisions of Christendom. / Let us pray for the peace of the whole world. / Let us pray for missionary workers, and for God's blessing upon their labours. / Let us pray for catechumens and inquirers. / Let us pray for the conversion of all unbelievers. / Let us pray for the coming of God's kingdom in this world. / Let us pray for preservation from sickness, pestilence and famine. / Let us pray for the supply of all our manifold necessities. / Let us pray for all in need, sickness, or suffering. / Let us pray for the faithful departed. / *The Priest, meantime, standing in the sanctuary with his attendants, shall make silent intercession to Almighty God; and, the Litany ended, he shall say this collect following:* / O Lord, who hast given us grace with one accord to make our common supplications unto thee, and dost promise, that if two or three shall be agreed together in thy name thou wilt grant their requests; fulfil now the desires and petitions of thy servants, as may be most expedient for them; granting us in this world knowledge of thy truth, and in the world to come life everlasting. Amen.

10 *Priest.* Peace be with you;
People. And with thy spirit.
Priest. Let us pray.

Then shall be said the Collect of the Day.

11 *It is customary for the people to stand throughout the Liturgy, but they may sit for the Lesson and the Epistle, and kneel for the Great Intercession.*

OMIT

12 *A Deacon, or other fit person appointed for the purpose, shall read the Lesson from the Old Testament, saying:*

The Lesson is written in the ..... Chapter of ..... beginning at the ..... verse. *And the Lesson ended, he shall say,* Here endeth the Lesson.

PREF. *And immediately after the Collect, the people being seated,*

13 *Then shall a Psalm or portion of a Psalm be sung.*

14 *Then shall the Deacon read the Epistle, saying:*

The Epistle is written in the ..... Chapter of ..... beginning at the ..... verse. *And the Epistle ended, he shall say,* Here endeth the Epistle.

15 *Then shall be sung a hymn, the people standing. And during this singing the Priest shall say privately:*

Grant us, O Lord God, the knowledge of thy divine words, and fill us with the understanding of thy holy gospel; that we may in all things fulfil thy blessed will, and be accounted worthy of the merits which proceed from thee, now and for ever. Amen.

16 [*Then shall he again set on and bless the incense, which shall be burned during the reading of the Gospel.*]

⟦This rubric is not bracketed in **1923**⟧

17 *Then shall the Deacon say:*

In silence stand and give heed unto the Holy Gospel.

18 *And the Priest shall read the Gospel, saying first:*

Peace be with you;
People. And with thy spirit.

Priest. The Holy Gospel is written in the . . . . . Chapter of . . . . . beginning at the . . . . . verse.
People. Glory be to thee, O Lord.

And after the Gospel they shall say:
Praise be to thee, O Christ.

Praise be to thee] Thanks be to thee

19 *Then shall the Priest, or other minister, declare unto the people what holy-days, or fasting days, are in the week following to be observed. He shall publish banns of marriages, and shall inform the people of all matters concerning which notice is needed to be given.*

20 *Then shall follow the Sermon or Instruction.*

21 *And the Sermon ended, the churchwardens shall receive the alms and other devotions of the people, and shall bring them to the Deacon, who shall say:*

Let us pray for them that bring an offering.
People. Accept the offering of the brethren, accept the offering of the sisters, accept the offering of us all.

22 *Then shall the Deacon bring the alms and devotions to the Priest, who shall present them before God at the altar, saying this prayer following:*

We beseech thee, Almighty Lord, for them that bring an offering within thy one holy Catholic Church, an oblation, first-fruits, a thank-offering, a vow, in secret or openly, whether much or little; and for them that desire but have not wherewith to give. Accept the ready mind of all, and grant them thy blessing both now and always.

23 *Then shall the Deacon say:*

Let us pray unto God for the Catechumens, that he may reveal unto them the gospel of truth, and may unite them unto his holy Church.

24 *And the Priest shall say:*

O Lord our God, who dwellest in the heavens, and lookest in mercy upon all thy works: Look down upon thy servants, the catechumens, who have bowed their heads before thee; grant them gladly to bear thine easy yoke, and make them to be members of thy holy Church; account them worthy of the washing of regeneration for the remission of their sins, and clothe them in the incorruptible garment of thy salvation, that they may know thee, the only true God, and may with us exalt thy mighty and all-glorious name, with the name of thy blessed Son, and of thy Holy Spirit, now and ever, and world without end. *Amen.*

25 *Then shall the Deacon give notice to the catechumens and to all unbaptized or excommunicate persons that they forthwith depart from the church, saying:*

Let all catechumens now depart.

Let none that is excommunicate or unbaptized remain in the church.

And he shall take good heed that none remain.

But if there be no catechumens present, the Prayer for the Catechumens together with the Deacon's bidding and the Dismissal shall be omitted.

[See note to no. 2 above]

26   THE PRAYERS OF THE FAITHFUL

Then the people standing, the Deacon shall say:

Let us humbly acknowledge before Almighty God that we have sinned in thought, word, and deed, by our fault, our own fault, our own most grievous fault.

People. Merciful Lord, we confess our sins, have mercy upon us, and help us.

Priest. O Lord God, Absolver, Sanctifier, Forgiver, who rememberest thy mercy and rememberest not our iniquities: Blot out our manifold sins and offences; pardon and deliver us, and give grace of amendment to us and to all thy faithful people; make us worthy to offer unto thee glory and thanksgiving now and for evermore.

People. Amen.
Priest. O Lord Almighty, who receivest sacrifices of praise from those who call upon thee with all their heart, draw us close to thy holy altar and enable us to make spiritual offerings and sacrifices for our sins and those of thy people. Make us worthy to be ourselves an acceptable sacrifice. May thy good Spirit brood over us, and over these oblations, and over all who believe in our Lord Jesus Christ, to whom with thee and the Holy Spirit be ascribed all honour and power, now and for evermore.
People. Amen.

[*After putting on incense, the Priest blesses the censer as follows:*
Priest. Holy ✣ is the Holy Father.
People. Amen.
Priest. Holy ✣ is the Holy Son.
People. Amen.
Priest. Holy ✣ is the living and Holy Spirit, who sanctifieth the incense of his sinful servant, having mercy upon us, and upon our fathers, our brethren, our leaders, our departed, and upon all the children of the Holy Church, living and departed, now and for evermore.
People. Amen.]

OMIT

27 *Deacon.* Let us who are of the household of faith together make profession of our Christian belief, and say:

Priest and People.
I believe in one God . . . 〚CF 4〛 . . . world to come. Amen.

〚But reading 'the Lord, and the Giver', and 'One Holy Catholic'.〛   *Deacon*]
Then, the people standing, the Deacon shall say:

28 *Then shall the Deacon say.*
Give we the Peace.

Priest. Grant, O Lord, that free from all guile and hypocrisy, we may greet one another with an holy kiss.

And, turning to the people, he shall say:
The peace of the Lord be always with you;
People. And with thy spirit.
Then shall the Peace be given.

The Bombay Liturgy

29 *And in the meanwhile, a basin of water being brought to him, the Priest shall wash his hands therein, saying privately:*

Wash away, O Lord God, the foul pollution of my soul, and cleanse me with the water of life; that in all purity and holiness I may be accounted worthy to enter thy holy of holies.

30 *Then shall he remove the veil from the sacred vessels, saying privately:*

O God our Father, who of thy tender love towards mankind didst send thy Son into the world to bring back the sheep that had gone astray: Reject not us who offer unto thee this bloodless sacrifice, for we trust not in our own righteousness but in thy mercies; and grant that this mystery which is administered for our salvation be not turned to our condemnation; but that we may thereby receive remission of our sins, and may render unto thee due praise and thanksgiving; as also unto thine only-begotten Son, and to thine all-holy and quickening Spirit, now and ever, and world without end. Amen.

31 [*And thereafter shall he cense the oblation, unless it has been previously censed, saying:*

We offer unto thee incense, O Lord our God, for a savour of spiritual sweetness; beseeching thee to accept it before thine altar in heaven, and to send down upon us the grace of thy Holy Spirit, now and ever. Amen.]

unless . . . censed] OM

32   THE ANAPHORA

Then the Priest, turning to the people, shall say:

The love of God the ✠ Father; the grace of the only-begotten ✠ Son; and the fellowship and indwelling of the Holy ✠ Spirit be with you all, my brethren, for ever;
People. And with thy spirit.
Priest. Your hearts be with Christ on high;
People. Our hearts are with the Lord.
Priest. Let us give thanks unto our Lord God;
People. It is meet and right so to do.

33 *And turning again to the altar, the Priest shall proceed, saying:*

It is very meet, right, and our bounden duty, that we should at all times, and in all places, give thanks unto thee, O holy Lord, Father Almighty, Everlasting God.

Here shall follow the Proper Preface¹ according to the season. After each of which Prefaces shall be said:

Therefore with martyrs and apostles, and with the great company of thy saints triumphant, we laud and magnify thy glorious Name: and we worship and adore thy Majesty with angels and archangels, and with all the host of heaven, who ever fly before thy throne, praising thee, and chanting, and saying,

34 [*Here the Priest may set on incense.*]

People. Holy, holy, holy, Lord God of hosts, heaven and earth are full of thy glory. Glory be to thee, O Lord most High.

Here . . . incense] OM

35 [*And here it is to be noted, that from the singing of* Holy, holy, holy, *until the end of the Great Intercession, incense is to be burned within the Sanctuary.*]

36 *Then shall the Priest proceed, saying:*

Holy in truth art thou, O Father Almighty, Eternal King, and in thine every gift and work dost thou reveal thy holiness unto men. Holy is thine only-begotten Son, our Saviour Jesus Christ, by whom thou framedst the worlds; and holy thine ever-blessed Spirit, who searcheth out thy secret things.

37 Even as in truth thou art holy, O Lord, so also that he might dwell in holiness before thee, didst thou create man in thine own image; whom, when he transgressed thy commandments and fell, thou didst not abandon nor despise, but didst chasten him as a merciful Father, speaking unto him by thy priests and by thy prophets; and, when the fulness of time was come, thou spakest unto us also by thine only-begotten Son, whom thou didst send into the world to take our nature upon him, that he might become man like as we are, and might renew thine image within us;

38 Who, in the same night that he gave himself to suffer death upon the Cross for our redemption, took bread into his holy and spotless hands, and, looking heavenward unto thee (*here the Priest is to look upward*), O God our Father, ✠ blessed, brake, and gave it to his apostles, saying: Take, eat; this is my Body which is given for you for the remission of sins and for life everlasting.

And the People shall say: Amen.

¹ [[For Proper Prefaces, see Appendix A.]]

The Bombay Liturgy

39 Likewise after supper he took the cup, and, when he had given thanks, he ✠ blessed and gave it to them, saying: Drink ye all of this; for this is my Blood of the New Testament, which is shed for you and for many, for the remission of sins and for life everlasting.
And again the People shall say: Amen.

40 Do this in remembrance of me; for as oft as ye eat this bread and drink this cup, ye do show forth my death and proclaim my resurrection until I come.
People. Thy death, O Lord, we commemorate; thy resurrection we confess; and thy second coming we await. We ask of thee also mercy and compassion, and implore forgiveness of our sins.

And the Priest shall proceed, saying:
41 Wherefore, O heavenly Father, we thine humble servants, being mindful of the precious death of thy Son, our Saviour Jesus Christ; as also of his glorious resurrection from the dead; his triumphant ascension into heaven; and his session in majesty at thy right hand; do offer unto thee this our reasonable service and sacrifice, making with these thy creatures of bread and wine the memorial which thy Son hath willed us to make, and rendering unto thee most hearty thanks for all thy dispensation towards us.

42 *People.* We give thanks to thee, we praise thee, we glorify thee, O Lord our God, and we pray thee to show thy mercy upon us, and to hearken unto the voice of our prayer.

43 *Then the Deacon shall give warning to the people, saying:*
How solemn, O my brethren, is this time, wherein we implore the holy and quickening Spirit to descend and hallow this our Eucharist. Let us worship in holy fear.

holy fear] ADD / *And therewith they shall all fall prostrate with their faces to the ground, and shall so continue until the Great Intercession be ended. And the people being thus prostrate,*

44 *The Priest shall say the Invocation of the Holy Spirit:*
Show us thy mercy, we pray thee, O Lord, and upon us and upon these gifts here set before thee send down thy Holy Spirit, that by his power this bread and this wine may become unto us the ✠ Body and the ✠ Blood of thy Son, our Saviour Jesus Christ, and may hallow the spirits, the souls, and the bodies of all who partake of them, to the bringing forth of the fruit of good works

and to the strengthening of thy Church upon the rock of faith; through the same Jesus Christ thy Son our Lord, to whom with thee and the Holy Spirit be all honour and glory, world without end.
People. Amen.

45 *Then shall silence be kept for a space, the people worshipping. And thereafter the Deacon shall say:*
Let us pray unto the Lord for his grace and mercy.
　Let us pray for the whole state of Christ's Church.
　Let us pray, at this dread time, for all men both living and departed.
People. Lord, have mercy.

the Deacon] ADD *standing and turning to the people · People . . . mercy]* OM

46 *And the Priest shall proceed with the Great Intercession, saying:*
O Almighty Lord God and Maker of all things, whose blessed Son, by his death upon the Cross, made one, perfect, and sufficient sacrifice for all mankind, that with boldness they might draw nigh unto the throne of grace and find acceptance in his name: Receive our supplications and prayers, which through him we now offer unto thy Majesty; making intercession before all things for thy holy Church throughout the world, and entreating thee to endue her with the gifts of thy Holy Spirit, and to grant unto her that peace and unity which are agreeable to thy will.
People. Amen.

47 *Deacon.* Let us remember our Fathers in God, and the sacred ministers of the holy Church.
People. Lord, have mercy.
Priest. And therein we pray for all Bishops, Priests, Deacons, and other orders of thy Church, and specially for *NN.*; beseeching thee to grant them thy grace, that both by their life and doctrine they may set forth thy true and lively Word, and rightly and duly fulfil the ministry which thou hast committed to their charge.
People. Amen.

Deacon . . . Priest] OM

48 *Deacon.* Let us remember those who travel, and those in any special affliction or distress.
People. Lord, have mercy.
Priest. And we humbly beseech thee, O Lord, to remember for good all them that travel by land, by water, or by air; as also to be mindful of them that suffer oppression, captivity, bondage,

The Bombay Liturgy

want, sickness, or any other adversity; and to show thy pity upon them that are vexed by unclean spirits. Send unto them the angel of thy mercy to comfort and relieve them according to their several necessities, and to preserve them to the attainment of eternal life.
People. Amen.
Deacon . . . Priest] OM

49 *Deacon.* Let us remember one another, and our fellow members in Christ's Body.
People. Lord, have mercy.
Priest. To us also thy servants, O Lord, and to all thy Christian people, vouchsafe thy grace and thy mercy; that we may be preserved from all things hurtful both to our souls and bodies, and may be delivered from those afflictions which through our sins are fallen upon us. Grant us to continue in the true faith of thy holy Church, and to walk stedfastly in the ways of thy commandments unto our lives' end.
People. Amen.
Deacon . . . Priest] OM

50 *Deacon.* Let us remember those who bear the burdens of authority, especially Christian Kings and Rulers.
People. Lord, have mercy.
Priest. We pray thee also, O Lord, to remember all Christian governors, and those in authority under them, specially *NN.*; aid them with the armour of thy Spirit, that in all things they may seek thy honour and glory, and that under them thy people may joyfully serve thee in all quietness and godly fear.
People. Amen.
Deacon . . . Priest] OM

51 *Deacon.* Let us remember all men, that the needs of every one may be supplied.
People. Lord, have mercy.
Priest. And we entreat thee also, O Lord, mercifully to bless the air and the dews, the rains and the winds; that through thy heavenly benediction we may be saved from dearth and famine, and may enjoy the fruits of the earth in all abundance and plenty; for the eyes of all wait upon thee, O Lord, and thou givest them their meat in due season.
People. Amen.
Deacon . . . Priest] OM

52 *Deacon.* Let us remember those who have gone before us, especially the glorious saints of God.
People. Lord, have mercy.
Priest. And here, O heavenly Father, we yield unto thee praise and thanksgiving for thy great glory declared in thy saints from the beginning of the world, but specially in the glorious and ever-blessed Virgin Mary, Mother of Jesus Christ, our Lord and God, as also in thy holy Apostle Saint Thomas, (*and, if it be the Festival of any other saint, or saints, or confessor, or martyr, here shall be added:* thy blessed Saint *N.,* or Saints *NN.,* or thy blessed Confessor *N.,* or Martyr *N.,*) and in all thine evangelists and doctors, who have been thy witnesses unto the uttermost parts of the earth; and we beseech thee so to unite us to their holy fellowship, that they may share with us in the communion of this our Eucharist, and continually assist us by their prayers.
People. Amen.
Deacon . . . Priest] OM

53 *Deacon.* Let us remember the faithful departed.
People. Lord, have mercy.
Priest. Finally, we commend to thy fatherly goodness the souls of thy servants who have departed hence from us with the sign of faith, and now repose in the sleep of peace. Grant unto them, we beseech thee, O Lord, thy tender mercy and everlasting rest.
People. Rest eternal grant unto them, O Lord, and let light perpetual shine upon them.
Priest. And vouchsafe unto us their brethren an end both Christian and free from sin, and gather us beneath the feet of thine elect, when thou wilt and as thou wilt, only without shame by reason of our faults; that in this, as in all things, thy blessed name may be exalted and glorified, together with the name of our Lord Jesus Christ and of thine all-holy and quickening Spirit, now and ever, and world without end.
People. Amen.
Deacon . . . mercy. Priest] OM

54 *Priest.* Peace be with you;
People. And with thy spirit.
Priest. May the grace of Almighty ✠ God and our Saviour Jesus Christ, be with you all.
OMIT

The Bombay Liturgy

55 *Then shall the Priest perform the Fraction, saying privately:*

Grant, we beseech thee, merciful Lord, that, as the body of thy blessed Son was broken (*here the Priest shall break the Host*) on the Cross (*here the Priest shall make the sign of the Cross over the chalice with a portion of the broken Host*) that we might become one with him; so we who now partake of these holy mysteries may be united in the fellowship of his mystical Body and (*here the Priest shall place the portion of the Host in the chalice*) share with him in the glory of his resurrection; through the same Jesus Christ our Lord. Amen.

56 *And, if the number of those desiring to communicate be large, the Deacon shall assist the Priest in breaking the bread.*

57 *And while the Priest performs the Fraction, the people shall in the meantime sing the anthem following:*

We have known the Lord, alleluia: in the breaking of the bread, alleluia.
   The bread which we break, alleluia: is the Body of our Lord Jesus Christ, alleluia.
   The cup which we bless, alleluia: is the Blood of our Lord Jesus Christ, alleluia.

58 *And the anthem ended, the Priest shall say:*

As our Saviour Christ hath commanded and taught us, we are bold to say:

And all together shall say,

Our Father, which art . . . ⟦CF 1⟧ . . . from evil.

59 *And the Priest shall proceed.*

Yea, Lord, we pray thee, suffer us not to be tempted above that we are able, but deliver us from the power of the evil one: for thine is the kingdom, the power, and the glory, for ever and ever. Amen.

60 [*Here the Priest may set on incense.*]

Priest. Peace be with you;
People. And with thy spirit.

[*Here . . . incense*]] OM

61 *Then shall the Deacon say:*

Let us pray unto the Lord that he make us worthy to partake of these his holy mysteries.

62 *And the Priest shall say the prayer following:*

Grant us thy blessing, we beseech thee, O Lord; and of thy mercy vouchsafe that in all purity of heart and mind we may receive the Communion of the Body and Blood of thy Son: who with thee and the Holy Spirit liveth and reigneth for ever. Amen.

63 *And turning himself to the people, he* (or *the Bishop, if he be present*) *shall bless them, saying:*

May the mercy ✠ of our God and Saviour Jesus Christ be with you all, my brethren, for ever.

64 *Then shall the Deacon say:* Give we heed in fear.

And the Priest, lifting the Gifts above the altar, shall say: Holy things for holy persons.

65 *And the People shall answer:*

There is none other holy save the Holy Father, the Holy Son, and the Holy Spirit. Amen.

  Praise be to the Father and to the Son and to the Living and Holy Spirit, One God, for ever and ever. Amen.

  Glory to God in the Highest. Amen.

  Hosanna to the Son of David. Blessed is he that cometh in the name of the Lord. The Lord is God and hath shined upon us. Hosanna in the highest.

There is none ... Son of David] OM · The Lord is God ... upon us] OM

66 *Then shall he first receive the Gifts in both kinds himself, saying when he partakes of the bread:*

The Body of Christ, the Bread of Life.

And when he partakes of the cup:

The Blood of Christ, the Chalice of Life.

And to whomsoever the Gifts be administered these same words shall be used therewith.

67 *And thereafter he shall deliver the same to such of the Deacons, and other persons within the sanctuary, as shall be minded to partake of the Holy Communion. Meanwhile a hymn may be sung.*

sanctuary] ADD *and of the choir*

The Bombay Liturgy

Meanwhile ... sung] *And afterwards the people shall receive thereof, as they may be disposed. And to the words of administration, both of the bread and of the cup, the communicant shall answer,* Amen. [[Cf. no. 72 below]]

68 *The Priest shall turn to the west, and descend to the Sanctuary step, bearing the Holy Gifts, and saying:*

May the blessings of our great God and Saviour Jesus Christ be on those who bear these Holy Gifts, and on those who dispense them, on those who receive them, and all who have partaken and do partake of them. May the grace of God be on us and on them here and hereafter for ever.

SUBST *And during the administration of the Holy Sacrament to the people shall be sung:*

69 *People.* O Lamb of God, that takest away the sins of the world, have mercy upon us.

O Lamb of God, that takest away the sins of the world, have mercy upon us.

O Lamb of God, that takest away the sins of the world, grant us thy peace.

People] OM · *thy peace*] ADD / *Or some other hymn. And when all have communicated, the Priest shall return to the altar, and shall reverently consume what remaineth of the Consecrated Elements (except such as he may wish to reserve for the Communion of the sick), and thereafter he shall cleanse the sacred vessels after the usual manner, and again cover them with the veil.*

70 *Priest.* Praise be to thee, O Lord our God, for ever. Praise be to thee. Praise be to thee. O Lord Jesu Christ, may thy Holy Body which we eat, and thy holy Blood which we drink, be not for our condemnation, but for our life and salvation. Have mercy upon us.

OMIT

71 *Then shall the Priest return to the altar.*

People. All the earth shall bow down before thee, and adore thee. Every tongue shall praise thy holy Name. Thou art the raiser of the dead and the good hope of those who lie in the grave. We give thanks to thee, O Lord, for thy gracious mercy towards us.

Here shall those of the people who desire to partake of the Gifts come forward.

OMIT

72 *And to the words of administration, both of the bread and of the cup, the communicant shall answer,* Amen.

[[Cf. note to no. 67 above]]

73 *And during the administration of the Holy Sacrament to the people shall be sung:*

> Strengthen, Lord, for holy service hands which took thy mysteries here;
> Be the ears which heard thy praises shielded from the voice of fear;
> Eyes which saw thy great compassion see thy blessed hope appear.
>
> May the tongues which chanted 'Holy' ever unto truth incline;
> Grant the feet which walked thy temple in the land of light to shine;
> Bodies, by the Body nourished, quicken thou with life divine.
>
> With thy worshippers abide thou; may thy love direct our ways;
> Hear the prayers we lift before thee, and accept our thankful praise.
> May thy peace and mercy keep us safe from harm through all our days.
>
> In the hour of thine appearing may we stand before thy face;
> Raise we ever glad hosannas for the wonder of thy grace;
> For thy love hath shined upon us to redeem our mortal race.
>
> Lord, who deign'st on our offences mercy's pardoning streams to pour,
> Grant us grace to own thy Godhead and in reverent faith adore.
> To thy sovereignty uplifting praise and blessing evermore. Amen.
>
> *Or some other Hymn.*

[[1923] places this after no. 76]] *Or some other hymn*] *Or this,* From glory to glory. [[see no. 79 below]] *Or this, when the service is not sung:* Finished and perfected [[see no. 77 below]]

74 *And turning to the people, he shall say:*

> Peace be with you;
> *People.* And with thy spirit.

75 *Then shall the Deacon say:*

> Let us give thanks unto the Lord, for that he hath vouchsafed us to partake of his holy mysteries, and hath refreshed us with food from his heavenly table.

And the People shall answer: Thanks be to him for his gift.

<small>gift] unspeakable gift</small>

76 *Then shall the Priest say this prayer following:*
Merciful Father, who of thine abundant goodness towards us hast vouchsafed to feed and strengthen us with the precious Body and Blood of thy Son our Saviour Jesus Christ, and dost thereby make us one with him and with all the members of his mystical body, and dost enable us in the power of that sacred communion to overcome sin and to walk as children of light: For these thy bountiful mercies we most heartily thank thee, we praise and worship thee. And we beseech thee to give us grace so to continue in that holy fellowship, that we may ever walk in the steps of thy blessed Son, and offer ourselves a living sacrifice acceptable unto thee; through the same Jesus Christ our Lord, to whom, with thee and thy quickening Spirit, be ascribed, as is most justly due, all praise and thanksgiving, now and ever, and world without end. Amen.

<small>⟦See note under no. 73⟧</small>

77 *Then shall the people say:*
Finished and perfected is the mystery of thy dispensation, as far as in us lies. We have made the memorial of thy Death, we have seen the symbol of thy Resurrection, we have been filled with thine inexhaustible bounty, and enriched with thine undying life; of the which do thou vouchsafe to count us worthy in the world to come, O Christ our God; to whom with thy Father eternal and thine all-holy and quickening Spirit be ascribed, as is mostly due, all praise and thanksgiving, now and ever, and world without end. Amen.

<small>Then shall . . . say] OM</small>

78 *Then the Priest, turning to the people, shall let them go, saying:*
Unto the mercies of the holy and glorious Trinity, brethren, we commit you; go ye with the food of your pilgrimage in ✠ peace and gladness.

The Ablutions may be taken after the Communion of the people, or at this place.

<small>The Ablutions . . . this place] SUBST And, the people being thus dismissed, the Priest and those with him in the sanctuary shall forthwith return to the vestry.</small>

79 *Meanwhile a Hymn may be sung, the following or some other:*

From glory unto glory advancing on our way,
We hymn thee, Christ our Saviour, our soul's eternal stay.

From strength to strength advancing, as from thy house we go,
We pray thee in our weakness thy perfect strength to show.

Direct our way before thee; preserve us in thy love;
And grant us through thy mercy thy heavenly realm above.

From glory unto glory advancing on our way,
We hymn thee, Christ our Saviour, our soul's eternal stay.

⟦See note under no. 73⟧

80   THE PRAYERS AFTER THE SERVICE

The Priest shall say:

O Lord, who hast vouchsafed unto us to be sanctified by the participation of the most holy Body and precious Blood of thine only-begotten Son Jesus Christ our Lord: Grant us also the grace of thy Holy Spirit, that we may be preserved unblameable in the faith, and lead us into our perfect sonship and redemption, and to the attainment of everlasting felicity; who with the same thine only-begotten Son and thine all-holy Spirit art our sanctification and light, now and always. *Amen.*

THE PRAYERS ... SERVICE] THE VESTRY PRAYERS · Priest] ADD *having returned to the vestry,*

81 *Then shall the Deacon say:*

Be we preserved in the peace of Christ.

Priest. Blessed be God, who blesseth and sanctifieth us by the receiving of his holy and spotless mysteries, now and for ever, and world without end. *Amen.*

82 *If a shortened form of the Liturgy is desired for weekdays, the following may be omitted: the incense prayers, the Old Testament Lesson and Psalm, the hymns, the prayers of the Alms, and some sections of the Great Intercession, at the discretion of the Priest. The Deacon's Biddings may be said by the Priest, and the Kiss of Peace given by touch of hands.*
OMIT

83 *The Kiss of Peace. The deacon takes the chains of the censer just above the lid into his left hand, and in his right holds them at the top. He then approaches the altar to the right of the celebrant, and kissing it, presents the centre of the hanging chains. The celebrant takes the centre of the chains into his right hand, and kissing them, offers his hand to the deacon*

The Bombay Liturgy

to kiss. The deacon kisses it, and the priest makes the sign of the cross on his (the deacon's) forehead. He then relinquishes his hold of the chains, and the deacon, again kissing the altar, goes to the bishop and other priests in the sanctuary, if any be present, and receives from them the kiss in the same way. Still holding the chains as described above, the deacon next approaches any other deacon or deacons in the sanctuary, and turning his palms inwards takes the right hand of the other between them, and so receives the kiss from him. Finally, relinquishing his hold of the chains above the lid, he holds the censer in his right hand only, and going to the nearest layman of the congregation, takes the layman's outstretched right hand between his joined palms, and so gives him the kiss. The layman passes the kiss to his neighbour in the same way, and he to his, and so on until all in the church have received it.

OMIT

〚Although **1923** omits 82 and 83, it is worth noting that the original (1920) edition of this liturgy did provide in Appendix III a shortened form for weekdays〛

CHAPTER X

THE INDIAN LITURGY, 1960

This liturgy was first published in the *Proposed Prayer Book*, authorized by the Episcopal Synod of C.I.P.B.C. in 1951. A revised text was printed in the draft edition of the new Indian Prayer Book (1957). The definitive text received the concurrence of the General Council of C.I.P.B.C. on 13 January 1960, and was published in the new Prayer Book in 1961. It is this text that is printed below.

1   THE ORDER FOR
    THE ADMINISTRATION OF
    THE LORD'S SUPPER

    THE ORDER OF 1960

2   A DEVOTION

which may be said by the Priest and people immediately before the celebration of the Lord's Supper on weekdays other than Greater Festivals.

In the name of the Father, and of the Son, and of the Holy Spirit. Amen.

3   *Priest.* I will go unto the altar of God;
    Answer. Even unto the God of my joy and gladness.
    [[Psalm 43 responsorially, with *Gloria Patri*[1]]]
    Priest. I will go unto the altar of God;
    Answer. Even unto the God of my joy and gladness.

4   *Priest.* Our help standeth in the name of the Lord;
    Answer. Who hath made heaven and earth.

5   Then shall the Priest and people say this Confession:
    We confess to God Almighty, the Father, the Son, and the Holy

---

[1] [[Reading 'Holy Spirit' for 'Holy Ghost', as throughout this liturgy.]]

Spirit, That we have sinned in thought, word, and deed, Through our own grievous fault. Wherefore we pray God to have mercy upon us.

6 Almighty God have mercy upon us, Forgive us all our sins, Deliver us from all evil, Confirm and strengthen us in all goodness, And bring us to everlasting life; Through Jesus Christ our Lord. Amen.

7 *Then turning towards the Congregation, the Priest (or the Bishop, being present) shall say this Absolution:*
May the Almighty and merciful Lord grant unto you pardon and remission of all your sins, time for true repentance, amendment of life, and the grace and comfort of the Holy Spirit.
Answer. Amen.

8 *Priest.* Wilt thou not turn again and quicken us;
Answer. That thy people may rejoice in thee?
Priest. O Lord, show thy mercy upon us;
Answer. And grant us thy salvation.
Priest. O Lord, hear our prayer;
Answer. And let our cry come unto thee.
Priest. The Lord be with you;
Answer. And with thy spirit.

Let us pray.

THE ORDER FOR THE LORD'S SUPPER

9 *The holy Table at the Communion time, having a fair white linen cloth upon it, shall stand in the chancel or in the body of the church.*

On Sundays and Festivals, when Morning Prayer is not read publicly before the Holy Eucharist, an Introit Psalm at the beginning of the Order, and an Old Testament Lesson, as appointed by authority, and a Canticle, may be read before the Epistle. When this is done, the obligation to read Morning Prayer is set aside.

The Deacon's part may be taken by any ordained Minister, or any layman, in so far as he may be duly authorized by the Bishop. In the absence of any such to assist at the Service, the Priest shall say the portions assigned to the Deacon.

It is fitting for the Priest to stand at the midst of the holy Table for the Creed, the Offertory, the Intercession, the Consecration, and the Gloria in Excelsis

The Service may begin with the Lord's Prayer, said by the Priest alone.

10 *The Priest, standing at the Table, shall say in a distinct and audible voice, the people devoutly kneeling,*
Almighty God unto whom . . . 〚CF 2〛 . . . Lord. Amen.

11 *Then shall the Priest, turning to the people, read all the TEN COMMANDMENTS; and the people, still kneeling, shall after every commandment ask God mercy for their transgression of every duty therein (either according to the letter or according to the spiritual import thereof) for the time past, and grace to keep the same for the time to come, as follows:*

And Note, that in reading the Ten Commandments, the Priest may leave unsaid those portions which are inset.

Priest. God spake these words . . . 〚CF 3〛 . . . we beseech thee.

〚Portions of four Commandments are inset as follows: (2) 'For I the Lord . . . commandments', (3) 'For the Lord . . . in vain', (4) 'In it thou shalt . . . hallowed it', (5) 'that thy days . . . God giveth thee'〛

---

12 *Provided that the Ten Commandments are read on at least one Sunday in every month, they may be omitted at other times. When they are so omitted, there shall be said in place thereof either our Lord's Summary of the Law, or else the Ninefold Kyrie.*

The Summary of the Law

Our Lord Jesus Christ said: Hear O Israel, The Lord our God is one Lord; and thou shalt love the Lord thy God with all thy heart, and with all thy soul, and with all thy mind, and with all thy strength. This is the first commandment. And the second is like, namely this: Thou shalt love thy neighbour as thyself. There is none other commandment greater than these. On these two commandments hang all the Law and the Prophets.

Answer. Lord, have mercy upon us, and write these thy laws in our hearts, we beseech thee.

13 *Or,* the Kyries

Lord, have mercy.	Kyrie eleison.
Lord, have mercy.	*Kyrie eleison.*
Lord, have mercy.	Kyrie eleison.
Christ, have mercy.	*Christe eleison.*
Christ, have mercy.	Christe eleison.
Christ, have mercy.	*Christe eleison.*

Lord, have mercy.	Kyrie eleison.
Lord, have mercy.	*Kyrie eleison.*
Lord, have mercy.	Kyrie eleison.

14 *Then shall the Priest say,*
   The Lord be with you;
Answer. And with thy spirit.
                              Let us pray.
And, turning to the holy Table, he shall say the Collect of the Day, and after it any Memorials or other Collects which are either appointed or permitted to be said.

THE MINISTRY OF THE WORD

15 *Immediately thereafter an Old Testament Lesson may be read, in which case the reader of the Old Testament Lesson shall say,* The Lesson is written in . . . ., in the . . . . chapter, beginning at the . . . . verse. *And the reading ended, he shall say,* Here endeth the Lesson.

16 *Then the reader of the Epistle shall say,* The Epistle (*or,* The Lesson) is written in . . . ., in the . . . . chapter, beginning at the . . . . verse. *And the reading ended, he shall say,* Here endeth the Epistle (*or,* the Lesson).

17 *Then the Deacon or Priest that reads the Gospel (the people all standing) may say,* The Lord be with you; *to which shall be answered,* And with thy spirit. *After which,* The Holy Gospel is written in the Gospel according to Saint . . . ., in the . . . . chapter, beginning at the . . . . verse.
Answer. Glory be to thee, O Lord.

The Gospel ended, there may be said. Praise be to thee, O Christ.

Alleluia *may be added to the responses before and after the Gospel from Easter Day until the Saturday after Whitsunday.*

He that reads the Epistle or Gospel shall so turn to the people that all may hear.

18 *Then shall be sung or said the Creed following, the people still standing as before: except that at the discretion of the Minister it may be omitted on any day, not being a Sunday or a Greater Festival.*
I believe in one God . . . ⟦CF 4⟧ . . . world to come. Amen.

⟦But reading 'Through whom all things were made', 'incarnate by the Holy Spirit', 'the Holy Spirit, The Lord, The giver of life', 'One Holy Catholic', 'the Life of the world to come'⟧

19 Then the Priest shall declare unto the people what Festivals or Days of Fasting, Abstinence, or Special Supplication are in the week following to be observed. And then also, if necessary, shall notice be given of the Lord's Supper or of other Services; Banns of Matrimony may be published, and Briefs, Citations, and Excommunications shall be read, and Bidding of Prayers may be made. And nothing shall be proclaimed or published in the church during the time of Service, but by the Minister; nor by him anything but what is prescribed in the rules of this Book, or enjoined or permitted by the Bishop. Then may follow the Sermon.

20   THE OFFERTORY

Then the Priest at the Lord's Table, turning to the people, shall say,

Let us present our offerings to the Lord with reverence and godly fear.

After which he shall begin the Offertory, saying one or more of the Sentences following.

⟦For Offertory Sentences, see Appendix B⟧

21 Then shall the Priest take of the Bread and Wine prepared for the Sacrament so much as he shall think sufficient, and place them upon the holy Table.

22 On Sundays and Festivals two members of the congregation, chosen by the Priest, may bring forward from the midst of the congregation Bread and Wine for this purpose.

23 In the mean while the Churchwardens, or other fit persons appointed for the purpose, shall receive the alms and other offerings of the people, and reverently bring them to the Priest, who shall humbly present them and place the alms upon the Table. Then shall the Priest say,

24   Let us pray.

All things come of thee, and of thine own do we give unto thee, O Creator of the world, who art ever adored by the holy Angels. We humbly beseech thee to accept at our hands these (alms and) oblations, which we present at thy holy Table, and with them the offering of ourselves to the service of thy divine Majesty; through Jesus Christ our Lord. Amen.

The People may say this Prayer with the Priest.

25 And after this, water being brought, the Priest may wash his hands therein.

THE INTERCESSION

26 *And the Priest, or Deacon, shall begin the Litany, as follows.*

Almighty God, who hast taught us to make prayers, supplications, and intercessions, for all men; hear us when we pray:

That it may please thee to inspire continually the universal Church with the spirit of truth, unity, and concord;
Hear us, we beseech thee.

That it may please thee to grant that all they that do confess thy holy name may agree in the truth of thy holy Word, and live in unity and godly love;
Hear us, we beseech thee.

That it may please thee to give grace to all Bishops, Priests, and Deacons, especially to thy servants, N. our Metropolitan and N. our Bishop, that by their life and doctrine they may set forth thy true and life-giving Word, and rightly and duly administer thy Holy Sacraments;
Hear us, we beseech thee.

That it may please thee to bless in their several callings all other thy servants, who are labouring for the building up of thy Church and the spread of thy Gospel, and grant that the whole world may be filled with the knowledge of thy truth;
Hear us, we beseech thee.

That it may please thee to give thy heavenly grace to all thy people, and specially to this congregation here present; that, with meek heart and due reverence, they may hear, and receive thy holy Word; truly serving thee in holiness and righteousness all the days of their life;
Hear us, we beseech thee.

That it may please thee to lead all nations in the way of righteousness and peace; and so to guide their rulers, especially our President (*or*, Governor-General), the Prime Minister, the Governor of this State (*or*, Province), and all in authority under them, that thy people may be justly and quietly governed;
Hear us, we beseech thee.

That it may please thee through thy heavenly benediction to save us from scarcity and famine, that with thankful hearts we may enjoy the fruits of the earth in their season:
Hear us, we beseech thee.

That it may please thee of thy goodness, O Lord, to comfort and succour all those, who in this transitory life are in trouble, sorrow, need, sickness, or any other adversity;
Hear us, we beseech thee.

That it may please thee to grant that with all the faithful departed we may receive the unsearchable benefits of thy Son's passion.
Hear us, we beseech thee.

That it may please thee to give us grace to follow the good examples of thy Saints, that with them we may be partakers of thy heavenly kingdom;
Hear us, we beseech thee.

Priest. Let us pray.

Hasten, O Father, the coming of thy kingdom; and grant that we and all thy servants, being quickened together in the eternal fellowship of thy Holy Spirit, may behold thy Son at his coming again in glorious Majesty, even Jesus Christ, our only Mediator and Advocate.
Answer. Amen; come, Lord Jesus.

---

27 *Or the Priest may say,*

Let us pray for the whole Church of Christ, and for all men according to their needs.

Almighty and everliving God, who by thy holy Apostle hast taught us to make prayers, and supplications, and to give thanks, for all men: We humbly beseech thee most mercifully to receive these our prayers, which we offer unto thy Divine Majesty: beseeching thee to inspire continually the universal Church with the spirit of truth, unity, and concord: And grant, that all they that do confess thy holy name may agree in the truth of thy holy Word, and live in unity, and godly love.

Give grace, O heavenly Father, to all Bishops, Priests, and Deacons, especially to thy servants, N. our Metropolitan and N. our Bishop, that by their life and doctrine they may set forth thy true and life-giving Word, and rightly and duly administer thy Holy Sacraments.

And bless, we beseech thee, in their several callings all other thy servants, who are labouring for the building up of thy Church and the spread of the Gospel, and grant that the whole world may be filled with the knowledge of thy truth.

And to all thy people give thy heavenly grace; and specially to this congregation here present; that, with meek heart and due reverence, they may hear, and receive thy holy Word; truly serving thee in holiness and righteousness all the days of their life.

We beseech thee to lead all nations in the way of righteousness and peace; and so to guide their rulers, that thy people may be justly and quietly governed; and more especially we remember our President (*or* Governor-General), the Prime Minister, the Governor of this State (*or* Province), and all in authority under them.

We entreat thee also, that through thy heavenly benediction we may be saved from scarcity and famine, and may with thankful hearts enjoy the fruits of the earth in their season.

We most humbly beseech thee of thy goodness, O Lord, to comfort and succour all those, who in this transitory life are in trouble, sorrow, need, sickness, or any other adversity.

We entrust to thy fatherly keeping all thy servants departed this life in thy faith and fear; and give unto thee most high praise and hearty thanks for the wonderful grace and virtue declared in all thy Saints; beseeching thee to enable us so to follow the example of their stedfastness in the faith, and obedience to thy holy commandments, that at the last day we, and all they who are of the mystical body of thy Son, may be partakers of thy heavenly kingdom.

Grant this, O Father, for Jesus Christ's sake, our only Mediator and Advocate; who liveth and reigneth with thee in the unity of the Holy Spirit, one God, world without end. *Amen.*

---

28   PREPARATION FOR COMMUNION

Then shall the Priest, or Deacon, say to them that intend to receive the Holy Communion,

Ye that do truly ... 〚CF 6〛 ... your knees.

29 *And then shall the following General Confession be said by all, kneeling,*

Almighty God, Father of our Lord ... 〚CF 7〛 ... our Lord. Amen.

30 *Then shall the Priest (or the Bishop, being present) stand up, and turning himself to the people, pronounce this Absolution.*

Almighty God, our heavenly Father ... 〚CF 8〛 ... our Lord. Amen.

31 *Then shall the Priest, or Deacon, say,*

Hear what comfortable ... 〚CF 9〛 ... our sins.

〚But reading 'Christ Jesus' in 1 Tim. 1. 15〛

32 *This Preparation of the communicants, consisting of the short Exhortation, together with the Confession, Absolution, and Comfortable Words, shall always be said on Sundays and Greater Festivals; but at other times it may be omitted, provided that the opening Devotion has been said with the congregation.*

33   THE CONSECRATION

The people standing or kneeling, the Priest shall stand at the Table and begin the Consecration, as follows.

      The Lord be with you;
Answer. And with thy spirit.
Priest. Lift up your hearts;
Answer. We lift them up unto the Lord.
Priest. Let us give thanks unto our Lord God;
Answer. It is meet and right so to do.

Then shall the Priest turn to the Lord's Table and continue,

It is very meet, right, and our bounden duty, that we should at all times, and in all places, give thanks unto thee, O Lord, Holy Father, Almighty, Everlasting God.

Here shall follow the Proper Preface,[1] *according to the time, if there be any specially appointed; or else immediately shall be said or sung by the Priest,*

Therefore with Angels and Archangels, and with all the company of heaven, we laud and magnify thy glorious name; evermore praising thee, and saying,

Holy, Holy, Holy, Lord God of hosts, heaven and earth are full of thy glory. Glory be to thee, O Lord most High. Amen. *Priest and people* Blessed is he that cometh in the name of the Lord: Hosanna in the highest.

---

[1] 〚For Proper Prefaces, see Appendix A.〛

34 *The people kneeling, the Priest shall then continue,*
Holy in truth art thou, and blessed in truth, O Almighty God, our heavenly Father, for that thou of thy tender mercy didst give thine only Son Jesus Christ to take our nature upon him, and to suffer death upon the Cross for our redemption; who made there, by his one oblation of himself once offered, a full, perfect, and sufficient sacrifice, oblation, and satisfaction, for the sins of the whole world; and did institute, and in his holy Gospel command us to continue, a perpetual memorial of that his precious death, until his coming again:

35   Who, in the same night that he was betrayed, [a]took Bread; and when he had given thanks to thee, he [b]brake it, and gave it to his disciples, saying, Take, eat, [c]this is my Body which is given for you: Do this in remembrance of me.

    Likewise after supper he [d]took the Cup; and, when he had given thanks, he gave it to them, saying, Drink ye all of this; for [e]this is my Blood of the New Covenant, which is shed for you and for many for the remission of sins: Do this, as oft as ye shall drink it, in remembrance of me. *People.* Amen.

[a] *Here the Priest is to take the Bread into his hands:*
[b] *And here to break the Bread:*
[c] *And here to lay his hand upon all the Bread.*
[d] *Here he is to take the Cup into his hand:*
[e] *And here to lay his hand upon every vessel in which there is any Wine to be consecrated.*

36   Wherefore, O Lord and heavenly Father, we thy humble servants do celebrate and make here before thy Divine Majesty, with these thy holy gifts, the memorial thy Son hath commanded us to make; having in remembrance his blessed passion, and precious death, his mighty resurrection, and glorious ascension; rendering unto thee most hearty thanks for the innumerable benefits procured unto us by the same, and looking for his coming again with power and great glory.

37   And we entirely desire thy fatherly goodness mercifully to accept on high this our sacrifice of praise and thanksgiving, beseeching thee to grant, that by the merits and death of thy Son Jesus Christ, and through faith in his blood, we and all thy whole Church may obtain remission of our sins, and all other benefits of his passion.

38   And we humbly beseech thee, most merciful Father, to send down thy holy and life-giving Spirit upon us and upon these thy gifts, that the Bread which we break may be the communion of

the Body of Christ, and the Cup which we bless may be the communion of his Blood; and grant, that all we who are partakers of this Holy Communion may be fulfilled with thy grace and heavenly benediction, and made one body in thy Son, our Saviour Jesus Christ.
People. Amen.

39 And here we offer and present unto thee, O Lord, ourselves, our souls and bodies, to be a reasonable, holy, and lively sacrifice unto thee.

And although we be unworthy, through our manifold sins, to offer unto thee any sacrifice, yet we beseech thee to accept this our bounden duty and service; not weighing our merits, but pardoning our offences, through Jesus Christ our Lord;

40 By whom, and with whom, and in whom, in the unity of the Holy Spirit, all honour and glory be unto thee, O Father Almighty, world without end.
People. Amen.

41 THE COMMUNION

As our Saviour Christ hath commanded and taught us, we are bold to say, Our Father, who art ... [[CF 1]] ... ever. Amen.
[[With inset rubric '*Priest and people*']]

42 *Then may the Priest say,*

The peace of the Lord be always with you;
Answer. And with thy spirit.
Then shall silence be kept for a space.

43 *Then shall this Prayer of Humble Access be said by the Priest and those who are to communicate with him, all kneeling,*

Let us pray.

We do not presume ... [[CF 10]] ... in us. *Amen.*

44 *And this Hymn may be said or sung:*

O Lamb of God, that takest away the sin of the world, Have mercy upon us.

O Lamb of God, that takest away the sin of the world, Have mercy upon us.

O Lamb of God, that takest away the sin of the world, Grant us thy peace.

The Indian Liturgy, 1960

45 *Then shall the Priest first receive the Communion in both kinds himself, saying the Words of Administration.*

And turning to the people, he may say to them that come to receive the Holy Communion,

Draw near and receive the Body and Blood of our Lord Jesus Christ, which were given for you, and feed on him in your hearts by faith with thanksgiving.

And when he delivers . . . 〚CF 11〛 . . . *and be thankful.*

Note, that when the words Draw near and receive . . . . thanksgiving *have been used as above, the Minister may omit the second sentence in the Words of Administration of the Bread and the Cup.*

46 *Where and when Communion is administered in both kinds together, either by intinction or with a spoon, at a public Service of the Lord's Supper, or to the sick by intinction, the following form of words shall be used at the administration to each communicant:* The Body and Blood of our Lord Jesus Christ preserve thy body and soul unto everlasting life.

47 *When all have communicated, the Priest, returning to the holy Table, may either at once reverently consume what remains of the consecrated Elements, and thereafter cleanse the sacred vessels in the usual manner and cover them with a veil; or else, replacing the Elements upon the Table, he shall cover them with a fair linen cloth; in this case, immediately after the Blessing he shall consume what remains and cleanse the vessels.*

THE THANKSGIVING

48 *Then shall the Priest say,*

   The Lord be with you;
Answer. And with thy spirit.
    Let us pray.

Almighty and everliving God . . . 〚CF 12〛 . . . without end. *Amen.*
〚But reading 'Holy Spirit' for 'Holy Ghost'〛

49 *Here shall be said or sung the* Gloria in Excelsis:
Glory be to God on high . . . 〚CF 13〛 . . . the Father. Amen.
〚But reading 'sin of the world' (thrice) and 'Holy Spirit' for 'Holy Ghost'〛

This hymn may be omitted on any day, not being a Sunday or a Greater Festival, save that it shall be said or sung on every day from Easter to Trinity Sunday.

50 *Immediately before the Blessing may be said one of the Prayers given below;*[1] *and then the Priest (or the Bishop, if he be present) shall let them depart with this Blessing:*

The peace of God . . . 〚CF 14〛 . . . always. Amen.
〚But reading 'Holy Spirit'〛

51 *When there is no Communion, on a Sunday or Festival, the first part of this Order (up to the Intercession, omitting the Offertory) may be used instead of Morning Prayer; it shall not be read from the holy Table, but from the customary place for reading Morning and Evening Prayer, and the passages of Scripture shall be read as Lessons from the lectern. In the absence of a Priest, the first part of this service may be conducted by a Deacon, or by a layman if authorized by the Bishop. After the Intercession a Hymn may be sung, during which the alms may be taken, and the Service may be ended with one of the Conclusions to Morning and Evening Prayer.*

[1] 〚See Appendix C.〛

CHAPTER XI

THE JAPANESE LITURGY

A DRAFT Liturgy for Nippon Seikokai was approved for permissive use for three years in 1953. A revised draft was authorized by the General Synod for a further three years in 1956. It was adopted by the General Synod in 1959. This liturgy was composed in Japanese. An English translation by the Right Reverend Kenneth Abbott Viall, S.S.J.E., Acting Bishop of Tokyo, and the Reverend Cyril H. Powles, was published by Japan Missions in 1957. This is the text printed here, but we have the advantage of a number of corrections of the translation communicated privately by Bishop Viall.

HOLY COMMUNION

1   THE EXHORTATION

The Priest shall read this exhortation from time to time (at the least once during Lent) during divine service. The People are seated.
〚Adaptation of the first **1662** exhortation〛

2   THE PREPARATION

This preparation is used before the Holy Communion. It may be used on the evening before a celebration together with the Exhortation, or an address or meditation.

The People kneel.

3 *All together say the Lord's Prayer.*
   Our Father, who art . . . 〚CF 1〛 . . . evil. Amen.

4 *The Minister says the following prayer.*
   Almighty God, unto whom . . . 〚CF 2〛 . . . our Lord. ℟ Amen.
   〚But omitting the words 'the thoughts of' and 'the inspiration of'〛

5   *The Ten Commandments*[1]

After each response there is space for self-examination.
Minister. God spake . . . 〚CF 3〛 . . . beseech thee.

[1] 〚This section includes the 'Summary of the Law' *as well as* the Decalogue.〛

⟦But some commandments are shortened as follows: (2) end at 'worship them', (3) end at 'in vain', (4) end at 'Lord thy God', (5) end at 'mother', (10) read 'Thou shalt not covet'⟧

Minister. Hear also what our Lord Jesus Christ saith: Thou shalt love the Lord thy God with all thy heart, and with all thy soul, and with all thy mind. This is the first and great commandment. And the second is like unto it; thou shalt love thy neighbour as thyself. On these two commandments hang all the Law and the Prophets.
People. Lord, have mercy upon us, and write this law in our hearts, we beseech thee.
Minister. Let us pray.
Almighty and everlasting God: vouchsafe, we beseech thee, to direct, sanctify, and govern, both our hearts and bodies, in the ways of thy laws, and in the works of thy commandments; that, through thy most mighty protection, both here and ever, we may be preserved in body and soul; through our Lord and Saviour Jesus Christ. ℞ Amen.

6 *If the Holy Communion is to follow immediately, the Priest, omitting what follows, begins the Liturgy.*

7 *The Confession*

Minister. Let us confess our sins unto Almighty God.

The following confession is said by all together.
Almighty God, Father of our Lord Jesus Christ ... ⟦CF 7⟧ ... Lord. Amen.

8 *The Comfortable Words*

The Minister says,
Hear what comfortable ... ⟦CF 9⟧ ... our sins.
⟦But reading 'Christ Jesus' in 1 Tim 1. 15⟧

Here may be used suitable prayers, or the Litany. When this Preparation is not used immediately before the Holy Communion, the Celebrant uses the following prayers before the Lord, have mercy, *or* Kyrie eleison *in the Liturgy. Note, however, that if the Liturgy is used with other offices and the Lord's Prayer has already been said, this Lord's Prayer may be omitted. The Celebrant alone says the* Amen *at the end of this Lord's Prayer.*

10 Our Father, who art . . . 〚CF 1〛 . . . evil. Amen.
11 Almighty God, unto whom . . . 〚CF 2〛 . . . our Lord. *Amen.*
   〚Variants as in no. 4 above〛

THE LITURGY
The Introduction

12 *Here may be used a Hymn, or one or more verses from the Psalms, as the Introit. All standing, the following words are sung or said. Each verse may be repeated three times.*

13   Lord, have mercy   *Or,*   Kyrie Eleison
       Christ, have mercy   Christe eleison
       Lord, have mercy   Kyrie eleison

14 *On Sundays and on other Holy Days, all sing or say the following Canticle, except that it is not used on Sundays in Advent, Pre-Lent, and Lent.*

Glory be to God . . . 〚CF 13〛 . . . Father. Amen.
〚Omitting 'Thou that takest away . . . upon us' and reading 'only, O Jesus Christ, art holy' and 'only, with the Holy Ghost'〛

15   *The Collects*

Priest. The Lord be with you.
People. And with thy spirit.

Priest. Let us pray.
Here he uses the collect(s) of the day.

16   *The Epistle*

The People being seated, the assistant, or the Priest, sings or says the Epistle, first saying, The Epistle is written in the —— Chapter of ——, beginning at the —— verse. *At the end he says,* Here endeth the Epistle. *Next all stand. Here may be used a Hymn, or one or more verses from the Psalms as the Gradual.*

17   *The Gospel*

The Deacon, or the Priest, after making the following response, sings or reads the Gospel.

Reader. The Lord be with you.
People. And with thy spirit.

Reader. The Holy Gospel is written in the —— Chapter of the Gospel according to Saint ——, beginning at the —— verse.

130   *The Liturgy in English*

People. Glory be to thee, O Lord.

After the Gospel the following is sung or said.
People. Thanks be to thee, O Lord.

18   The Sermon

Before or after the Sermon the Priest gives notice of Holy Days, Days of Abstinence, and Fast Days to be observed during the week; also of days on which there is to be a celebration of Holy Communion; of other matters such as communications from the Bishop, Banns of Marriage, and notices of excommunication.

After the Sermon, prayers for Evangelism, for Catechumens, or for other intentions may be used.

19   The Nicene Creed

On Sundays and other Holy Days, all, standing, together sing or say the following Creed.

I believe in one God ... [[CF 4]] ... to come. Amen.

[[But reading: 'substance with the Father;'; 'The Lord, the Giver of Life'; 'one Holy Catholic']]

20 *Here a Hymn may be sung.*

21   The Confession and Absolution

The Deacon or Priest says,

Let us confess our sins, that we may offer a sacrifice acceptable to the Lord, and worthily celebrate this Holy Sacrament.

The People kneel.

22 *Priest.* I confess to God Almighty, Father, Son, and Holy Spirit, before the whole company of heaven and you, my brethren, that I have sinned exceedingly in thought, word, and deed. Wherefore, I beseech God to have mercy upon me, and you, my brethren, to pray for me to the Lord our God.

23 *People.* Almighty God have mercy upon thee, forgive thee all thy sins, and bring thee to everlasting life.
    Priest. Amen.

24 *People.* We confess [[&c., *mutatis mutandis*, as above]] our God.

25 *Then the Priest (the Bishop of the Diocese if he be present), turning to the People, says,*

The Almighty and Merciful Lord grant you absolution and

remission of all your sins, time for true repentance, amendment of life, and the grace and comfort of his Holy Spirit.
People. Amen.

Here all stand.

The Offertory

26 *Priest.* The Lord be with you.
People. And with thy spirit.

Here the Deacon or the Priest sings or says as follows:
Let us make our offering unto the Lord.

Then one or more of the following sentences, or the Offertory, shall be used.

[For Offertory Sentences see Appendix B]

27 *Here the Alms of the People are collected. During the collection a Hymn may be sung. Representatives of the People bring the Alms, and the Bread and Wine, to the Priest.*

When the Priest offers the Alms and Oblations, he uses the following prayer. When there are no Alms, the words in brackets are omitted.
O God, the Father Almighty, accept, we beseech thee, our (Alms and) Oblations; and vouchsafe to bless us and grant us grace; through Jesus Christ, thy Son our Lord. ℟ Amen.

28 *Alternatively, the following sentence may be sung or said by all.*
All things come of thee, O Lord, and of thine own have we given thee. (1 Chron. 29. 14)

The Intercession

29 *The People kneel.*

Here the Priest, saying, Let us pray for . . ., *may ask the silent intercessions of the People.*

Then the Priest says.
Let us pray for the whole Church.
Almighty and everliving God, who by thy holy Apostle hast taught us to make prayers and supplications, and to give thanks for all men; we humbly beseech thee to receive these our prayers, which we offer to thy Divine Majesty; beseeching thee to inspire

continually the Universal Church with the spirit of truth, unity, and concord: And grant, that all they that do confess thy holy Name may agree in the Truth of thy holy Word, and live in unity and godly love.

Give grace, O heavenly Father, to all Bishops, Priests, and Deacons, especially to . . . our Bishop, that they may both by their life and doctrine set forth thy true and living word, and rightly and duly administer thy holy Sacraments.

And to all thy people give thy heavenly grace; and especially to this congregation here present; that with due reverence they may hear thy holy Word, truly serving thee in holiness and righteousness all the days of their life.

And we most humbly beseech thee, of thy goodness, O Lord, to strengthen and succour all them who in this transitory life are in trouble, sorrow, sickness, need, or any other adversity.

And we commend to thy gracious keeping, O Lord, all thy servants departed this life in thy faith and fear, beseeching thee to grant them everlasting light and peace.

And here we give thee most high praise and hearty thanks for all thy saints, who have been the chosen vessels of thy grace, and lights of the world in their several generations.

Through Jesus Christ, thy Son, our Lord. ℟ Amen.

The Consecration

30 *Priest.* The Lord be with you.
People. And with thy spirit.
Priest. Lift up your hearts.
People. We lift them up unto the Lord.
Priest. Let us give thanks unto our Lord God.
People. It is meet and right so to do.

Then the Priest sings or says,

It is very meet, right, and our bounden duty that we should at all times and in all places, give thanks unto thee, Most Holy Father, Almighty and Everlasting God.

Here follows the Proper Preface.

⟦For Proper Prefaces, see Appendix A⟧

Therefore with Angels and Archangels, and with all the company of heaven, we laud and magnify thy glorious Name, evermore praising thee, and saying:

The Japanese Liturgy 133

All together sing or say,

Holy, Holy, Holy, Lord God of Hosts. Heaven and earth are full of thy Glory: Hosanna in the highest.

Continuing, they may sing or say the following. Alternatively these words may be used immediately before the People's Communion.

Blessed is he that cometh in the Name of the Lord. Hosanna in the highest.

Then the Priest says,

31 Unto thee, O God, the Father almighty, be thanksgiving, and blessing, and glory, and wisdom, and honour, and power, and might, for ever and ever; for that thou by thy Word didst create all things, and for us men, and for our salvation didst give thine only Son Jesus Christ verily to take our nature upon him, and to be born into this world; Who did make upon the Cross (by his one oblation of himself once offerred) the only perfect sacrifice, oblation, and satisfaction for the sins of the whole world; and did institute, and in his holy Gospel command us to continue, a perpetual memory of that his precious sacrifice and death until his coming again.

32 Hear us, O merciful Father, we most humbly beseech thee, and vouchsafe to bless and sanctify with thy Word and Holy Spirit these gifts of Bread and Wine, that we may be partakers of the most precious Body and Blood of thy Son Jesus Christ; Who in the same night in which he was betrayed, took Bread*a* and when he had given thanks, he brake it, and gave it to his disciples, saying, Take, eat, this is my Body, which is given for you. Do this in remembrance of me.

a Here the Priest takes the Bread into his hands.

b Here he takes the Cup into his hands.

33 Likewise, after supper, he took the Cup*b* and when he had given thanks, he gave it to them, saying, Drink ye all of this: for this is my Blood of the New Covenant, which is shed for you and for many, for the remission of sins. Do this, as oft as ye shall drink it, in remembrance of me.

34 Wherefore, O heavenly Father, according to the institution of thy dearly beloved Son, our Saviour, Jesus Christ, in remembrance of his blessed passion and precious death, his mighty resurrection and glorious ascension, rendering unto thee most hearty thanks for the innumerable benefits procured unto us by the same, we do celebrate and make here the memorial thy Son hath

commanded us to make, and in the Lord's presence offer this holy Bread of Heaven and Cup of Salvation, looking unto the day when he shall come again.

35 And we humbly beseech thee to lift up to the heavenly altar this sacrifice of praise and thanksgiving; that we and all others who shall be partakers of this Holy Communion may be made one body with Christ, that we may dwell in him, and he in us; and thereby keep us in the fellowship of thy servants who have departed this life in thy faith and fear, that with thy Saints we may be partakers of thy heavenly Kingdom; through Jesus Christ our Lord.

36 And now unto thee, O Father Almighty, who art able to do exceeding abundantly above all that we ask or think, according to the power that worketh in us, unto thee be glory in the Church by Christ Jesus throughout all ages, world without end. ℟ Amen.

37   *The Communion*

The Priest sings or says,
As our Saviour Christ hath taught us, let us pray.
All together sing or say,
Our Father, who art . . . ⟦CF 1⟧ . . . evil. Amen.

38 *Here the Priest breaks the consecrated Bread.*
Next may be used the following response.
Priest. The Peace of the Lord be alway with you.
People. And with thy spirit.

39 *Continuing, they may sing or say the following anthem.*
Note, however, that in celebrations in memory of the Departed, instead of, Have mercy upon us *is said* Grant them rest, *and instead of* Grant us thy peace, Grant them rest eternal.

O Lamb of God, that takest away the sins of the world: have mercy upon us.

O Lamb of God, that takest away the sins of the world: have mercy upon us.

O Lamb of God, that takest away the sins of the world: grant us thy peace.

All together say the following prayer.

40 We do not presume . . . ⟦CF 10⟧ . . . in us. Amen.
⟦But reading 'that our sinful bodies and souls may be made clean by his most precious Body and Blood'⟧

41 *The Priest first receives the Holy Communion then those in Holy*

Orders, afterwards the People in their turn. When he administers Holy Communion, he says to each person.

The Body of our Lord Jesus Christ, which was given for thee.
The Blood of our Lord Jesus Christ, which was given for thee.

42 *Here may be sung a Hymn; or one or more verses from the Psalms may be used for the Communion.*

The Thanksgiving

All together say the following prayer.

43 Almighty and everliving God, we most heartily thank thee, for that thou dost vouchsafe to feed us who have duly received these holy mysteries, with the spiritual food of the most precious Body and Blood of thy Son our Saviour Jesus Christ; and dost assure us thereby of thy favour and goodness towards us; and that we are very members incorporate in the mystical body of thy Son, which is the blessed company of all faithful people; and are also heirs through hope of thy everlasting kingdom, by the merits of the most precious death and passion of thy dear Son. And we most humbly beseech thee, O heavenly Father, so to assist us with thy grace, that by his merits we may present ourselves, our souls and bodies, to be a living sacrifice; and that we may continue in that holy fellowship, and do all such good works as thou hast prepared for us to walk in; through Jesus Christ our Lord, to whom, with thee and the Holy Ghost, be all honour and glory, world without end. ℟ Amen.

44 *Here may be used the Postcommunion Collect[1] proper to the season. If it is used, the following is said.*

45 *Priest.* The Lord be with you.
People. And with thy spirit.
Priest. Let us pray.

The Blessing

The Priest (the Bishop of the Diocese, if he be present) blesses the People, using the following words.

The blessing of God Almighty, the Father, the Son, and the Holy Ghost, be amongst you and remain with you always. ℟ Amen.

46 *Next the following Response may be used.*

Deacon, or Priest. Come, let us go forth.
People. In the name of the Lord. Amen.

---

[1] ⟦See Appendix C.⟧

CHAPTER XII

THE CANADIAN LITURGY, 1959

THE Liturgy of the Canadian Prayer Book (1918) will be found in Chapter III. In 1943 a Joint Committee of both houses of the General Synod on the revision of the Book of Common Prayer was appointed, and this Committee's Draft Report, containing a revised form of the Liturgy, was presented in 1955. The General Synod thereupon authorized the Draft Book for experimental use for a period of five years. With certain modifications made since 1955, the Liturgy was approved by the General Synod in 1959 and included in the *Book of Common Prayer* (1959), which was issued in 1960 for permissive use for an indefinite period. This is the text here printed.

1 ## THE HOLY COMMUNION
OR HOLY EUCHARIST

THE ORDER FOR THE ADMINISTRATION OF THE
LORD'S SUPPER OR HOLY COMMUNION

2 *The Lord's Table, at the Communion time, shall have a fair white linen cloth upon it.*

3 *An Introit may be sung or said as the Priest proceeds to the holy Table.*

4 *The Priest, standing at the Table, shall say in an audible voice the Lord's Prayer with the Collect following, the people kneeling.*

Our Father who art in heaven . . . ⟦CF 1⟧ . . . evil. Amen.

5 ### THE COLLECT

Almighty God, unto whom . . . ⟦CF 2⟧ . . . Lord. *Amen.*

6 *Then shall the Priest, facing the people, rehearse the* TEN COMMANDMENTS *or else the Two Great Commandments of the Law. The Ten Commandments shall always be read at least once in each month on a Sunday at the chief Service of the day.*

It shall suffice to read the first paragraph of the Second and of the Fourth Commandment.

〚The effect of this rubric is to end (2) after 'worship them' and (4) after 'thy God'〛

7 *The people, still kneeling, shall after every Commandment sing or say the Kyrie, asking God's mercy for their transgressions in the past, and grace to keep his laws in time to come.*

Minister. Hear the Law of God which was given to Israel in old time. God spake ... 〚CF 3〛 ... beseech thee.

8 *Or he may rehearse, instead of these Commandments, the following:*

Minister. Our Lord Jesus Christ said: Hear O Israel, The Lord our God is one Lord; and thou shalt love the Lord thy God with all thy heart, and with all thy soul, and with all thy mind, and with all thy strength. This is the first and great commandment. And the second is like unto it: Thou shalt love thy neighbour as thyself. On these two commandments hang all the Law and the Prophets.

People. Lord, have mercy upon us, and write both these thy laws in our hearts, we beseech thee.

9 *Then may be sung or said:*

Lord, have mercy upon us.
   Christ, have mercy upon us.
Lord, have mercy upon us.

10 *Then the Priest shall say:*

    The Lord be with you;
People. And with thy spirit.

Let us pray.

11 *Then may follow this Collect for the Queen.*

Almighty God, whose kingdom is everlasting ... 〚as Chapter III no. 7, but reading '*ELIZABETH*', &c.〛 ... end. *Amen.*

12 *Then shall be said* THE COLLECT OF THE DAY, *together with any other Collects appointed to be said.*

13 *Then, the people being seated, the Priest or other person appointed shall read* THE EPISTLE, *saying:* The Epistle [or The Lesson] is written

in the ... chapter of ... beginning at the ... verse. *And the reading ended, he shall say:* Here endeth the Epistle [*or* the Lesson].

14 *Here may follow a Psalm or a Hymn.*

15 *Then shall the people stand for* THE GOSPEL; *and the Deacon or Priest who reads shall say:* The Holy Gospel is written in the ... chapter of the Gospel according to Saint ... beginning at the ... verse.

16 *Then shall the people sing or say:* Glory be to thee, O Lord. *And after the reading of the Gospel they shall sing or say:* Praise be to thee, O Christ.

17 *Then shall be sung or said this Creed by the Priest and people. It may, however, at the discretion of the Minister, be omitted on weekdays which are not Holy-days.*

I believe in one God ... 〚CF 4〛 ... to come. Amen.

〚*But reading* 'Begotten of the Father'; 'one substance with the Father;'; 'through whom all things'; 'The Lord, The Giver of Life'; 'One, Holy, Catholic'〛

18 *Here on Sundays the Minister shall announce what Holy-days and what days of Fasting, Abstinence, and Solemn Prayer are to be observed during the week, and publish Banns of Marriage and such other communications as are enjoined by lawful authority.*

THE SERMON

19 *Then shall the Priest, standing at the Lord's Table, begin*

THE OFFERTORY

saying one or more of the following Sentences:[1]

The Churchwardens, or others appointed by them, shall collect the offerings of the people, and reverently bring them to the Priest, who shall humbly present and place them upon the holy Table.

20 *The Priest shall also at the time of the Offertory present and place on the Lord's Table so much Bread and Wine as he shall think sufficient, the same being brought to him, if so desired, by the Churchwardens or other representatives of the people.*

---

[1] 〚For Offertory Sentences see Appendix B.〛

21 *Then may be said or sung:*

Blessed be thou, Lord God of Israel, for ever and ever. All that is in the heaven and in the earth is thine.

All things come of thee, and of thine own have we given thee. 1 *Chronicles* 29. 10, 11, 14.

22 *Then shall one of the Ministers ask the prayers of the people, using always either the first or the last of the following Biddings, together with one or more others if so desired; and he may provide short periods for silent prayer.*

23 Let us pray for Christ's holy Catholic Church.

Let us pray for peace on earth and for the unity of all Christian people.

Let us pray for our missionaries at home and abroad.

Let us remember before God those of our brethren who have departed this life and are at rest.

Let us pray for the whole state of Christ's Church militant here in earth.

24 *Then the Priest shall say* THE INTERCESSION.

Almighty and everliving God, who by thy holy Apostle hast taught us to make prayers and supplications, and to give thanks, for all men: We humbly beseech thee most mercifully *to accept our alms and oblations, and* to receive these our prayers, which we offer unto thy Divine Majesty; beseeching thee to inspire continually the universal Church with the spirit of truth, unity and concord: And grant that all they that do confess thy holy Name may agree in the truth of thy holy Word, and live in unity and godly love.

25 We beseech thee also to lead all nations in the way of righteousness; and so to guide and direct their governors and rulers, that thy people may enjoy the blessings of freedom and peace: and grant unto thy servant *ELIZABETH* our Queen, and to all that are put in authority under her, that they may truly and impartially administer justice, to the maintenance of thy true religion and virtue.

26 Give grace, O heavenly Father, to all Bishops, Priests, and Deacons, *and specially to thy servant N. our Bishop,* that they may both by their life and doctrine set forth thy true and living Word, and rightly and duly administer thy holy Sacraments: Prosper, we

pray thee, all those who proclaim the Gospel of thy kingdom among the nations: And to all thy people give thy heavenly grace, and specially to this congregation here present, that, with meek heart and due reverence, they may hear and receive thy holy Word; truly serving thee in holiness and righteousness all the days of their life.

27 And we most humbly beseech thee of thy goodness, O Lord, to comfort and succour all them, who in this transitory life are in trouble, sorrow, need, sickness, or any other adversity, *especially those for whom our prayers are desired.*

28 We remember before thee, O Lord, all thy servants departed this life in thy faith and fear: and we bless thy holy Name for all who in life and death have glorified thee; beseeching thee to give us grace that, rejoicing in their fellowship, we may follow their good examples, and with them be partakers of thy heavenly kingdom.

29 Grant this, O Father, for Jesus Christ's sake, our only Mediator and Advocate, to whom, with thee and the Holy Ghost, be all honour and glory, world without end. *Amen.*

30 *Then shall the Priest or one of the Ministers say:*

Ye that do truly ... ⟦CF 6, but reading 'the new life'⟧ ... upon your knees.

31 *Then shall this general Confession be made by all those that are minded to receive the holy Communion, both Priest and people humbly kneeling.*

Almighty God, Father ... ⟦CF 7⟧ ... our Lord. Amen.

⟦But reading 'confess' for 'bewail' and omitting 'provoking ... against us' and 'The remembrance ... mercy upon us'⟧

32 *Then shall the Priest* (or *the Bishop if he be present*) *stand up, and turning himself to the people, pronounce this Absolution:*

Almighty God, our heavenly Father ... ⟦CF 8⟧ ... our Lord. *Amen.*

33 *Then shall the Priest say:*

Hear what comfortable words ... ⟦CF 9⟧ ... our sins.

⟦Reading 'eternal' for 'everlasting' in S. John 3. 16 and 'Christ Jesus' for 'Jesus Christ' in 1 Tim. 1. 15⟧

34 *The Priest shall then proceed with the holy Eucharist in* THANKSGIVING AND CONSECRATION *as follows:*

  The Lord be with you;
People. And with thy spirit.

The Canadian Liturgy, 1959

Priest. Lift up your hearts;
People. We lift them up unto the Lord.
Priest. Let us give thanks unto our Lord God;
People. It is meet and right so to do.

35 *Then shall the Priest turn to the Lord's Table, and say:*

It is very meet, right, and our bounden duty, that we should at all times, and in all places, give thanks unto thee, O Lord, Holy Father, Almighty, Everlasting God, Creator and Preserver of all things.

Here shall follow the Proper Preface,[1] *if there be any specially appointed, or else immediately shall be said or sung:*

Therefore with Angels and Archangels, and with all the company of heaven, we laud and magnify thy glorious Name; evermore praising thee and saying:

Holy, Holy, Holy, Lord God of hosts, Heaven and earth are full of thy glory. Glory be to thee, O Lord Most High. *Priest and People*

36 *Either here, or immediately before the Communion, the Priest and people may say or sing:*

Blessed is he that cometh in the Name of the Lord: Hosanna in the highest.

37 *Then shall the Priest proceed with the Prayer of Consecration and the Breaking of the Bread before the people.*

Blessing and glory and thanksgiving be unto thee Almighty God, our heavenly Father, who of thy tender mercy didst give thine only Son Jesus Christ to take our nature upon him, and to suffer death upon the Cross for our redemption; who made there, by his one oblation of himself once offered, a full, perfect, and sufficient sacrifice, oblation, and satisfaction, for the sins of the whole world; and did institute, and in his holy Gospel command us to continue, a perpetual memorial of that his precious death, until his coming again.

38   Hear us, O merciful Father, we most humbly beseech thee; and grant that we receiving these thy creatures of bread and wine, according to thy Son our Saviour Jesus Christ's holy institution, in remembrance of his death and passion, may be partakers of his

---

[1] [[For Proper Prefaces, see Appendix A.]]

most blessed Body and Blood; who, in the same night that he was betrayed, ᵃtook Bread; and, when he had given thanks, ᵇhe brake it; and gave it to his disciples, saying, Take, eat; ᶜthis is my Body which is given for you: Do this in remembrance of me. Likewise after supper ᵈhe took the Cup; and, when he had given thanks, he gave it to them, saying, Drink ye all, of this; for ᵉthis is my Blood of the new Covenant, which is shed for you and for many for the remission of sins: Do this, as oft as ye shall drink it, in remembrance of me.

^ᵃ *Here the Priest is to take the Paten into his hands:*
^ᵇ *And here to break the Bread:*
^ᶜ *And here to lay his hand upon all the Bread:*
^ᵈ *Here he is to take the Cup into his hands:*
^ᵉ *And here to lay his hand upon every vessel (be it Chalice or Flagon) in which there is any Wine to be consecrated.*

39   Wherefore, O Father, Lord of heaven and earth, we thy humble servants, with all thy holy Church, remembering the precious death of thy beloved Son, his mighty resurrection, and glorious ascension, and looking for his coming again in glory, do make before thee, in this sacrament of the holy Bread of eternal life and the Cup of everlasting salvation, the memorial which he hath commanded; And we entirely desire thy fatherly goodness mercifully to accept this our sacrifice of praise and thanksgiving, most humbly beseeching thee to grant, that by the merits and death of thy Son Jesus Christ, and through faith in his blood, we and all thy whole Church may obtain remission of our sins, and all other benefits of his passion; And we pray that by the power of thy Holy Spirit, all we who are partakers of this holy Communion may be fulfilled with thy grace and heavenly benediction; through Jesus Christ our Lord, by whom and with whom, in the unity of the Holy Spirit, all honour and glory be unto thee, O Father Almighty, world without end.

And all the people shall answer: Amen.

40   *After a short period of silence the Priest shall say:*

   The peace of the Lord be always with you;
People. And with thy spirit.

41   *Then shall the Priest kneel down at the Lord's Table, and shall, together with all that shall receive the Communion, humbly say this prayer following:*

We do not presume . . . ⟦CF 10⟧ . . . in us. Amen.

The Canadian Liturgy, 1959

42 *Then shall the Priest first receive*

THE COMMUNION

in both kinds himself, and then proceed to deliver the same to the Bishops, Priests, and Deacons, in like manner, (if any be present,) and after that to the people also in order, into their hands, all meekly kneeling. And, as he delivers the Bread . . . [[CF 11]] . . . be thankful.

43 *In the Communion time, Hymns or Anthems such as the following may be used:*

O Lamb of God, that takest away the sin of the world, have mercy upon us.
   O Lamb of God, that takest away the sin of the world, have mercy upon us.
   O Lamb of God, that takest away the sin of the world, grant us thy peace.

44 *When all have communicated, then shall the Priest say the Lord's Prayer, the people repeating with him every petition.*

Let us pray.

Our Father who art in heaven . . . [[CF 1]] . . . ever and ever. Amen.

45 *Then shall the Priest say:*

Almighty and everliving God, we most heartily thank thee that thou dost graciously feed us, in these holy mysteries, with the spiritual food of the most precious Body and Blood of thy Son our Saviour Jesus Christ; assuring us thereby of thy favour and goodness towards us; and that we are living members of his mystical body, which is the blessed company of all faithful people; and are also heirs through hope of thy everlasting kingdom.

   And here we offer and present unto thee, O Lord, ourselves, our souls and bodies, to be a reasonable, holy, and living sacrifice unto thee. And although we are unworthy, yet we beseech thee to accept this our bounden duty and service, not weighing our merits, but pardoning our offences; through Jesus Christ our Lord, to whom, with thee and the Holy Ghost, be all honour and glory, world without end. *Amen.*

46 *Then shall be said or sung Gloria in Excelsis. On a weekday which is not a festival it may be omitted.*

Glory be to God . . . ⟦CF 13⟧ . . . Father. *Amen.*

⟦Omitting 'Thou that takest . . . mercy upon us'⟧

47 *Then the Priest (or the Bishop if he be present) shall let them depart with this Blessing.*

The peace of God . . . ⟦CF 14⟧ . . . always. *Amen.*

CHAPTER XIII

THE LITURGIES OF THE DIOCESES OF NYASALAND AND NORTHERN RHODESIA[1]

THESE two liturgies are sufficiently alike in order and in text to be printed together in one chapter. Each has been authorized by the Bishop in Synod for the diocese concerned; but neither has been published in England. In the case of the Nyasaland liturgy, local editions both in English and in vernaculars have been printed; but the rite of Northern Rhodesia has not been printed in English at all, and the text which follows is taken from a typed translation used for the information of missionaries who are about to take up work in the diocese. For this reason, trivial differences of wording between the two rites (especially in rubric) have been ignored. The aim has been to print the text continuously and in one column as far as possible, the portions which are not found in Nyasaland being enclosed in square [brackets] and those not found in Northern Rhodesia in pointed ⟨brackets⟩. However, in some passages the two rites have divergent forms for the same purpose; in such cases they have been printed in parallel columns.

1

[THE LITURGY]

[MASS OF THE CATECHUMENS]

2

THE PREPARATION

[*This may be omitted in part or whole at the discretion of the Priest*]

Priest. In the Name of the Father, and of the Son, and of the Holy Ghost. *Amen.*

Priest. I will go unto the Altar of God:
People. Even unto the God of my joy and gladness.
⟦Psalm 43 said responsorially by Priest and People⟧
⟨*The Psalm is omitted at Requiems, and in Passiontide.*⟩
Priest. I will go unto the Altar of God:
People. Even unto the God of my joy and gladness.

[1] See note on p. 161.

3 *Priest.* Our help is in the Name of the Lord;
People. Who hath made heaven and earth.

⟨*Priest.* I confess to God Almighty, to all the Saints, and to you, brethren, that I have sinned exceedingly in thought, word and deed, by my fault, my own fault, my own most grievous fault. Wherefore I beg all the Saints to pray for me, and you, brethren, to pray for me to the Lord, our God.⟩

⟨*People.* Almighty God have mercy upon you, forgive you your sins, and bring you to everlasting life.⟩

⟨*Priest.* Amen.⟩

⟨*People.* I confess to God Almighty, to all the Saints, and to you, Father, that I have sinned exceedingly in thought, word, and deed, by my fault, my own fault, my own most grievous fault. Wherefore I beg all the Saints to pray for me, and you, Father, to pray for me to the Lord our God.⟩

⟨*Priest.* Almighty God have mercy upon you, forgive you your sins, and bring you to everlasting life.⟩

⟨*People.* Amen.⟩

⟨*Priest.* The Almighty and merciful Lord grant us pardon, absolution, and remission of our sins.⟩

⟨*People.* Amen.⟩

4 *Priest.* Wilt thou not turn again and quicken us, O Lord;
People. That thy people may rejoice in thee.

Priest. Shew us thy mercy, O Lord;
People. And grant us thy salvation.

Priest. Lord, hear my prayer;
People. And let my cry come unto thee.

⟨*Priest.* The Lord be with you;⟩
⟨*People.* And with thy spirit.⟩

5 ⟨THE SERVICE⟩
⟨*The Priest goes up to the Altar and says:*⟩
Almighty God, unto whom . . . ⟦CF 1⟧ . . . Lord. Amen.

Nyasaland and Northern Rhodesia

Rhod

6 *Then the Priest, standing in the midst of the Altar, shall say the Ten Commandments; these shall always be read on Sundays; at the discretion of the Priest on Holy Days; and omitted on Ferias*

God spake these words and said: Thou shalt have none other Gods but me.

People. Lord, have mercy upon us, and incline our hearts to keep this law.

7 *Priest.* Thou shalt not make idols to worship them.

Thou shalt not take the Name of the Lord thy God in vain.

Remember the Lord's Day; that it may be holy.

Honour thy father and thy mother.

Thou shalt do no murder.

Thou shalt not commit adultery.

Thou shalt not steal.

Thou shalt not bear false witness against thy neighbour.

Do not covet anything belonging to your neighbour.

People. Lord, have mercy upon us, and write all these thy laws in our hearts, we beseech thee.

or,

8 Lord have mercy upon us
Lord have mercy upon us
Lord have mercy upon us
Christ have mercy upon us

Nyas

Then the Priest reads
THE INTROIT

Then shall follow
THE KYRIES
Lord have mercy
Lord have mercy
Lord have mercy
Christ have mercy

The Liturgy in English

Rhod	**Nyas**
Christ have mercy upon us	Christ have mercy
Christ have mercy upon us	*Christ have mercy*
Lord have mercy upon us	Lord have mercy
Lord have mercy upon us	*Lord have mercy*
Lord have mercy upon us	Lord have mercy

Then shall be said, or sung, if it is appointed

THE GLORIA IN EXCELSIS GLORIA IN EXCELSIS DEO

Glory be to God on high . . . ⟦CF 13⟧ . . . God the Father. Amen.

⟦**Nyas** omits 'Thou that takest . . . upon us'⟧

10   [*Then turning to the people the Priest shall say or sing*]

The Lord be with you;

People. And with thy spirit.

[*Then standing by the book at the Epistle corner the Priest shall say*]

Let us pray.

THE [PROPER] COLLECTS

11   [*Then shall he announce the Epistle thus*]

[The Epistle is written in the . . . Chapter of . . . beginning at the . . . verse.]

THE EPISTLE

[*To be said or sung by the Priest, or the sub-deacon at High Mass, which ended he shall say,* Here endeth the Epistle.]

[*And the people respond*] ⟨R⟩ Thanks be to God.

⟨*Then the Priest reads* THE GRADUAL⟩

12   [*Then shall the Priest say*]

⟨V⟩ The Lord be with you;

R And with thy spirit.

⟨*Before the Gospel*⟩

[*Priest.* The Holy Gospel is written in the . . . chapter of . . . beginning at the . . . verse.]

People. Glory be to thee, O Lord.

[*Then shall the Priest say or sing*]

THE HOLY GOSPEL

⟨*After the Gospel*⟩
People. Praise be to thee, O Christ.
[*On Sundays and great Feast Days here followeth the Sermon.*]¹

13   [THE DISMISSAL OF THE CATECHUMENS]
[*Note that the whole of this order of Dismissal shall be used on Sundays; but at other times the concluding prayer shall suffice*]

[*Priest*. You catechumens, pray to the Lord.
Catechumens. Lord, have mercy upon us.
   Lord, have mercy upon us.
   Lord, have mercy upon us.

Priest. You Christians, pray for the Catechumens.
People. Lord, have mercy upon them.

Priest. Make them to know thy truth.
People. Lord, have mercy upon them.

Priest. Reveal to them the Gospel of Righteousness.
People. Lord, have mercy upon them.

Priest. Grant them a new heart and a prepared spirit.
People. Lord, have mercy upon them.

Priest. Lead them into thy Holy Church.
People. Lord, have mercy upon them.

Priest. You Catechumens, worship the Lord.

Catechumens. Thou art our God; and we praise thee.
   Thou art our God; and we praise thee.
   Thou art our God; and we praise thee.]

14 [*Priest*. Let us pray.
Almighty God, who dost daily give to thy Church new Children; grant to these Catechumens that they truly increase in knowledge and in faith, till they are born again in Holy Baptism and made thy children by adoption and grace; through Jesus Christ, our Redeemer. *Amen*.

Priest. You Catechumens, depart in peace.]

¹ [There is no direction for a Sermon in **Nyas**.]

Rhod	Nyas

15 MASS OF THE FAITHFUL

Then shall be said or sung, always on Sundays and Great Festivals, but may be omitted on Ferias and certain other days, and always omitted at a Requiem Mass.   *Then shall be said or sung, if it is appointed:*

THE CREED   THE NICENE CREED

I believe in one God . . . ⟦CF 4⟧ . . . world to come. Amen.

⟦**Rhod** reads 'the Lord, the Giver of life' and adds two rubrics: '*here all kneel*' after '*from heaven*' and '*here all rise*' after '*was buried*'. Both read 'One Holy Catholic'⟧

⟨℣ The Lord be with you;
℟ And with thy spirit.⟩

16   THE OFFERTORY

[*Then shall the Priest read*: I will offer in the Lord's dwelling an oblation with great gladness, I will sing and speak praises unto him. (Psalm xxvii. 7)]

[*or*, Offer unto God thanksgiving, and pay thy vows unto the most Highest. (Psalm l. 14)]

Rhod	Nyas

17 *The priest shall then put ready the bread, and the wine mixed with water. This done, he turns to the people and says:*   *When the Priest has offered the Bread and Wine he turns to the people and says:*

Brethren, pray that both my sacrifice and yours may be acceptable to God the Father Almighty.

Pray, Brethren, that my sacrifice and yours may be acceptable to God the Father Almighty.

People. The Lord receive this Sacrifice at thy hands to the praise and glory of his Name, to our benefit and the benefit of all his Church.

The people shall say:

The Lord accept this sacrifice at thy hands, to the praise and glory of his Name, for our benefit, and that of all his holy Church.

Priest. Amen.

Nyasaland and Northern Rhodesia

Rhod

℣ The Lord be with you;
℟ And with thy spirit.

Priest.

18   Let us pray for the whole

Almighty and everliving God, we beseech thee to accept these our prayers and offerings, and we pray thee to inspire the universal Church with the spirit of truth and concord.

Defend our King N. and grant that under him we may be godly and quietly governed. O heavenly Father, bless our Bishop N., and all the Bishops and Pastors, that both by their life and doctrine they may set forth thy true and living Word, and rightly and duly administer thy Holy Sacraments.

And to all thy people give thy heavenly grace, that they may serve thee truly all the days of their life. Comfort all those who are in trouble, sorrow, need, sickness, or any other adversity (especially N. and N.). We pray thee to bless those assembled here to celebrate the commemoration of the most glorious death of thy Son, Christ our Lord. *Amen.*

And here do we give unto thee most high praise and thanks for the wonderful grace and virtue declared in all thy saints; and chiefly in the glorious and most Blessed Virgin

Nyas

The Priest shall then say,

state of Christ's Church.

Almighty and everliving God, who by thy holy Apostle hast taught us to make prayers and supplications, and to give thanks for all men; We humbly beseech thee most mercifully to accept our (alms and) oblations, and to receive these our prayers, which we offer unto thy Divine Majesty; beseeching thee to inspire continually the universal Church with the spirit of truth, unity, and concord: And grant that all they that do confess thy holy Name may agree in the truth of thy holy Word, and live in unity, and godly love.

We beseech thee also to save and defend all Christian Kings, Princes, and Governors; and specially thy Servant Elizabeth, our Queen; that under her we may be godly and quietly governed; And grant unto her whole Council and to all that are put in authority under her, that they may truly and faithfully minister justice, to the punishment of wickedness and vice, and to the maintenance of thy true religion, and virtue.

Give grace, O heavenly Father, to all Bishops, Priests and Deacons and especially to thy

Rhod

Mary, mother of thy Son Jesus Christ our Lord and our God; and in the holy Patriarchs, Prophets, Apostles, and Martyrs, whose examples, O Lord, and steadfastness in thy faith, and keeping of thy holy Commandments, grant us to follow; through Christ our Lord. *Amen.*

We commend unto thy mercy, O Lord, all other thy servants which are departed hence from us, with the sign of faith (especially . . .), grant unto them, we beseech thee, thy mercy and everlasting peace, that at the day of the general resurrection thou wilt bring us all together to the glory of thy Son. Grant this, O Father, for Jesus Christ's sake, our only Mediator and Advocate. *Amen.*

Nyas

Servants N. our Archbishop and N. our Bishop, that they may both by their life and doctrine set forth thy true and living Word, and rightly and duly administer thy holy Sacraments: And to all thy people give thy heavenly grace; and especially to this congregation here present, that with meek heart and due reverence they may hear and receive thy holy Word, truly serving thee in holiness and righteousness all the days of their life.

And we most humbly beseech thee of thy goodness, O Lord, to comfort and succour all those who are travelling, and all who are in trouble, sorrow, need, sickness or any other adversity, and to bring into the way of Truth all such as have erred, and to grant to the excommunicate, and to all impenitent sinners, the grace of true repentance.

And we commend to thy gracious keeping, O Lord, all thy servants departed this life in thy faith and fear, beseeching thee to grant them mercy, light and peace, both now and at the day of Resurrection.

And here we do give unto thee, O Lord, most high praise and hearty thanks for the wonderful grace and virtue declared

Nyas

in all thy Saints, and chiefly in the Blessed Virgin Mary, Mother of thy Son Jesus Christ, our Lord and God, and in the holy Patriarchs, Prophets, Apostles and Martyrs; and in all other thy righteous servants, known to us or unknown, beseeching thee to give us grace that we, rejoicing in the Communion of the Saints and following the good examples of those who have served thee here and are at rest, may be partakers with them of thy heavenly kingdom: Grant this, O Father, for Jesus Christ's sake, our only Mediator and Advocate, who with thee and the Holy Ghost liveth and reigneth One God, world without end. *Amen.*

19 [*Then shall the Priest say*]
[Confess your sins unto the Lord.]

[*And the server and people shall say*][1]
[We confess to God Almighty, in the sight of the whole company of Heaven, that we have sinned exceedingly, in thought, word, and deed, through our own fault. Wherefore we beseech God Almighty to have mercy upon us.]

[May the Almighty God have mercy upon us, forgive us our sins, and bring us to everlasting life.]

20 [*Then shall the Priest turn to the people and say*]
[The Almighty and merciful Lord grant you forgiveness, absolution, and remission of your sins. *Amen.*]

---

[1] [[Cf. no. 28 below.]]

[*Then shall be said, on Sundays at least*]
[THE COMFORTABLE WORDS]
[Hear what comfortable . . . 〚CF 9〛 . . . our sins.]

〚Reading 'Christ Jesus' in 1 Tim. 1. 15〛

21 [SURSUM CORDA]

℣ The Lord be with you;
℟ And with thy spirit.
℣ Lift up your hearts;
℟ We lift them up unto the Lord.
℣ Let us give thanks unto our Lord God;
℟ It is meet and right so to do.

Priest. It is very meet, right, and our bounden duty, that we should at all times and in all places give thanks unto thee, [O] Holy Lord, Almighty Father, Everlasting God. 〚Father Almighty, **Nyas**〛

[*Here follows the Proper Preface,*[1] *if any*]

Therefore with Angels and Archangels, and with all the company of Heaven, we laud and magnify thy glorious Name, evermore praising thee and saying:

22 [*Priest and people.*]
Holy, Holy, Holy, Lord God of Hosts, Heaven and earth are full of thy glory. [Hosanna in the highest.] Blessed is he that cometh in the Name of the Lord. Hosanna in the highest.

23 [THE PRAYER OF CONSECRATION]

Rhod	**Nyas**
All glory and thanksgiving be to thee, Almighty God, our heavenly Father, for that thou of thy tender mercy didst give thine only Son Jesus Christ to suffer death upon the Cross for our redemption; who made there (by his one oblation of himself once offered) a full,	Truly thou art Holy, O Almighty God and Heavenly Father, and to thee do we give thanks for that thou didst give thine only Son Jesus Christ, to take our nature upon him and to suffer death upon the cross for our redemption; who made there one all-sufficient sacrifice

[1] 〚For Proper Prefaces see Appendix A.〛

Nyasaland and Northern Rhodesia

Rhod

perfect, and sufficient sacrifice, oblation, and satisfaction for the sins of the whole world; and didst institute, and in his Holy Gospel command us to continue, a perpetual memory of that his precious death, until his coming again.

Who, in the same night that he was betrayed, took bread, and, when he had given thanks, he brake it, and gave it to his disciples, saying, TAKE, EAT, THIS IS MY BODY WHICH IS GIVEN FOR YOU: DO THIS IN REMEMBRANCE OF ME.

Likewise after supper he took the cup, and, when he had given thanks, he gave it to them saying, DRINK YE ALL OF THIS: FOR THIS IS MY BLOOD OF THE NEW TESTAMENT, WHICH IS SHED FOR YOU AND FOR MANY FOR THE REMISSION OF SINS: DO THIS, AS OFT AS YE SHALL DRINK IT, IN REMEMBRANCE OF ME. *Amen.*

Wherefore, O Lord and heavenly Father, we thy humble servants, having in remembrance the blessed Passion of the same Christ thy Son our Lord, his mighty Resurrection and glorious Ascension, and rendering unto thee most

Nyas

for the sins of the whole world, and did institute and in his holy Gospel command us to continue a perpetual memory of that his precious death, until his coming again.

Hear us, O merciful Father, we humbly beseech thee, and with thy Holy Spirit and with thy Word vouchsafe to sanctify these thy creatures of bread and wine, that they may be unto us the Body and Blood of thy most dearly beloved Son Jesus Christ. Who in the same night that he was betrayed took bread, and when he had blessed and given thanks he brake it and gave it to his disciples, saying, Take, eat, THIS IS MY BODY WHICH IS GIVEN FOR YOU. DO THIS IN REMEMBRANCE OF ME; Likewise after supper he took the cup, and when he had blessed and given thanks he gave it to them saying, Drink ye all of this, for THIS IS MY BLOOD OF THE NEW TESTAMENT WHICH IS SHED FOR YOU AND FOR MANY FOR THE REMISSION OF SINS. DO THIS AS OFT AS YE SHALL DRINK IT IN REMEMBRANCE OF ME.

Wherefore, O Lord and Heavenly Father, we thy humble servants, together with all

Rhod

hearty thanks for the innumerable benefits procured unto us by the same, do offer unto thy Divine Majesty these sacred gifts and creatures of thine own, this holy Bread of eternal life and this Cup of everlasting salvation; and we humbly beseech thee to pour thy Holy Spirit upon us and upon these thy gifts, that he may hallow this oblation, and that all we who are partakers of this Holy Communion may worthily receive the most precious Body and Blood of thy Son, and be fulfilled with thy grace and heavenly benediction. *Amen.*

And we entirely desire thy fatherly goodness mercifully to accept this our sacrifice of praise and thanksgiving; most humbly beseeching thee to grant, that by the merits and death of thy Son Jesus Christ, and through faith in his Blood, we and all thy whole Church may obtain remission of our sins and all other benefits of his Passion. *Amen.*

And here we offer and present unto thee, O Lord, ourselves, our souls and bodies, to be a reasonable, holy, and living sacrifice unto thee.

And although we be unworthy, we beseech thee, O Father, to accept this our

Nyas

thy holy people, having in remembrance the Blessed Passion of the same thy Son Christ our Lord, as also his mighty Resurrection and glorious Ascension, do offer unto thy Divine Majesty of these thy Holy Gifts a pure and holy Victim, this holy Bread of eternal life, and this Cup of everlasting salvation; beseeching thee to grant that by the merits and death of thy Son Jesus Christ and through faith in his Blood we and all thy whole Church may obtain remission of our sins and all other benefits of his Passion.

And here we offer unto thee, O Lord, ourselves, our souls and bodies, to be a holy and living sacrifice unto thee, humbly beseeching thee that whosoever shall receive the sacred Body and Blood of thy Son may be filled with thy grace and heavenly benediction. And although we be unworthy through our manifold sins to offer unto thee any sacrifice, yet we beseech thee to command that this our Sacrifice, together with our prayers, be brought to thy Holy Altar on high, before the sight of thy Divine Majesty; through Jesus Christ our Lord, by whom and with whom and in whom, in

Rhod	**Nyas**
sacrifice, not weighing our merits but pardoning our offences: through Jesus Christ our Lord, by whom, and with whom, in the unity of the Holy Ghost, all honour and glory be unto thee, O Father Almighty, world without end. *Amen.*	the unity of the Holy Ghost, all honour and glory be unto thee, O Father Almighty, world without end. *Amen.*
24 *Priest.* As our Saviour Christ hath commanded and taught us, we are bold to say,	And now, as our Saviour Christ has taught us, we are bold to say,

[*Priest and People*]

Our Father ... ⟦CF 1⟧ ... from evil. [For thine is the kingdom, the power and the glory; for ever and ever.] Amen.

Rhod	**Nyas**
25 *Then, the priest, kneeling upon his knees, shall say,*	
Lord, we are not worthy to come to this thy table. We pray thee, grant us so to eat the Flesh of thy dear Son Jesus Christ, and to drink his Blood, that our sinful bodies may be cleansed by his Body, and our souls washed by his most precious Blood; through the same Jesus Christ our Lord. *Amen.*	
26 *When the Priest breaks the Host, he shall say,*	*The Priest makes the Fraction and Commixture and says aloud,* World without end. ℟ Amen.
The peace of the Lord be always with you;	The peace of the Lord be with you always;

℟ And with thy spirit.

Rhod	Nyas
27 *In an audible voice together with the people:*	*Then shall be said or sung by the Priest and people together:*

O Lamb of God that takest away the sins of the world, have mercy upon us.

O Lamb of God that takest away the sins of the world, have mercy upon us.

O Lamb of God that takest away the sins of the world, grant us thy peace.

Or in Requiem Masses:

O Lamb of God that takest away the sins of the world, grant them rest.

O Lamb of God that takest away the sins of the world, grant them rest.

O Lamb of God that takest away the sins of the world, grant them rest eternal.

28 ⟨*When there are Communicants, the bell is rung once. Then those who are to communicate shall kneel at the altar, and say the Confession*⟩[1]

⟨I confess to God Almighty, to all the Saints, and to you, Father, that I have sinned exceedingly in thought, word and deed, through my fault, my own fault, my own most grievous fault. Wherefore I beg all the Saints to pray for me, and you, Father, to pray for me to the Lord our God.⟩

⟨*The Priest, facing the Epistle side, shall say*⟩

⟨Almighty God have mercy upon you, forgive you your sins, and bring you to everlasting life. *Amen.*⟩

⟨May the Almighty and merciful Lord grant you pardon, absolution, and remission of your sins. *Amen.*⟩

Rhod	Nyas
29 *When the Priest turns to the people to give them their Communion, let him say,*	*The Priest then faces the people and raising the Blessed Sacrament says,*

Behold the Lamb of God that taketh away the sins of the world. ⟨*Priest.* Lord, I am not worthy that thou shouldest come under my roof, but speak the word only and my soul shall be healed.⟩

---

[1] [[Cf. no. 19 above.]]

⟨*People.* Lord, I am not worthy that thou shouldest come under my roof, but speak the word only and my soul shall be healed.⟩

⟨*Priest.* Lord, I am not worthy that thou shouldest come under my roof, but speak the world only and my soul shall be healed.⟩

Rhod	**Nyas**
30 *When he communicates them, he shall say,*	*When he communicates the people, he says,*

The Body of our Lord Jesus Christ, which was given for thee, preserve thy body and soul unto everlasting life.

The Blood of our Lord Jesus Christ, which was shed ⟦given, **Rhod**⟧ for thee, preserve thy body and soul unto everlasting life.

Rhod	**Nyas**
31 *Then*	*When he has cleansed the vessels,*

the Priest goes to the Epistle corner and reads,

THE COMMUNION

[I am crucified with Christ; but I live. Yet it is not I that live, but Christ who liveth in me.]

[*or other words of Holy Scripture as appointed*]

32 *Then, returning to the midst of the altar, he* ⟨*kisses it, and*⟩ *turns to the people, and says,*

℣ The Lord be with you;
℞ And with thy spirit.

He goes to the book and says ⟦*reads* **Rhod**⟧,

⟨Let us pray⟩

⟨*Then follow*⟩

THE POST-COMMUNION ⟨COLLECTS⟩

Rhod	**Nyas**
Let us pray	*Instead of, or in addition to, the post-communion Collect of the day, the Priest may, if he wishes, say the following thanksgiving.*
33 Remember, O Lord, what thou hast wrought in us and not what we deserve; and as thou hast called us to thy service, do thou make us worthy of thy calling; through Jesus Christ our Lord.	Almighty and everliving God, we most heartily thank thee, for that thou dost vouchsafe to feed us, who have duly re-

Rhod	Nyas

34 *And if many have made their Communion he may add,*

Almighty God, heavenly Father, we most heartily thank thee for that thou hast vouchsafed to feed us in these Holy Mysteries with the Body and Blood of thy Son Jesus Christ. We most humbly beseech thee so to assist us with thy grace that we may do all such good works as thou hast prepared for us to walk in. Through the same Jesus Christ our Lord, who liveth and reigneth with thee in the Unity of the Holy Spirit, God world without end. *Amen.*

ceived these holy mysteries, with the spiritual food of the most precious Body and Blood of thy Son, our Saviour Jesus Christ: and dost assure us thereby of thy favour and goodness towards us: and that we are very members incorporate in the mystical body of thy Son, which is the blessed company of all faithful people: and are also heirs through hope of thy everlasting kingdom, by the merits of the most precious death and passion of thy dear Son. And we most humbly beseech thee, O Heavenly Father, so to assist us with thy grace, that we may continue in that holy fellowship, and do all such good works as thou hast prepared for us to walk in; through Jesus Christ our Lord, to whom, with thee and the Holy Ghost, be all honour and glory, world without end. *Amen.*

35 *Then let the Priest turn to the people and say—except in Requiem Masses,*

The Peace of God . . . 〚CF 14〛 . . . always. *Amen.*

Then returning to the midst of the altar, he kisses it, and turning to the people, says,

THE BLESSING

The Blessing of God Almighty, the Father, the Son, and the Holy Ghost, be amongst you and remain with you always. *Amen.*

	Rhod	Nyas
36	In Requiem Masses the Pax and the Blessing are omitted, but the Priest, still turned towards the Altar, says,	In Requiem Masses instead of the Blessing, is said,

℣ May they rest in peace.
℟ Amen.

37 ⟨*The Priest then reads the Last Gospel.*⟩

NOTE

From July 1964 the former Diocese of Nyasaland will be known as the Diocese of Malawi and from October 1964 the former Diocese of Northern Rhodesia will be known as the Diocese of Zambia. For the purposes of this chapter the old names, in use when the rites concerned were authorized, have been retained.

CHAPTER XIV

THE SWAHILI MASS

This liturgy was compiled in Swahili and has never been published in English. It was authorized for the diocese of Zanzibar[1] by the Bishop in Synod during the episcopate of Frank Weston and has been used there ever since. It is now used also in the dioceses of Masasi and South-West Tanganyika. The text here printed is taken from a typed English translation which is used at the headquarters of U.M.C.A. for the information of new missionaries. This explains the presentation of the liturgy simply in outline with the complete text of the Canon. It should, however, be pointed out that even the text of the Canon is simply a literal translation made for the purpose mentioned; it was not intended for liturgical use and has no liturgical authority.

A. THE MASS OF THE CATECHUMENS

    The Preparation: *said by priest and whole congregation.*
    Collect for Purity
    The Introit
    Nine-fold Kyrie
    Gloria (*when ordered*)
    The Collect(s)
    The Epistle
    Gradual
    The Gospel
    The Sermon (*on Sundays and Greater Festivals*)
    The Dismissal of the Catechumens (*on Sundays and Greater Festivals*)

B. THE MASS OF THE FAITHFUL

    Nicene Creed (*when ordered*)
    Offertory
    'Pray, Brethren. . . . .'
    The Secret Prayer(s)
    Sursum Corda

[1] Now Zanzibar and Dar-es-Salaam.

Preface (*Proper Prefaces*[1] *as in* The English Missal)
Sanctus
Benedictus
The Canon (*the whole being said aloud*) [[The text of the Canon is printed below]]
The Lord's Prayer, *said by the whole congregation.*
The Pax
The Agnus Dei
> *Communicants now approach the altar rail; and while the priest is making his Communion they say together a form of*

The Prayer of Humble Access
Confession
Absolution
'Behold the Lamb of God'
'Lord I am not worthy' (*three times*)
> *Communion usually received directly into the mouth.*

Communion Sentence
Post Communion Collect(s)
Blessing
Last Gospel.

THE CANON OF THE SWAHILI MASS

Almighty and Everlasting God, we beseech thee that thou accept these our offerings together with our prayers.

We beg thee that thou wouldest breathe upon thy Catholic Church the spirit of truth and concord.

Guard our Queen, *N.*, grant to us that we may be ruled under her as thou willest.

Heavenly Father, bless our Bishop *N.*, bless all bishops and all who shepherd the souls of men that they may preach thy word by their teaching and by their pure way of life.

Give grace to all thy people that they may serve thee truly all their days. Also, help those in trouble, sorrow, sickness, or any other need, especially *N.*, and *N.*

We beg thee also to bless us who are here, making remembrance of the glorious death of thy Son, Christ our Lord. *Amen.*

[1] [[See Appendix A.]]

And we give thee great thanks because thou hast shown us the power of thy grace in all thy Saints; especially in the glorious Blessed Virgin Mary, Mother of thy Son Jesus Christ our Lord and our God; and in the Holy Patriarchs, Prophets, Apostles and Martyrs.

We beg thee, Lord, that we may follow them, their faith and their obedience, through Christ our Lord. *Amen.*

Again, Lord, we desire mercy for all thy servants who have departed from the world in the faith: especially *N.*, and *N.* Do thou grant them, we beseech thee, thy mercy and everlasting peace, and do thou bring them, together with us, at the day of resurrection to the glory of thy Son.

Grant us these things, Father, for the sake of him, Jesus Christ our Mediator and Advocate. *Amen.*

[Down to this point the prayer may be taken as a litany]

O God, Father of Heaven, through thy goodness and mercy thou gavest us thine Only-Begotten Son, Jesus Christ, that he might die upon the Cross for our salvation; and he gave himself to be an offering which has no equal, to be a full sacrifice, a perfect oblation and a sufficient satisfaction for the sake of the sins of the whole world. And he ordered a memorial of his precious death, and in his Holy Gospel he commanded us that we should keep on doing this for ever until he shall come again.

Hear us, we beg thee, O Father of mercy, bless these thy creatures of bread and wine and cleanse them by thy Holy Spirit and by thy Word, that they may be to us the Precious Body of thy Son Jesus Christ and his Blood.

He in the very night that he was given up took bread, and he raised his eyes to thee, God the Father Almighty, and gave thanks, and blessed it and brake it and gave to his disciples, saying: Take, eat, THIS IS MY BODY WHICH WAS GIVEN FOR THE SAKE OF YOU. Do this for my memorial.

And in the same way, after eating, he took the Cup, and he gave thanks, and he blessed it, and gave to his disciples, saying, Drink ye all of this, for THIS IS MY BLOOD OF THE NEW TESTAMENT, WHICH IS SHED FOR THE SAKE OF YOU AND FOR ALL MEN THAT IT MAY BE THE REMISSION OF SINS. Do this every time when you shall drink it for my memorial. *Amen.*

Therefore, O Lord, Father of Heaven, we thy servants are

offering gifts to thee, who art by thyself Holy, thy gifts which thou gavest us, this pure offering, holy offering, offering without spot, the Bread of eternal life, and the Chalice of everlasting salvation; making memorial of the Blessed Passion of him, Christ, thy Son our Lord, and his powerful Resurrection and glorious Ascension, and thanking thee for all the good which it [the Passion &c.] obtained for us. *Amen.*

We beg thee, Father, who art good, that thou accept this our sacrifice which gives thee praise and which thanks thee; grant us, together with thy Church also, forgiveness of our sins, and all the good that was obtained through the Passion of thy Beloved Son.

And, O Lord, we are offering ourselves as a sacrifice to thee, ourselves, our souls and our bodies. We beg thee that whoever shall receive these holy things may truly share the Precious Body of thy Son, Jesus Christ, and his Blood, and that he may be filled with thy grace and heavenly benediction and made One Body with him.

And we who are not worthy beg, O Father, That thou command our offering to be carried by thy Holy Angel, together with our prayers, to the altar on high before thee, God, who art Holy; through Christ our Lord, through the unity of the Holy Ghost, all honour and glory throughout all ages for ever and ever. *Amen.*

Let us pray: As our Saviour Christ commanded us and taught us, we are bold to say:
Our Father ... (*said by whole congregation*)

The priest continues aloud:

Deliver us, we beg thee, O Lord, from all evil. Accept the prayers which Mary, Ever-Virgin, the Mother of God, prays for us, together with [the prayers which] thy blessed Apostles and all thy Saints [pray for us]. Give us peace in our days, help us by thy mercy that we may dwell far from sin in our days and that we may not be distressed by anything whatsoever. Through him, our Lord Jesus Christ thy Son, who liveth and reigneth with thee in the unity of the Holy Ghost, God for ever and ever. *Amen.*

CHAPTER XV

THE LITURGY OF THE CHURCH IN KOREA

THE compiling of the Korean Liturgy was initiated at a conference of the clergy of the diocese in 1922. Several interim forms were issued in Korean and in English, including an English draft printed for private circulation and criticism in 1933. The Korean forms were used experimentally at diocesan synods. The text resulting from this procedure was finally approved by the Diocesan Synod on 6 May 1938; and it became the sole use of the diocese by order of the Bishop from 1 February 1939. It was first published in English in a bilingual edition, omitting the manual acts of the celebrant during the Prayer of Consecration, in Lent 1962; and this translation is authorized for use in churches which have English-speaking congregations. For this reason, the translation is not everywhere a literal rendering of the Korean original; but great care has been taken to combine accuracy with felicity of wording in rendering the Prayer for the Church and the Prayer of Consecration. The text here printed is that of 1962, corrected in consultation with the Reverend Richard Rutt. The missing rubrics referred to above have been inserted. Optional matter and prayers said by the priest in a low voice are printed in small type.

THE ORDER OF THE MASS

I. INTRODUCTORY WORSHIP

THE PREPARATION

1 *During the preparation a hymn or psalm may be sung. The priest, standing before the altar with the assistants, says:*

Priest. In the name of the Father . . . Amen.
    I will go unto the altar of God;
Assistants. Even unto the God of my joy and gladness.

⟦Psalm 43 is said responsorially. But at Requiems and during Passiontide the psalm and the antiphon at the end are omitted.⟧

Priest. I will go . . . *Assistants.* Even unto the God . .

The Liturgy of the Church in Korea

2 *Priest.* Our help is in the name of the Lord;
Assistants. Who hath made heaven and earth.
Priest (bowing his body). I confess to almighty God, to blessed Mary, to all the saints, and to you: that I have sinned exceedingly in thought, word, and deed: through my fault, through my fault, through my most grievous fault. Therefore I beg blessed Mary, all the saints, and you, to pray to God for me.
Assistants. Almighty God have mercy upon thee, forgive thee all thy sins, and bring thee to everlasting life.
Priest (standing erect). Amen.
Assistants (bowing low). I confess ... [[as above, *mutatis mutandis*]]
Priest. Almighty God have mercy ... [[as above, *mutatis mutandis*]]
R⁊ Amen.
The Assistants become erect.

3 *Priest.* Wilt thou not turn again, and quicken us, O Lord;
Assistants. That thy people may rejoice in thee?
Priest. O Lord, show thy mercy upon us;
Assistants. And grant us thy salvation.
Priest. O Lord, hear our prayer;
Assistants. And let our cry come unto thee.
Priest. The Lord be with you;
Assistants. And with thy spirit.

4 *Priest (ascending to the altar).* Let us pray.
Almighty God, unto whom ... [[CF 2]] ... our Lord. Amen.

5 *If incense is used, the priest now blesses it, saying:*
Lord, bless this incense which is offered for the honour of thy name.

6 *When the English language is used the priest may here say:*
Hear what our Lord Jesus Christ saith: Thou shalt love the Lord thy God with all thy heart and with all thy soul and with all thy mind. This is the first and great commandment. And the second is like unto it: Thou shalt love thy neighbour as thyself. On these two commandments hang all the Law and the Prophets.

7 <center>KYRIE ELEISON</center>

The priest and people say alternately:

Priest.	Kyrie, eleison.	(Lord, have mercy.)
People.	Kyrie, eleison.	(Lord, have mercy.)

Priest.	Kyrie, eleison.	(Lord, have mercy.)
People.	Christe, eleison.	(Christ, have mercy.)
Priest.	Christe, eleison.	(Christ, have mercy.)
People.	Christe, eleison.	(Christ, have mercy.)
Priest.	Kyrie, eleison.	(Lord, have mercy.)
People.	Kyrie, eleison.	(Lord, have mercy.)
Priest.	Kyrie, eleison.	(Lord, have mercy.)

8   GLORIA IN EXCELSIS

Except for the Sundays of Advent and all the Sundays from Septuagesima to Palm Sunday inclusive, the Gloria is said on all Sundays and feasts. It is also said daily from Christmas Day to the 13th of January inclusive, and from the first mass of Easter until the Feast of the Holy Trinity (except in the Rogation masses).

Glory be to God . . . 〚CF 13〛 . . . Father. Amen.

〚*But reading 'on earth peace', and 'prayer' for 'prayers'. There is no division into paragraphs. And each of the sentences beginning 'We' or '[For] Thou only' ends with a full stop.*〛

9   THE COLLECT OF THE DAY

Priest. The Lord be with you; ℞ And with thy spirit.
Priest. Let us pray. *He then reads the collect.*

II. INSTRUCTION IN THE FAITH

10   THE EPISTLE

The epistle [lesson] is written in the —— chapter of —— beginning at the —— verse.

11   PREPARATION FOR THE GOSPEL

After the epistle a psalm or hymn may be sung. If incense is used, the priest now blesses it as before. Then the priest says in a low voice:

Cleanse my heart and lips, almighty God, who didst cleanse the lips of the prophet Isaiah with a live coal: that I may worthily proclaim thy holy Gospel. [*or,* Almighty God, who did cleanse the lips of the prophet Isaiah with a live coal, cleanse thy heart and thy lips, that thou mayest worthily proclaim his holy Gospel.]

THE HOLY GOSPEL

12

Deacon or Priest. The Lord be with you; ℟ And with thy spirit.

Deacon or Priest. The holy gospel is written in the —— chapter of Saint —— beginning at the —— verse.

℟ Glory be to thee, O Lord.

After the gospel the people say: Thanks be to God.

THE SERMON

13

On Sundays notice is given of holy days and fast days occurring during the following week, and of other important matters. If there is a sermon, it follows here.

THE NICENE CREED

14

The creed is said on all Sundays and red-letter feasts, during the greater octaves, and on all feasts of doctors of the Church. At other times it is omitted.

I believe in one God . . . ⟦CF 4⟧ . . . to come. Amen.

⟦But not divided into paragraphs; reading 'only-begotten' and 'one holy, catholic'; adding '(*Here genuflect*)' before 'And was incarnate', '(*Arise*)' after 'made man'; and with the following variants in punctuation: 'one God,'; visible and invisible'; 'very God;'; 'begotten, not made'; 'things were made.'; 'Virgin Mary:'; 'made man.'; 'the dead.'; 'the Lord, and giver of life'; 'glorified;'.⟧

III. THE EUCHARISTIC OFFERING

THE OFFERTORY

15

Before the offertory the priest stands in the midst of the altar, and turning to the people says:

Priest. The Lord be with you; ℟ And with thy spirit.

During the offertory a psalm or hymn may be sung.
Here the offerings of the people are collected and the bread and wine are prepared.

16 *Offering the bread, the priest says:*

Receive, O holy Father, almighty and everlasting God, this bread which I thine unworthy servant offer unto thee, the living and true God, for my numberless sins and negligences, for all who stand around, and for the living and departed: that it may avail to us for salvation unto life eternal. Amen.

17 *He blesses the water which is to be mixed with the wine, saying:* [*In masses of the dead he does not make the sign of the cross:*]

Grant, O God, that by the mystery of this water and wine we may be sharers of his divinity, who vouchsafed to be made partaker of our humanity, Jesus Christ our Lord. Amen.

18 *Offering the chalice of wine, he says:*

We offer unto thee, O Lord, the cup of salvation, humbly beseeching thy mercy: that it may ascend before thee as a sweet-smelling savour for our salvation, and for that of the whole world. Amen.

19 *Bowing slightly, he says:*

In a humble spirit, and with a contrite heart, may we be accepted of thee, O Lord: and let our sacrifice be pleasing unto thee. Amen.

20 *Standing erect, he says:*

Come, O almighty eternal God, the source of holiness: and bless this sacrifice prepared for thy holy name.

21 *If incense is used, the priest blesses it saying:*

Hear, O Lord, the intercession of the angels and archangels, and bless this incense, that it may ascend before thee as a sweet-smelling savour. Through Jesus Christ our Lord. Amen.

22 *While washing his hands, the priest says:*

[Ps. 26, 6 with Gloria; but Gloria is omitted in masses of the dead and during Passiontide.]

23 *Bowing slightly in the midst of the altar, the priest says:*

Receive, O Holy Trinity, this oblation which we offer unto thee in memory of the passion, resurrection, and ascension of our Lord Jesus Christ, and in honour of blessed Mary and all the saints: and may they, whose memory we celebrate on earth, vouchsafe to intercede for us in heaven. Through the same Jesus Christ our Lord. Amen.
[Nos. 16–23 are read in a low voice.]

24 THE OFFERTORY COLLECT

The hymn or psalm being ended, the priest turns to the people and says:

Pray, brethren, that this our sacrifice may be acceptable to God for his praise and glory, and to the benefit of Christ's holy Church. ℟ May God receive this sacrifice to his praise and glory.

25 *Then the priest says over the offered bread and wine:*

Bless, O Lord, these gifts which we here offer unto thee, that we may be made partakers of the Body and Blood of thine only-begotten Son Jesus Christ, and preserved in body and soul unto everlasting life. Through the same Jesus Christ our Lord, who

The Liturgy of the Church in Korea

liveth and reigneth with thee in the unity of the Holy Ghost, ever one God, world without end. Amen.
⟦Some priests read this prayer in a low voice. Others read it aloud, in which case the people say the 'Amen'⟧
Or some other appointed collect may be said instead.
⟦Such a collect is ordered on rare occasions by the bishop.⟧

26   THE PRAYER FOR THE CHURCH

Let us pray.
Almighty and everlasting God, who hast taught us to make prayers . . . ⟦continuing as in **1662** no. 14, but omitting 'most mercifully . . . oblations and'⟧ . . . godly love. Give grace, O heavenly Father, to all bishops, priests, and deacons, especially to thy servant N. our bishop, that they may . . . ⟦as in **1662**, but omitting 'and specially . . . present'⟧ . . . days of their life.

We beseech thee also so to direct the hearts of all rulers, that they may truly and impartially administer justice, to the punishment of wickedness and vice, and to the maintenance of thy true religion and virtue.

And we most humbly beseech . . . ⟦=**1662**⟧ . . . other adversity.

And we devoutly commend to thy merciful goodness this congregation here gathered in thy name to celebrate the precious death of thy Son our Saviour. [*At Easter and Pentecost, when holy baptism is administered, here is added:* praying especially for those whom thou hast now vouchsafed to regenerate with water and the Holy Ghost, granting them remission of their sins.]

And here we do give unto thee, O Lord, most high praise and hearty thanks for the wonderful grace and virtue declared in all thy saints, and chiefly in the blessed Virgin Mary, Mother of thy Son, our Lord Jesus Christ, and in the holy patriarchs, prophets, apostles and martyrs: beseeching thee to give us grace to follow their good examples in steadfastness of faith and in keeping of thy commandments.

And we commend to thy gracious keeping, O Lord, all thy servants departed this life in thy faith and fear, who now rest in the sleep of peace, beseeching thee to grant them mercy, peace, and light, both now and in the day of resurrection.

Grant this, O Father, for Jesus Christ's sake, our only Mediator and Advocate. ℟ Amen.

27   ⟦*The Exhortation, General Confession, and Absolution (no. 43 below) may be said here at celebrations in English.*⟧

28

THE PREFACE

Facing the altar as before, the priest says:

Priest. The Lord be with you;   ℞ And with thy spirit.

Priest. Lift up your hearts;   ℞ We lift them up unto the Lord.

Priest. Let us give thanks unto our Lord God;   ℞ It is meet and right so to do.

Priest, with hands extended, says: It is very meet, right, and our bounden duty, that we should at all times, and in all places give thanks unto thee, O Lord, holy Father, almighty, everlasting God. 〚For Proper Prefaces, see Appendix A.〛

Therefore with angels and archangels and with all the company of heaven, we laud and magnify thy glorious Name, evermore praising thee, and saying:

[*The Sanctus is said by all together.*]

Holy, Holy, Holy, Lord God of Hosts. Heaven and earth are full of thy glory. Glory be to thee, O Lord most high. Blessed is he that cometh in the name of the Lord. Hosanna in the highest.

THE PRAYER OF CONSECRATION

29
[*The Canon*]

Thanks be to thee, Almighty God, our heavenly Father, for that thou of thy tender mercy didst give thine only Son to take our nature upon him, and to suffer death upon the cross for our redemption: who by his one oblation of himself once offered, made a full, perfect, and sufficient sacrifice, oblation, and satisfaction for the sins of the whole world; and did institute, and command us to continue, a perpetual memory of that his precious death, until his coming again. [*Stretching his hands over the offered gifts*]

30   Hear us, O merciful Father, we most humbly beseech thee, and by thy holy Spirit vouchsafe to bless and sanctify these thy creatures of bread and wine, according to our Lord Jesus Christ's holy institution, who, in the same night that he was betrayed, took bread, [*He takes the large host.*] and when he had given thanks, he brake it, and gave it to his disciples, saying: 'Take eat. [*Taking the large host between the thumb and forefinger of both hands he says reverently*] This is my body, which is given for you. Do this in remembrance of me.'

Holding the large host, he genuflects, rises, lifts the host high, replaces it on the corporal, and genuflects.

31   Likewise after supper he took the cup; [*He takes the cup in both hands.*] and when he had given thanks, he gave it to them, saying: 'Drink ye all of this: [*lifting the chalice slightly, he says reverently*] for this is my blood of the New Testament, which is shed for you and for many for the remission of sins. Do this as oft as ye shall drink it, in remembrance of me.'

He sets the chalice on the corporal. He genuflects, rises, lifts the chalice high, replaces it on the corporal, and genuflects.

32   Wherefore we thy humble servants, according to his holy ordinance, do now celebrate the memorial thy Son hath commanded us to make, and, having in remembrance his blessed passion and precious death, his mighty resurrection and glorious ascension, offer unto thy divine majesty these sacred gifts and creatures of thine own, the holy bread of eternal life, and the cup of everlasting salvation.

33   And we entirely desire thy fatherly goodness mercifully to accept this our sacrifice, humbly beseeching thee to grant that by the merits and death of thy Son Jesus Christ, we and all thy whole Church may obtain remission of our sins and all other benefits of his passion. [*Bowing his body, with hands joined on the altar, he says*:] And we beseech thee to pour thy holy and lifegiving Spirit on us and on all who in every place are partakers of this holy communion, that we may offer ourselves, our souls and bodies, to be a reasonable, holy, and lively sacrifice unto thee; that we may be fulfilled with thy grace and heavenly benediction; and made one body with thy Son Jesus Christ, that he may dwell in us, and we in him.

34   And although we be unworthy, through our manifold sins, to offer unto thee any sacrifice: yet we beseech thee to accept this our bounden duty and service, not weighing our merits, but pardoning our offences. [*He makes the sign of the cross three times over the Sacred Body and Precious Blood.*] Through Jesus Christ our Lord: [*He removes the pall from the chalice, genuflects, takes the large host in his right hand, and with it makes the sign of the cross over the chalice three times.*] by whom and with whom, in the unity of the holy Ghost, [*He makes the sign of the cross between the chalice and his breast, twice.*] all honour and glory be unto thee, [*Lifting the large host and chalice a little, he says:*] O Father almighty: world without end.   ℟ Amen.

IV. THE RECEIVING OF THE GIFTS

35 ### THE LORD'S PRAYER

The priest, with hands joined, says: Let us pray. As our Saviour Christ hath commanded and taught us, we are bold to say: [*with hands extended, he says*] Our Father, who art in heaven:
People. Hallowed ... ⟦=CF 1, but reading 'on earth'⟧ ... from evil.

The priest takes the paten, and says in a low voice: Deliver us, O Lord, we beseech thee, from all evils, past, present, and to come: and at the intercession of the blessed and glorious Virgin Mary and all the saints, grant peace in our days, that we may ever be free from sin and safe from all distress. [*He places the paten under the Sacred Body, removes the pall from the chalice, genuflects, and breaking the large host in halves over the chalice, says:*] Through Jesus Christ thy Son our Lord, [*He places on the paten the half of the host in his right hand; and, breaking a small particle from the other half, says:*] who liveth and reigneth with thee in the unity of the Holy Ghost, ever one God.

Throughout all ages, world without end. ℟ Amen.

36 ### THE KISS OF PEACE

Priest. Making the sign of the cross over the chalice three times with the particle of the Sacred Body, he says: The peace of the Lord be always with you;
People. And with thy spirit.

He puts the particle in the chalice, saying: May this commixture of the body and blood of our Lord Jesus Christ be unto us who receive it unto everlasting life.

37 ### AGNUS DEI

O Lamb of God, that takest away the sins of the world, have mercy upon us. [*twice*] (*At Requiems:* grant them rest.)

O Lamb of God, that takest away the sins of the world, grant us peace. (*At Requiems:* grant them rest everlasting.)

38 *The priest, bowing his body, with hands joined on the altar, says in a low voice:*
O Lord Jesus Christ, who didst say to thine apostles, 'Peace I leave with you, my peace I give unto you': regard not our sins, but the faith of thy Church, and grant her peace and unity according to thy will. Who livest and reignest world without end. Amen.

If the pax is given, the priest here kisses the altar, and gives the pax to the deacon, saying: Peace be to thee, and to the Church of God. ℟ And with thy spirit.

In masses of the dead the pax is not given, nor is the preceding prayer said.

39 THE PRIEST'S COMMUNION

O Lord Jesus Christ, Son of the living God, who by the will of the Father, and the co-operation of the Holy Ghost, hast through thy death given life unto the world: deliver me by this thy most sacred body and blood from all mine iniquities, and from every evil: make me ever obedient to thy commandments, and suffer me never to be separated from thee. Who with the same Father and the Holy Ghost livest and reignest God world without end. Amen.

40 Let the partaking of thy body, O Lord Jesus Christ, which I, unworthy, presume to receive, turn not to my judgement and condemnation: but of thy goodness let it avail unto me for healing and protection both of body and soul. Amen.

41 *He genuflects, rises, and says:* I will receive the bread of heaven, and call upon the name of the Lord.

Taking the two fragments of the host, and the paten, in his left hand, he beats his breast with his right hand three times, saying: Lord, I am not worthy that thou shouldest enter under my roof: but speak the word only and my soul shall be healed.

Making the sign of the cross before himself with the Sacred Body held in his right hand, he says: The Body of our Lord Jesus Christ.

42 *After receiving the two fragments of the large host, he prays silently for a brief while, removes the pall from the chalice, rises, gathers the crumbs on the paten, puts them into the chalice, and says:* What reward shall I give unto the Lord for all the benefits that he hath done unto me? I will receive the cup of salvation, and call upon the name of the Lord. *Making the sign of the cross before himself with the chalice held in his right hand,* he says: The Blood of our Lord Jesus Christ. *He receives the Precious Blood and the particle of the Sacred Body.*

43 THE COMMUNION OF THE FAITHFUL

If there are other communicants, the priest or deacon says:

[Ye that do truly ... neighbours,] Draw near ... ⟦CF 6⟧ ... almighty God, devoutly kneeling.

People. Almighty God, Father ... ⟦=CF 7, but reading 'most heartily'⟧ ... our Lord. Amen.

Then the priest or bishop, turning to the people, says the absolution:

Almighty God, [our heavenly Father ... unto him] ... ⟦CF 8⟧ ... our Lord. ℟ Amen.

⟦The bracketed passages in the invitation and absolution are usually omitted.⟧

44 *Delivering the Sacred Body to each one, he says:* The Body of our Lord Jesus Christ.

Administering the Precious Blood to each one, he says: The Blood of our Lord Jesus Christ.

During the communion a hymn or psalm may be sung.

45 THE ABLUTIONS

When all have communicated, the priest consumes any of the Blessed Sacrament which may remain, saying:

Grant, O Lord, that what we have taken with our mouths we may receive with our hearts; and by the grace we have received in time we may be strengthened unto eternity.

46 *Cleansing the sacred vessels with wine and water, he says:*

May the holy sacrament which we have now received cleanse us from all sin and be unto us for an everlasting refreshment. Through Jesus Christ our Lord. Amen.

V. CLOSING PRAYERS

47 THE THANKSGIVING COLLECT

Priest. The Lord be with you; ℟ And with thy spirit.

Priest. Let us pray. Almighty and everlasting God, we most heartily ... ⟦CF 12⟧ ... without end. ℟ Amen.

⟦But reading 'hast vouchsafed'; 'through the merits of his most precious death and passion' for 'by the merits of the most precious death and passion of thy dear Son'; 'hast assured' for 'hast prepared'.⟧

If other prayers are appointed, they may be said.

⟦Five such prayers are given in the Korean BCP; and one or more of these is sometimes read in addition to, or in substitution for, the above text.⟧

48 THE DISMISSAL

The priest stands before the altar, turning to the people, and says:
The Lord be with you; ℟ And with thy spirit.

Deacon or priest. Depart in peace.

If the Gloria in excelsis *has not been said, he faces the altar and says:*
Let us bless the Lord. ℟ Thanks be to God.

In masses of the dead, after The Lord be with you, *the deacon or priest, facing the altar, says instead:* May they rest in peace. ℟ Amen.

From the first mass of Easter till Easter Saturday, Alleluia *is added twice to* Depart in peace *and* Thanks be to God *by priest and people respectively.*

49 *The priest, bowing himself in the midst of the altar, says in a low voice:*

May the homage of my service be pleasing to thee, O Holy Trinity: grant that the sacrifice which I, though unworthy, have offered before thee, may be acceptable to thee: and of thy mercy may we obtain remission of our sins. Through Jesus Christ our Lord. Amen.

50 ## THE BLESSING

The priest or bishop gives the blessing. In masses of the dead the blessing is not given.

The peace of God, which passeth all understanding, keep your hearts and minds in the knowledge and love of God, and of his Son Jesus Christ our Lord: *Turning to the people, he blesses them, saying:* And the blessing of God Almighty, the Father, the Son, and the Holy Ghost, be amongst you, and remain with you always. ℟ Amen.

51 ## THE LAST GOSPEL

The priest goes to the gospel side of the altar, and says: The Lord be with you; ℟ And with thy spirit.

Priest. The beginning of the Holy Gospel according to Saint John.
People. Glory be to thee, O God.

Priest. In the beginning . . . ⟦S. John 1. 1–14⟧ . . . grace and truth.
People. Thanks be to God.

The priest and other ministers leave together.

CHAPTER XVI

THE LITURGY OF THE CHURCH OF THE PROVINCE OF THE WEST INDIES

THIS liturgy was published in English in London in 1959. It is authorized by the Provincial Synod of the West Indies 'for permissive use as directed in each Diocese by the Bishop' for a period of three years. It is understood that there are various diocesan editions which differ from this standard text; but it has not been possible to collect these variations. In 1962 it was decided to postpone any further revision for three years, and that the 1959 liturgy should continue in use under the same conditions during that period.

1   GENERAL RUBRICS

If there be no Deacon or Reader the parts assigned to them shall be taken by the Priest.

The manner of celebrating the Liturgy is set forth in the Directory of Ceremonial authorized by the Bishop.

Hymns from a book approved by the Bishop may be sung at customary places during the Service.

2   AN ORDER FOR THE CELEBRATION OF
THE HOLY EUCHARIST
AND THE ADMINISTRATION OF
THE HOLY COMMUNION

3   THE INTRODUCTION

At the entry of the Priest and his Assistants, or after the Collect for Purity, an Introit Psalm may be sung or said.

4   THE COLLECT FOR PURITY

Let us pray.

Almighty God, unto whom ... ⟦CF 2⟧ ... Lord. ℞ Amen.

The Liturgy in English

5   KYRIE ELEISON

⟦Ninefold, in English or in Greek. In place of this may be said the TEN COMMANDMENTS or the SUMMARY OF THE LAW with their responses. These texts are printed in an appendix, the *Decalogue* having the second, third, fourth, fifth, ninth, and tenth commandments curtailed⟧

6   GLORIA IN EXCELSIS

On Sundays and other Holy Days (except Sundays in Advent and Sundays from Septuagesima to Palm Sunday, inclusive) and daily from Easter Day to Trinity Sunday, the following Hymn is sung or said, unless it is to be sung or said before the Blessing.
Glory be to God on high ... ⟦CF 13⟧ ... the Father. Amen.
⟦Omitting 'Thou that takest ... mercy upon us'⟧

7   ℣ The Lord be with you;
     ℟ And with thy spirit.
              Let us pray.

THE COLLECT OF THE DAY
which may be followed by other Collects.

8   THE MINISTRY OF THE WORD
                THE EPISTLE
The people being seated, the Reader shall read the Epistle or Lesson. Here may follow a Psalm or portion of a Psalm, or a Hymn.

9   THE GOSPEL
The Deacon shall read the Gospel, the People standing and facing towards him.
     ℣ The Lord be with you;
     ℟ And with thy spirit.
After he has announced the Gospel,
     ℟ Glory be to thee, O Lord.
The Gospel ended, there shall be said,
     ℟ Praise be to thee, O Christ.

10   THE NICENE CREED
On Sundays and other Holy Days this Creed shall be sung or said:
I believe in one God ... ⟦CF 4⟧ ... world to come. Amen.
⟦But reading 'Begotten of the Father', 'Through whom all things were made', 'The Lord, the Giver of life', and 'One, Holy, Catholic', agreeing with **CanR**. **WInd** also punctuates with semi-colons: 'God of God;' &c. with Canada, but it does not insert a comma after the first member of these phrases⟧

Then one of the Ministers shall announce any Holy Days, Days of Abstinence, or Fast Days to be observed during the week. And Notices, Banns of Marriage, or Pastorals from the Bishop shall be published.

Biddings for special thanksgiving and prayer shall be made, unless they are to be made before the Intercession. Then shall follow the Sermon.

11 THE OFFERTORY

℣ The Lord be with you;
℟ And with thy spirit.

12 *Then shall the priest begin the Offertory, saying one or more of the Sentences,¹ or some other appropriate Sentence from Holy Scripture.*

The offerings of bread and wine shall be brought to the Priest by representatives of the People, or by one of the Assistants, and the Priest shall present them and place them upon the Altar.

When alms are offered they shall be received by the Churchwardens or other fit persons and shall be presented on the Altar by the Priest.

The Offerings having been made, the Priest shall wash his hands.

13 *Then he shall begin the Intercession.*

THE INTERCESSION

Let us pray for the whole state of Christ's Church.

Almighty and everliving God, who by thy holy Apostle hast taught us to make prayers and supplications, and to give thanks, for all men: We humbly beseech thee most mercifully to accept our (alms and) oblations . . . ⟦as in 1662⟧ . . . unity and godly love.

14 We beseech thee also to save and defend all Christian Kings, Princes, and Governors, especially thy servant *Elizabeth* our Queen and all that are put in authority under her, that thy people may be godly and quietly governed.

15 Give grace, O heavenly Father, to all Bishops, Priests, and Deacons, especially thy servants *N.* our Archbishop, and *N.* our Bishop, that they may by their life and doctrine set forth thy true and lively Word, and rightly and duly administer thy holy Sacraments.

16 And to all thy people give thy heavenly grace; that with meek heart . . . ⟦as in 1662⟧ . . . days of their life.

17 Increase, we pray thee, the number of thy servants who pro-

¹ ⟦For the text of the Offertory Sentences, see Appendix B.⟧

claim among the nations the Gospel of thy kingdom, and enlighten with thy Spirit all places of education and learning; that the whole world may be filled with the knowledge of thy truth.

18 And we most humbly beseech ... ⟦as in **1662**⟧ ... adversity.

19 We also commend unto thy mercy, O Lord, all thy servants departed this life in thy faith and fear; beseeching thee to grant them everlasting light and peace.

20 And here we do give unto thee most high praise and hearty thanks for the wonderful grace and virtue declared in all thy Saints; chiefly in the Blessed Virgin Mary, Mother of thy Son Jesus Christ, our Lord and God, and in the holy Patriarchs, Prophets, Apostles, and Martyrs; beseeching thee to give us grace that we, rejoicing in the Communion of thy Saints, and following their good examples, may be partakers with them of thy heavenly kingdom:

Grant this, O Father, for Jesus Christ's sake, our only Mediator and Advocate. R̷ Amen.

21 THE EUCHARISTIC PRAYER

V̷ The Lord be with you;
R̷ And with thy spirit.
V̷ Lift up your hearts;
R̷ We lift them up unto the Lord.
V̷ Let us give thanks unto our Lord God;
R̷ It is meet and right so to do.

Then shall the Priest continue,

It is very meet, right ... ⟦as in **1662**⟧ ... O Lord most high.
⟦No 'Amen'⟧

Blessed is he that cometh in the Name of the Lord, Hosanna in the Highest.
⟦For Proper Prefaces, see Appendix A⟧

22 *Then shall the Priest proceed, saying,*

All glory, praise, and thanksgiving be unto thee, O Lord, Holy Father, Almighty, Everlasting God, for that thou hast created the world and all mankind, and of thy tender mercy didst give thine only Son Jesus Christ to take our nature upon him, and to suffer death upon the cross, for our redemption; who made there, by his own oblation of himself once offered, a full, perfect, and sufficient sacrifice, oblation, and satisfaction for the sins of the whole world;

and did institute, and in his holy Gospel command us to continue, a perpetual memory of that his precious death, until his coming again.

23 *He extends his hands over the Oblations.*

Hear us, O merciful Father, we most humbly beseech thee; and vouchsafe to accept, bless, and sanctify these thy gifts and creatures of bread and wine, that they may be unto us the Body and Blood of thy Son, our Saviour Jesus Christ: Who in the same night . . . ⟦as in **1662** but with 'Covenant' for 'Testament' ('Testament' as alternative in margin) and with the omission of fraction and imposition of hand upon the elements⟧ . . . in remembrance of me.

24 Wherefore, O Lord and heavenly Father, we thy servants with all thy holy people, having in remembrance the blessed passion, mighty resurrection, and glorious ascension of thy beloved Son, do offer unto thy Divine Majesty this holy Bread of eternal life and this Cup of everlasting salvation, rendering thanks unto thee for the wonderful redemption which thou hast wrought for us in him. And we beseech thee, O Father, to accept upon thy heavenly altar this our Sacrifice of praise and thanksgiving; and to grant that by the merits and death of thy Son Jesus Christ, and through faith in his blood, we and all thy whole Church may obtain remission of our sins and all other benefits of his passion.

25 And we pray that by the power of thy Holy Spirit all who shall be partakers of this holy Communion may be fulfilled with thy grace and heavenly benediction, and be numbered in the glorious company of thy Saints.

26 And here we offer and present . . . ⟦as in **1662** *Prayer of Oblation*⟧ . . . pardoning our offences;

Through Jesus Christ our Lord, by whom, and with whom, and in whom, in the unity of the Holy Ghost, all honour and glory be unto thee, O Father Almighty, throughout all ages, world without end.

Here shall all the People answer **Amen.**

27 Let us pray.

As our Saviour Christ hath commanded and taught us, we are bold to say,

Then shall the Priest and the People sing or say together,
Our Father . . . ⟦CF 1⟧ . . . and ever. Amen.
⟦But reading 'who art'⟧

28   THE FRACTION
Here the Priest is to break the Sacrament of Christ's Body.
℣ The peace of the Lord be always with you;
℟ And with thy spirit.

29   A<small>GNUS</small> D<small>EI</small>
Here shall be said or sung this anthem,
O Lamb of God, that takest away the sins of the world; have mercy upon us. ⟦twice⟧
  O Lamb of God, that takest away the sins of the world; grant us thy peace.

At Memorials of the Departed instead of, have mercy upon us, *is said,* grant them rest, *and instead of* grant us thy peace, grant them rest eternal.

30   THE COMMUNION
              T<small>HE</small> I<small>NVITATION</small>
The Deacon shall say,
Ye that do truly . . . ⟦CF 6⟧ . . . to Almighty God.
⟦But omitting 'following . . . holy ways' and 'meekly . . . knees'⟧

31   T<small>HE</small> G<small>ENERAL</small> C<small>ONFESSION</small>
All who intend to receive the Holy Communion shall say,
Almighty God . . . ⟦CF 7⟧ . . . Christ our Lord. Amen.
⟦Reading 'confess' for 'bewail'⟧

32   T<small>HE</small> A<small>BSOLUTION</small>
The Priest (or the Bishop, if he be present) shall say,
Almighty God . . . ⟦CF 8⟧ . . . Christ our Lord.   ℟ Amen.

33   T<small>HE</small> C<small>OMFORTABLE</small> W<small>ORDS</small>
Then may be said,
Hear what comfortable . . . ⟦CF 9⟧ . . . our sins.
⟦But reading 'Christ Jesus' in 1 Tim. 1. 15 as usual⟧

34 ### THE PRAYER OF HUMBLE ACCESS
Let us pray.

We do not presume to come to this thy Table, O merciful Father, trusting in our own righteousness, but in thy manifold and great mercies. We are not worthy so much as to gather up the crumbs under thy Table. But thou art the same Lord, whose property is always to have mercy: Grant us therefore, gracious Lord, so to eat the flesh of thy dear Son Jesus Christ, and to drink his blood, that with bodies and souls made clean from every stain of sin, we may evermore dwell in him, and he in us. ℞ Amen.

The Priest shall receive Holy Communion in both kinds and then proceed to administer the same.

35 ### THE ADMINISTRATION OF HOLY COMMUNION

The Deacon shall say,

Draw near and receive the Body and Blood of our Lord Jesus Christ, which were given for you, and feed on him in your hearts by faith with thanksgiving.

When the Priest delivers the Sacrament of Christ's Body he shall say,

The Body of our Lord Jesus Christ preserve thy body and soul unto everlasting life.

36 *The Deacon in administering the Cup shall say,*

The Blood of our Lord Jesus Christ preserve thy body and soul unto everlasting life.

37 *When all have communicated, if any of the holy Sacrament remain apart from that which is to be reserved, the Priest shall consume the same. He shall then cleanse the sacred vessels in the accustomed manner.*

38 *A Communion Sentence may be sung or said during the administration, or be said by the Priest immediately before the following prayer.*

THE THANKSGIVING

and other collects, when they are so appointed.

℣ The Lord be with you;
℞ And with thy spirit.

Let us pray.

Almighty and everliving God, we most heartily thank thee for that thou dost graciously feed us in these holy mysteries with the spiritual food of the most precious Body and Blood of thy Son our Saviour Jesus Christ, assuring us thereby that we are very members incorporate in the mystical body of thy Son and are also heirs, through hope, of thy everlasting kingdom. And we most humbly beseech thee so to assist us . . . [[as in CF 12]] . . . without end. ℟ Amen.

Gloria in Excelsis *shall be sung or said here as directed on page* [[179]], *unless it has already been sung or said before the Collect of the Day.*

THE BLESSING

The Priest (or the Bishop if he be present) shall let the People depart with this Blessing,

The peace of God . . . [[CF 14]] . . . always.   ℟ Amen.

At Memorials of the Departed the Blessing may be omitted and the following may be said,

℣ The Lord be with you;
℟ And with thy spirit.
℣ May they rest in peace.
℟ Amen.

PART II

CHAPTER XVII

THE DIRECTORY

THE text printed in this chapter is not strictly speaking a liturgy, but rather instructions to enable the Minister to order the service for himself. *A Directory for the Publique Worship of God* was ordered to be printed and published by Parliament on 13 March 1644, at the time when the Book of Common Prayer was ordered to be 'taken away'. It remained in force until the Restoration, when it in turn was taken away; but it has continued to influence those who have dissented from the Act of Uniformity of 1661 and has influence in some quarters today. The text is printed from the edition of the *Directory* published by Evan Tyler, Alexander Fifield, Ralph Smith, and John Field, London, 1644.

OF THE CELEBRATION OF THE COMMUNION, OR SACRAMENT OF THE LORD'S SUPPER

[This chapter of the Directory deals simply with the Communion strictly so called. The 'Ante-Communion', as is implied by the first sentence printed below, is contained in earlier chapters. From these we learn that the 'Ante-Communion' was to consist of an opening prayer, readings from both Testaments, a prayer before the Sermon, the Sermon, and a prayer after the Sermon]

When the day is come for administration, the Minister having ended his Sermon and Prayer, shall make a short Exhortation,

Expressing the inestimable benefit we have by this Sacrament; together with the ends and use thereof: setting forth the great necessity of having our comforts and strength renewed thereby in this our pilgrimage and warfare: How necessary it is that we come to it with Knowledge, Faith, Repentance, Love, and with hungring and thirsting souls after Christ and his benefits: How great the danger, to eat and drink unworthily.

Next, he is, in the Name of Christ, on the one part, to warn all such as are Ignorant, Scandalous, Profane, or that live in any sin or offence against their knowledge or conscience, that they presume not to come to that holy Table, shewing them, That he that eateth and drinketh unworthily, eateth and drinketh judgement unto himself: And on the other part, he is in especiall manner to invite and encourage all that labour under the sense of the burden of their sins, and fear of wrath, and desire to reach out unto a greater progresse in Grace than yet they can attain unto, to come to the Lord's Table; assuring them, in the same Name, of ease, refreshing and strength to their weak and wearied souls.

After this Exhortation, Warning, and Invitation, the Table being before decently covered, and so conveniently placed, that the Communicants may orderly sit about it, or at it, The Minister is to begin the action with sanctifying and blessing the elements of Bread and Wine set before him (the Bread in comely and convenient vessels, so prepared, that being broken by him, and given, it may be distributed amongst the Communicants: The Wine also in large Cups;) having first in a few words shewed, That those elements, otherwise common, are now set apart and sanctified to this holy use, by the word of Institution and Prayer.

Let the words of Institution be read out of the Evangelists, or out of the first Epistle of the Apostle *Paul* to the Corinthians. Chap. 11. verse 23. *I have received of the Lord, etc.* to the 27. verse, which the Minister may, when he seeth requisite, explaine and apply.

Let the Prayer, Thanksgiving, or Blessing of the Bread and Wine, be to this effect;

With humble and hearty acknowledgement of the greatnesse of our misery, from which neither man nor Angel was able to deliver us, and of our great unworthinesse of the least of all God's mercies; To give thanks to God for all his benefits, and especially for that great benefit of our Redemption, the love of God the Father, the sufferings and merits of the Lord Jesus Christ the Son of God, by which we are delivered; and for all means of Grace, the Word and Sacraments, and for this Sacrament in particular, by which Christ and all his benefits are applied and sealed up unto us, which, notwithstanding the deniall of them unto others, are in great mercy continued unto us, after so much and long abuse of them all.

To professe that there is no other name under Heaven, by which we can be saved, but the Name of Jesus Christ, by whom alone we receive liberty and life, have accesse to the throne of Grace, are admitted to eat and drink at his own Table, and are sealed up by his Spirit to an assurance of happinesse and everlasting life.

Earnestly to pray to God, the Father of all mercies, and God of all consolation, to vouchsafe his gracious presence, and the effectuall working of his Spirit in us, and so to sanctifie these Elements both of Bread and

Wine, and to blesse his own Ordinance, that we may receive by Faith the Body and Blood of Jesus Christ crucified for us, and so to feed upon him that he may be one with us, and we with him, that he may live in us, and we in him, and to him, who hath loved us, and given himself for us.

All which he is to endeavour to performe with suitable affections answerable to such an holy Action, and to stir up the like in the people.

The Elements being now sanctified by the Word and Prayer, The Minister, being at the Table, is to take the Bread in his hand, and say, in these expressions (or other the like, used by Christ, or his Apostle upon this occasion:)

According to the holy Institution, command, and example of our blessed Saviour Jesus Christ, I take this Bread, and having given thanks, I break it, and give it unto you (There the Minister, who is also himselfe to communicate, is to breake the Bread, and give it to the Communicants:) *Take yee, eat yee; This is the Body of Christ which is broken for you, Do this in remembrance of him.*

In like manner the Minister is to take the Cup, and say, in these expressions (or other the like, used by Christ, or the Apostle upon the same occasion;)

According to the Institution, command, and example of our Lord Jesus Christ, I take this Cup, and give it unto you (Here he giveth it to the Communicants,) *This Cup is the new Testament in the Blood of Christ, which is shed for the remission of the sins of many; Drink ye all of it.*

After all have communicated, the Minister may, in a few words, put them in mind

Of the grace of God, in Jesus Christ held forth in this Sacrament, and exhort them to walk worthy of it.

The Minister is to give solemn thanks to God

For his rich mercy, and invaluable goodnesse vouchsafed to them in that Sacrament, and to entreat for pardon for the defects of the whole service, and for the gracious assistance of his good Spirit, whereby they may be enabled to walk in the strength of that Grace, as becometh those who have received so great pledges of salvation.

The Collection for the poore is so to be ordered, that no part of the publique worship be thereby hindred.

CHAPTER XVIII

THE BOOK OF COMMON ORDER

THE *Book of Common Order* of the Church of Scotland (1940) provides five alternative Orders for the Lord's Supper. That which is printed below is the first in order; and it appears that the remaining four are either abbreviations of or alternatives to this Order. It is, however, stated in the Preface to the book that 'the General Assembly by authorizing these books have recognized that the provision of such forms implies no desire to supersede free prayer'; and there is a passage in the Preface to the edition of 1928, quoted in 1940, stating that a service book is necessary 'to express the mind of the Church with regard to its offices and worship, in orders and forms which, while not fettering individual judgement in particulars, will set the norm for the orderly and reverent conduct of the various public services in which ministers have to lead their people'. This first Order of Communion is similar to that used at the Communion at the General Assembly and may therefore presumably be regarded as the 'standard' form for the celebration of the Lord's Supper.

ORDER FOR THE CELEBRATION OF THE SACRAMENT OF THE LORD'S SUPPER OR HOLY COMMUNION

The Congregation being assembled, the Minister shall solemnly call them to worship, saying: Let us worship God.

And the service shall begin with a Psalm or Hymn (*such as* Psalm 43. 3–5)

Then shall be said a Call to Prayer in words of Holy Scripture, such as:[1]

What shall we render unto the Lord for all His benefits towards us? We will take the cup of salvation, and call upon the name of the Lord. We will pay our vows unto the Lord now in the presence of all His people.

[1] ⟦A collection of sentences suitable to the seasons of the Christian Year is given later in the book.⟧

Christ our Passover is sacrificed for us; therefore let us keep the feast.

O taste and see that the Lord is good. Blessed is the man that trusteth in Him.

Let us pray.

Almighty God, unto whom all hearts . . . ⟦CF 2⟧ . . . our Lord. *Amen.*

Eternal God, our heavenly Father, who admittest Thy people into such wonderful communion that, partaking by a divine mystery of the body and blood of Thy dear Son, they should dwell in Him, and He in them; we unworthy sinners, approaching Thy presence and beholding Thy glory, do repent us of our transgressions. We have sinned, we have grievously sinned against Thee, in thought, word, and deed. We have broken our past vows, and have dishonoured Thy holy name.

Yet now, most merciful Father, have mercy upon us; for the sake of Jesus Christ, forgive us all our sins; deliver us, by Thy Holy Spirit, from all uncleanness in spirit and in flesh; and enable us heartily to forgive others, as we beseech Thee to forgive us, and to serve Thee henceforth in newness of life, to the glory of Thy holy name. *Amen.*

O God, who hast prepared for them that love Thee such good things as pass man's understanding; pour into our hearts such love toward Thee, that we, loving Thee above all things, may obtain Thy promises, which exceed all that we can desire; through Jesus Christ our Lord, to whom, with Thee and the Holy Spirit, be all honour and glory, world without end. *Amen.*

Then shall be sung a Canticle, Psalm, or Hymn.

Then a Lesson from the Old Testament shall be read, after which a Psalm, such as Psalm 116, *in the prose version of the Psalter, shall be sung or read, ending with the Gloria; or a metrical Psalm, such as* Psalm 116. 13-19, *shall be sung.*

Then Lessons from the New Testament (Epistle and Gospel) shall be read.

Before each Lesson the words shall be used: Hear the Word of God, as it is written in . . . the . . . chapter, at the . . . verse.

And at the end of each: The Lord bless to us the reading of His holy Word, and to His name be glory and praise.

After the Gospel may be said the Nicene Creed,[1] *and the Intercessory Prayer shall follow.*

I believe in one God ... ⟦CF 4⟧ ... world to come. *Amen.*
⟦But reading 'the Lord and Giver of Life' and 'one Holy Catholic'⟧

Let us pray.

Almighty God, the Father of our Lord Jesus Christ, of whom the whole family in heaven and earth is named; we Thy children, gathered round Thy Holy Table, remember before Thee all with whom we have part in the communion of Thy saints, and we beseech Thee to hear our humble intercessions.

We pray for Thy Church, Holy, Catholic, and Apostolic. Increase and sanctify her more and more; reveal Thy glory among the nations; and hasten the victory of Thine eternal kingdom.

We pray for this parish and congregation, that Thou wouldst be pleased to pour out the riches of Thy grace upon this people.

[We pray for all those who come to Thy Table for the first time, beseeching Thee to perfect the good work Thou hast begun in them, and to keep them ever faithful to Thee.]

We pray for our country, for Thy servant George our King, Elizabeth our Queen, Mary the Queen Mother, the Princess Elizabeth, and the other members of the Royal Family. Give grace and guidance to those who rule and defend us, and establish our nation in righteousness.

Give and preserve to our use the kindly fruits of the earth; and keep us from war, pestilence, and famine.

Remember in Thy mercy, O Lord, the sick and the suffering, the aged and the dying, all who are in trouble and bereavement, especially those known to us, whom we name in our hearts before Thee ... Visit them with Thy love and consolation, and grant them Thy peace.

We pray for our own loved ones, whether at home, or absent from us, upon the sea ..., or in far-off lands ..., that Thy presence may be their strength and stay. Bless them, and keep them, and cause Thy face to shine upon them. *Amen.*

[1] *Or, the Creed may be said as part of the following prayer, thus:* Hear us, O Lord, as, with Thy whole Church, we make confession of our faith: We believe ...; *or, it may be said after the bringing in of the elements.*

The Book of Common Order

Eternal God, with whom are the issues of life; we give Thee thanks for all Thy saints who, having in this life witnessed a good confession, have left the light of their example to shine before Thy people; especially those beloved by us who are now with Thee. Bring us into communion with them here in Thy holy presence; and enable us so to follow them in all godly living, that hereafter we may with them behold Thy face in glory, and in the heavenly places be one with them for ever; through Jesus Christ our Lord, to whom, with Thee and the Holy Spirit, be all honour and glory, world without end. *Amen.*

Then shall be sung a Psalm or Hymn.

Here the Banns of Marriage may be proclaimed, and Intimations made.

Before the Sermon this or other Prayer for Illumination shall be offered:

Let us pray.

Almighty God, with whom are hid all the treasures of wisdom and knowledge; open our eyes, that we may behold wondrous things out of Thy law; and draw us with the cords of everlasting love; through Jesus Christ our Lord. *Amen.*

The Sermon shall then be preached, ending with the following or other Ascription:

Unto Him that loved us, and washed us from our sins in His own blood, and hath made us kings and priests unto God and His Father; to Him be glory and dominion for ever and ever. *Amen.*

The Offerings shall be given, during which the Minister shall go to the Holy Table.

Then shall the Minister give an Invitation in words of Holy Scripture:

Beloved in the Lord, draw near to the Holy Table, and hear the gracious words of the Lord Jesus Christ:
Come unto me [[Matt. 11. 28 f.]] . . . your souls.
I am the bread of life [[John 6. 35–37, abbreviated]] . . . in no wise cast out.
Blessed are they which do hunger and thirst [[Matt. 5. 6]] . . . filled.

Then shall be sung Psalm 24. 7–10, Para.[1] 35, Hymn 320,[2] *or other suitable Psalm or Hymn.*

[1] [[i.e. Metrical Paraphrase, from those appended to the Scottish *Metrical Psalter*: No. 35 = Matt. 26. 26–29.]]
[2] [[i.e. in Revised *Church Hymnary* = 'And now, O Father . . .', by W. Bright.]]

During the singing the elements of bread and wine shall be brought into the church and laid on the Holy Table.

Thereafter the Creed, if not already used, may be said.

Thereafter the Minister shall unveil the elements, and may offer these prayers:

Let us pray.

O God, who by the blood of Thy dear Son hast consecrated for us a new and living way into the holiest of all; grant unto us, we beseech Thee, the assurance of Thy mercy, and sanctify us by Thy heavenly grace; that we, approaching Thee with pure heart and cleansed conscience, may offer unto Thee a sacrifice in righteousness; through Jesus Christ our Lord, to whom, with Thee and the Holy Spirit, be all glory, world without end. *Amen.*

Almighty and most merciful Father, we offer unto Thee this bread and this cup; for all things come of Thee, and of Thine own do we give Thee. Blessed be Thy holy name for ever; through Jesus Christ our Lord. *Amen.*

Then shall the Minister say: THE GRACE OF THE LORD JESUS CHRIST BE WITH YOU ALL.

Beloved in the Lord, attend to the words of the institution of the Holy Supper of our Lord Jesus Christ, as they are delivered by Saint Paul.

I have received of the Lord ... ⟦1 Cor. 11. 23–26⟧ ... till he come.

Therefore, that we may fulfil His institution in righteousness and joy, let us follow His blessed example in word and action: IN THE NAME OF THE FATHER, AND OF THE SON, AND OF THE HOLY SPIRIT:

As the Lord Jesus, the same night in which He was betrayed, took bread, I take these elements of bread and wine to be set apart from all common uses to this holy use and mystery; and as He gave thanks and blessed, let us draw nigh to God, and present unto Him our prayers and thanksgivings.

The Lord be with you;
℟ And with thy spirit.

Lift up your hearts;
℟ We lift them up unto the Lord.

Let us give thanks unto our Lord God;
℟ It is meet and right so to do.

It is verily meet, right and our bounden duty that we should at all times and in all places give thanks unto Thee, O Holy Lord, Father Almighty, Everlasting God; who didst create the heavens and the earth and all that is therein; who didst make man in Thine own image and whose tender mercies are over all Thy works.[1]

Thee, mighty God, heavenly King, we magnify and praise. With angels and archangels and with all the company of heaven, we worship and adore Thy glorious name; evermore praising Thee, and saying:

Holy, Holy, Holy, Lord God of Hosts,
Heaven and earth are full of Thy glory:
Glory be to Thee, O Lord Most high.

Blessed is He that cometh in the name of the Lord:
Hosanna in the highest.

Verily holy, verily blessed, art Thou, Almighty and Merciful God, who didst so love the world that Thou gavest Thine only-begotten Son, that whosoever believeth in Him should not perish but have everlasting life.

Not as we ought, but as we are able, do we bless thee for His holy incarnation, for His perfect life on earth, for His precious sufferings and death upon the Cross, for His glorious resurrection and ascension, for His continual intercession and rule at Thy right hand, for the promise of His coming again, and for His gift of the Holy Spirit.

Wherefore, having in remembrance the work and passion of our Saviour Christ, and pleading His eternal sacrifice, we Thy servants do set forth this memorial, which He hath commanded us to make; and we most humbly beseech Thee to send down Thy Holy Spirit to sanctify both us and these Thine own gifts of bread and wine which we set before Thee, that the bread which we break may be the communion of the body of Christ, and the cup of blessing which we bless the communion of the blood of Christ; that we, receiving them, may by faith be made partakers of His body and blood, with all His benefits, to our spiritual nourishment and growth in grace, and to the glory of Thy most holy name.

---

[1] Here may be added the Preface according to the season of the Christian Year. ⟦See Appendix A.⟧

And here we offer and present unto Thee ourselves, our souls and bodies, to be a reasonable, holy, and living sacrifice; and we beseech Thee mercifully to accept this our sacrifice of praise and thanksgiving, as, in fellowship with all the faithful in heaven and on earth, we pray Thee to fulfil in us, and in all men, the purpose of Thy redeeming love; through Jesus Christ our Lord, by whom, and with whom, in the unity of the Holy Spirit, all honour and glory be unto Thee, O Father Almighty, world without end. Amen.

And now, as our Saviour Christ hath taught us, we humbly pray, Our Father . . .

Then the Minister shall say:

According to the holy institution, example, and command of our Lord Jesus Christ, and for a memorial of Him, we do this: who, the same night in which He was betrayed, TOOK BREAD

(*here the Minister shall take the bread into his hands*),

and when He had blessed, and given thanks, HE BRAKE IT

(*here he shall break the bread*),

and said,

TAKE, EAT; THIS IS MY BODY, WHICH IS BROKEN FOR YOU: THIS DO IN REMEMBRANCE OF ME.

After the same manner also, HE TOOK THE CUP

(*here he shall raise the cup*),

saying:

THIS CUP IS THE NEW COVENANT IN MY BLOOD: THIS DO YE, AS OFT AS YE DRINK IT, IN REMEMBRANCE OF ME.

Lamb of God, that takest away the sins of the world, have mercy upon us.

Lamb of God, that takest away the sins of the world, have mercy upon us.

Lamb of God, that takest away the sins of the world, grant us Thy peace.

Then the Minister shall himself receive in both kinds, and, in giving the bread, he shall say:

Take ye, eat ye; this is the body of Christ which is broken for you: this do in remembrance of Him.

And, in giving the cup:

This cup is the new covenant in the blood of Christ, which is shed for many unto remission of sins: drink ye all of it.

When all have received, and the bread and wine have been replaced on the Holy Table and covered, the Minister shall say:

THE PEACE OF THE LORD JESUS CHRIST BE WITH YOU ALL.

Then he shall call the People to thanksgiving, saying:

Let us pray.

Almighty and ever-living God, we most heartily thank Thee that in Thy great love Thou dost vouchsafe to feed us at Thy Table with this spiritual food, and dost thereby assure us of Thy favour and goodness towards us; and that we are very members incorporate in the mystical body of Thy Son, the blessed company of all faithful people, and are also heirs through hope of Thy everlasting kingdom. And we most humbly beseech Thee, O heavenly Father, to receive us as now again we dedicate ourselves to Thee, and so to assist us with Thy grace, that we may continue in this holy fellowship, and live henceforth to Thy glory; through Jesus Christ our Lord. *Amen.*

And rejoicing in the communion of saints, we thank and praise Thee for all Thy servants who have departed in the faith; the great cloud of witnesses by which we are compassed about; all Thy saints in every age who have loved Thee in life and continued faithful unto death; especially those dear to our own hearts. . . . Give us grace to follow them as they followed Christ; and bring us with them, at the last, to those things which eye hath not seen, nor ear heard, which Thou hast prepared for them that love Thee; through Jesus Christ our Lord, who liveth and reigneth, and is worshipped and glorified, with Thee, O Father, and the Holy Spirit, world without end. *Amen.*

Or,

Almighty God, we praise and bless Thy holy name for Thy great and wonderful goodness unto us in permitting us to shew the death of our Redeemer, and to receive through His blessed Sacrament the communion of His body and His blood. Wherefore, we humbly beseech Thee to enable us to live no longer unto ourselves, but unto Him who died for us and rose again. And because at best we cannot worthily praise Thee, we beseech Thee, Almighty God, that the offering of Thy only begotten Son, made once for all upon the Cross, may be accepted on our behalf, in expiation for all our sins, and in thanksgiving for all mercies vouchsafed through the glorious riches of Jesus Christ our Lord. *Amen.*

And rejoicing . . .

Or,

Heavenly Father, we give Thee thanks and praise that upon us, who are unworthy, Thou dost confer so rich a benefit as to bring us into fellowship of Thy Son Jesus Christ: whom Thou didst deliver up unto death, and dost give for the nourishment of our souls unto life eternal. Now also grant us grace that we, never being unmindful of these things, but having them engraven upon our hearts, may advance and grow in that faith from which all good works proceed; through Jesus Christ our Lord.

And rejoicing . . .

Then shall be sung Psalm 103. 1–5, Para. 60,[1] *or other Psalm or Hymn of Praise.*

Thereafter the Minister shall pronounce the Benediction.

The peace of God . . . [[CF 14]] . . . always. *Amen.*

As the elements are being removed from the church, Nunc dimittis (Hymn 716)[2] *or Para. 38. 8, 10, 11*[3] *may be sung.*

[1] [[Metrical Paraphrase No. 60 = Heb. 13. 20–21.]]
[2] [[Revised Church Hymnary, No. 716 = Nunc Dimittis.]]
[3] [[These verses = Luke 2. 29–32 = Nunc Dimittis.]]

CHAPTER XIX

A CONGREGATIONALIST LITURGY

THE liturgy here printed is not, of course, an official form ordered for use by Congregationalists; but it is taken from a book produced by Congregationalists of considerable influence and is believed to be widely used. The book in question is *A Book of Public Worship compiled for the use of Congregationalists* by John Huxtable, John Marsh, Romilly Micklem, and James Todd (London, 1948). The book contains, among other things, five orders of Service followed by four orders for the Lord's Supper. The liturgy here printed consists of the first order of Morning Service with the first order of the Lord's Supper linked to it in the way ordered by the rubrics.

FIRST ORDER OF SERVICE
The Service begins with a Call to Worship, the Minister saying,
Let us worship God.

Then, all standing, he reads one or more Sentences of Holy Scripture; and then follow Prayers of Adoration and of Confession.
Serve the Lord with gladness: come before his presence with singing.
   Enter into his gates with thanksgiving, and into his courts with praise.
   For the Lord is good; his mercy is everlasting; and his truth endureth to all generations.

Let us pray.

Great and marvellous are thy works, Lord God Almighty; just and true are thy ways, thou King of saints. Who shall not fear thee, O Lord, and glorify thy name? for thou only art holy. Wherefore with thy whole Church in heaven and on earth we worship and adore thee, Father, Son, and Holy Ghost: to whom be glory for ever and ever. *Amen.*

Have mercy upon us, O God, according to thy lovingkindness: according to the multitude of thy tender mercies blot out our transgressions. Wash us throughly from our iniquity and cleanse us from our sin. For we acknowledge our transgressions: and our sin is ever before us. Create in us a clean heart, O God: and renew a right spirit within us. Cast us not away from thy presence: and take not thy Holy Spirit from us. Restore unto us the joy of thy salvation: and uphold us with thy free Spirit: through Jesus Christ our Lord. *Amen.*

Then may follow an Absolution, or Assurance of Pardon, read by the Minister.

With everlasting kindness will I have mercy on thee, saith the Lord, thy Redeemer. I, even I, am he that blotteth out thy transgressions for mine own sake, and will not remember thy sins. Return unto me, for I have redeemed thee. *Amen.*

Then a Hymn is sung.

Then a Lesson from the Old Testament is read; after which a Psalm or a Canticle is sung; and then a Lesson from the New Testament is read.

The New Testament Lesson may consist of two passages of Scripture, the first taken from a book of the New Testament other than a Gospel, and the second from one of the Gospels.

Before each Lesson these words may be used:

Hear the Word of God in ——, the —— chapter, at the —— verse.

And at the close of the Lessons these words may be used:

May God bless to us the reading of his Word, and to him be the glory.

Then a Hymn or an Anthem is sung.

Then Prayers of Thanksgiving, of Supplication, and of Intercession are offered; after which Minister and People say together the Lord's Prayer.

Let us pray.

Most gracious God, our heavenly Father, who art good to all, and whose tender mercies are over all thy works; we lift our hearts to thee in gratitude and praise. We thank thee for the wonders of thy creation, for the care of thy providence, and for the riches of thy grace. Most of all, we praise thee for our salvation in Jesus Christ thy Son: for the grace and truth that came by him; for his obedience unto death, even the death of the Cross; and for his resurrection and everlasting reign. We bless thee for the coming of the Holy Spirit; for the Church, which is Christ's body; and for the promise of eternal life to all believers. Make our hearts to grow in thankfulness for all thy mercies; and enable us to present ourselves a living sacrifice to thee, that we may live in thy service and ever seek to praise thy glorious name.

Holy Father, who hast redeemed us with the precious blood of thy dear Son; keep us, we beseech thee, steadfast in faith, and enable us to live no longer unto ourselves, but unto him who died for us and rose again. Strengthen us by thy grace that we may fight the good fight, and finish our course, and keep the faith. Help us manfully to overcome our temptations, and faithfully to fulfil the work thou hast given us to do. Shed abroad thy love in our hearts; make us kind one to another, tender-hearted, forgiving one another, even as thou for Christ's sake hast forgiven us; and persuade us that neither death nor life, nor things present nor things to come, shall be able to separate us from thy love, which is in Christ Jesus our Lord.

Almighty God, who hast taught us in thy holy Word to make supplications, prayers, intercessions, and giving of thanks for all men; hear us, we beseech thee, in the name of Jesus Christ.

Send down thy blessing on thy whole Church, in all its communions and in every land. Confirm it in the faith of Christ; cleanse it from every fault and stain; unite it in the bond of thy Spirit; and strengthen its witness to thy truth. Enrich all Ministers with knowledge and understanding of thy Word, and enable them to open their mouths boldly to proclaim the mystery of the Gospel. Bestow the fulness of thy grace on all thy people, that they may walk worthy of the vocation wherewith they are called, and continue steadfast in thy service unto the end. Reveal thy glory among the nations; and hasten the time when in the name of Jesus every knee shall bow, and every tongue confess that he is Lord, to the glory of thy holy name.

Direct and govern all who bear rule among the peoples, especially our Sovereign Lord King George, our gracious Queen Elizabeth, Mary the Queen Mother, the Princess Elizabeth, the Duke of Edinburgh, and all the Royal Family. Give wisdom and understanding to our Ministers of State, to the High Court of

Parliament, and to all who are called to the public service. Let thy blessing rest continually upon the British Commonwealth of Nations: purge us of all sin and corruption; keep us faithful to the high trust thou hast laid upon us; and deepen our life in that righteousness which alone exalteth a nation. Unite men everywhere in justice, liberty, and peace; and let the reign of Christ be acknowledged throughout the world.

Show pity and mercy to all who are in trouble and distress, and give them courage and consolation. Protect all who are in danger by land, or sea, or air; provide for those who are poor and destitute; reclaim those who have wandered from thy ways; heal the sick; befriend the lonely; speak peace to the dying; and comfort all mourners with the eternal promises of Christ. Hear us especially for those whom we name in silence before thee. . . . God be merciful unto them, and bless them; and cause thy face to shine upon them, and be gracious unto them.

Finally, we thank thee for all thy faithful servants departed this life. . . . Bring us with them at last, we humbly pray thee, to those things which eye hath not seen, nor ear heard, which thou hast prepared for them that love thee: through Jesus Christ our Lord, to whom with thee, O Father, and the Holy Ghost, be all honour and glory, world without end. *Amen.*

Our Father. . . .

Then the Notices are given; after which the Offerings are received; and a Prayer of Dedication is offered. Or else, the Offerings may be received after the Sermon.

Let us pray.

O Lord our God, all things come of thee, and of thine own we give thee. Receive our offerings; and grant, by thy mercies, that we may present ourselves a living sacrifice, holy, acceptable to thee: through Jesus Christ our Lord. *Amen.*

Then a Hymn is sung.

Before the Sermon a Prayer for Illumination may be offered.

Let us pray.

O God, who hast called us unto thy kingdom and glory by Christ Jesus; let thy Gospel come unto us not in word only, but also in power and in the Holy Ghost, that it may be spoken and heard

A Congregationalist Liturgy

not as the word of men but as thy Word, which effectually worketh in all who believe: through Jesus Christ our Lord. *Amen.*

Then the Sermon is preached.

Then a Hymn is sung, during which those worshippers who are not remaining to the Sacrament may withdraw; or else, the Minister may dismiss them with a Blessing at the close of the Hymn.

The Minister and Deacons take their places at the Lord's Table; and the bread and wine, which have previously been prepared on the Table, are uncovered.

Where individual cups are used, one large cup should be in readiness on the Table for raising at the due point in the Service. There should also be one piece of bread suitable for breaking.

Then, a Communion Hymn having been sung, the Minister says:

Beloved in the Lord: Attend to the words of institution of the Holy Supper of our Lord Jesus Christ, as they are delivered by Saint Paul.

I have received of the Lord that which also I delivered unto you, That the Lord Jesus, the same night in which he was betrayed, took bread: and, when he had given thanks, he brake it, and said, Take, eat: this is my body, which is broken for you: this do in remembrance of me. After the same manner also he took the cup, when he had supped, saying, This cup is the new testament in my blood: this do ye, as oft as ye drink it, in remembrance of me. For as often as ye eat this bread, and drink this cup, ye do shew the Lord's death till he come.

Then the Minister says:

Hear now the words with which our Lord bids us come to him, that you may draw near to this Table in full assurance of faith.

Come unto me, all ye that labour and are heavy laden, and I will give you rest.

Blessed are they which do hunger and thirst after righteousness, for they shall be filled.

I am the bread of life: he that cometh to me shall never hunger, and he that believeth on me shall never thirst.... Him that cometh unto me I will in no wise cast out.

Behold, I stand at the door and knock: if any man hear my

voice and open the door, I will come in to him, and will sup with him, and he with me.

Let us pray.

Minister: Lift up your hearts;
People: We lift them up unto the Lord.
Minister: Let us give thanks unto our Lord God;
People: It is meet and right so to do.
Minister: It is very meet, right, and our bounden duty, that we should at all times, and in all places, give thanks unto thee, O Lord, Holy Father, Almighty, Everlasting God. Therefore with angels and archangels, and with all the company of heaven, we laud and magnify thy glorious name; evermore praising thee, and saying,

(*Minister and People*)
Holy, holy, holy, Lord God of Hosts,
Heaven and earth are full of thy glory:
Glory be to thee, O Lord most High. Amen.

Then follows the Prayer of Thanksgiving.
O Holy, Almighty, and Merciful God, who didst create the heavens and the earth and all that is therein, who didst make man in thine own image, and whose tender mercies are over all thy works; with thy whole Church we offer up to thee our worship and our praise.

For all thy bounties known to us, for all unknown, we give thee thanks; but chiefly that when through disobedience we had fallen from thee, thou didst not suffer us to depart from thee for ever, but hast redeemed us from sin and death, and given us the joyful hope of everlasting life, through Jesus Christ our Lord; who, being very and eternal God, came down from heaven in perfect love, and became man for our salvation.

We bless thee for his holy incarnation; for his life on earth; for his precious sufferings and death upon the Cross; for his glorious resurrection and ascension to thy right hand; and for the promise of his coming again in the glory of his kingdom. We bless thee tor the gift of the Holy Ghost; for the sacraments and ordinances of thy Church; for the communion of saints; and for the hope of everlasting life and glory in the kingdom of thy dear Son.

Thee, mighty God, heavenly King, we magnify and praise. We

worship and adore thy glorious name, Father, Son, and Holy Ghost: to whom be all honour and glory for ever and ever.

O merciful Father, we most humbly beseech thee to send down thy Holy Spirit to sanctify both us and these thine own gifts of bread and wine which we set before thee, that the bread which we break may be to us the communion of the body of Christ, and the cup of blessing which we bless the communion of the blood of Christ; that we, receiving them, may by faith be made partakers of his body and blood, with all his benefits, to our spiritual nourishment and growth in grace, and to the glory of thy holy name.

Mercifully accept, we beseech thee, O God, this our sacrifice of praise and thanksgiving; and, for the sake of him who loved us and gave himself for us, grant that we may present ourselves unto thee a living sacrifice: through the same Jesus Christ our Lord, to whom with thee, O Father, and the Holy Ghost, be all honour and glory, world without end. *Amen.*

Then the Minister and People may say together the Lord's Prayer, the Minister first saying:

And now, as our Saviour Christ hath taught us, we say,
Our Father, which art ... ⟦CF 1⟧ ... ever. *Amen.*

Then the Minister says:

In obedience to our Lord, and in remembrance of him, we do this: Who the same night in which he was betrayed took bread (*here the Minister takes the bread into his hands*), and when he had given thanks, as we give thanks, he brake it (*here the Minister breaks the bread*), and said, Take, eat: this is my body, which is broken for you: this do in remembrance of me. After the same manner also he took the cup (*here the Minister raises the cup in his hands*), saying, This cup is the new covenant in my blood: this do ye, as oft as ye drink it, in remembrance of me.

Then the Minister delivers the bread to the Deacons, who take it to the people. In giving the bread, he says:

Take ye, eat ye: this is the body of Christ which is broken for you: do this in remembrance of him.

Then the minister delivers the wine to the Deacons, who take it to the People. In giving the wine, he says:

This cup is the new covenant in the blood of Christ, which is shed for the remission of sins: drink ye of it.

When all have received, Prayer is offered.

Let us pray.

Heavenly Father, we give thee praise and thanks that upon us the unworthy thou dost confer so rich a benefit as to bring us into the communion of thy Son Jesus Christ; whom having delivered up to death, thou hast given for our nourishment unto eternal life. Now also grant us grace, that we may never be unmindful of these things; but bearing them about, engraven on our hearts, may advance and grow in that faith which is exercised in good works: through Jesus Christ our Lord. *Amen.*

An Offering for the poor may then be received.

Then a Hymn is sung; after which the Minister dismisses the People with the Blessing.

The grace of the Lord Jesus Christ, and the love of God, and the communion of the Holy Ghost, be with you all. *Amen.*

CHAPTER XX

THE LITURGY OF THE CHURCH OF SOUTH INDIA

THIS liturgy was used for the first time at the second Synod of the Church of South India in 1950. It was there authorized by the Synod 'for optional use on special occasions in accordance with the provisions contained in Rule 5, Chap. X, of the Constitution'. In 1954 the text printed below was approved by the Synod. Further small changes were made in 1962 and the resulting text was printed in the *Book of Common Worship* (1963), too late to be used here.

THE LORD'S SUPPER
OR THE HOLY EUCHARIST

A SERVICE THAT MAY BE USED BEFORE THE CELEBRATION OF THE LORD'S SUPPER

As often as possible, a special service shall be held the night before the celebration of the Lord's Supper, or at some other convenient time. Or it may be held before the celebration on the same day, with an interval for silent common prayer. Such a service may include, besides the praise of God and the confession of sin and the reading and preaching of God's Word:

1. The reading of 1 Corinthians 11: 23–29.
2. The reading, with responses, of the Ten Commandments or of our Lord's Summary of the Law and the Prophets.
3. An Exhortation.

THE TEN COMMANDMENTS

God spake all these words, saying:

I. I am the Lord thy God; thou shalt have none other gods before me.

II. Thou shalt not make unto thee a graven image, nor the likeness of any form that is in heaven above, or that is in the earth beneath, or that is in the water under the earth: thou shalt not bow down thyself unto them, nor serve them.

III. Thou shalt not take the name of the Lord thy God in vain.

IV. Remember the sabbath day, to keep it holy. Six days shalt thou labour, and do all thy work: but the seventh day is a sabbath unto the Lord thy God.

V. Honour thy father and thy mother.

VI. Thou shalt do no murder.

VII. Thou shalt not commit adultery.

VIII. Thou shalt not steal.

IX. Thou shalt not bear false witness.

After each commandment the people shall say:
Lord, have mercy upon us, and incline our hearts to keep this law.

X. Thou shalt not covet.

[[*People*]] Lord, have mercy upon us, and write all these thy laws in our hearts, we beseech thee.

OUR LORD'S SUMMARY OF THE LAW AND THE PROPHETS

Our Lord Jesus Christ said: Hear, O Israel, The Lord our God is one Lord; and thou shalt love the Lord thy God with all thy heart, and with all thy soul, and with all thy mind, and with all thy strength. This is the first commandment. And the second is like, namely this: Thou shalt love thy neighbour as thyself. There is none other commandment greater than these. On these two commandments hang all the Law and the Prophets.

[[*People*]] Lord, have mercy upon us, and incline our hearts to keep this law.

AN EXHORTATION

Dearly beloved, it is right that we who would come to the Lord's Table should take to heart the mystery of this sacrament. The mystery is this: that Christ truly gives unto us his body and blood as food and drink of everlasting life. The Good Shepherd has laid down his life for the sheep; he who was without guile has died for sinners, the Head for his members, the Bridegroom for his bride the Church; in obedience to the Father's will and in infinite love to us, the High Priest has offered himself as the perfect sacrifice. By his death he has done away with all that stood in the way of our fellowship with God the Father, that we may assuredly be his children, be upheld by his love, be guided by him all the days of our life, and rejoice in the hope of his glory. In the fellowship of his sufferings he calls us to crucify the old man with his lusts, and to bear trials and tribulations patiently, to the glory of his name. In the power of his resurrection he calls us to newness of life. In the fellowship of his Spirit he joins us together, and seeks to change us into his image. By the same Spirit he pours his love into our hearts, so that we may love one another, and our enemies for his sake.

If any man will not lay this to heart, but is minded to continue in sin and unrighteousness, let him not approach the Table of the Lord. Let a man examine himself and so let him eat of that bread and drink of that cup. The worthiness which the Lord requires from us is that we be truly sorry for our sins and find our joy and salvation in him. For we come to this supper not as righteous in ourselves, but trusting in the righteousness of Christ our Saviour. He invites us to partake of this holy meal.

THE PREPARATION

A hymn or psalm may be sung or said.

As the ministers come to the Lord's Table, the people shall stand. The presbyter, or one of those with him, shall carry in both hands the Bible from which the lessons are to be read, and shall place it on the Table or on a lectern. The presbyter may stand behind the Table, facing the people.

The presbyter shall say, the people standing:

>Let us pray.

Almighty God, unto whom ... [[CF 2]] ... Lord. ℟ Amen.

Then all shall sing or say:

Glory to God in the highest, and on earth peace among men in whom he is well pleased. We praise thee, we bless thee, we worship thee, we glorify thee, we give thanks to thee for thy great glory, O Lord God, Heavenly King, God the Father Almighty.

O Lord, the only-begotten Son Jesus Christ, O Lord God, Lamb of God, Son of the Father, that takest away the sin of the world, have mercy upon us; thou that takest away the sin of the world, receive our prayer. Thou that sittest at the right hand of God the Father, have mercy upon us.

For thou only art holy, thou only art Lord, thou only art most high, O Jesus Christ, with the Holy Spirit, in the glory of God the Father. Amen.

Or this ancient hymn, thrice repeated:
Holy God;
[[People]] Holy and mighty, holy and immortal, have mercy on us.

Or this litany, the deacon leading the responses:
Worthy is the Lamb that hath been slain to receive the power, and riches, and wisdom, and might, and honour, and glory, and blessing.
[[People]] Unto the Lamb be glory!
Unto him that sitteth on the throne, and unto the Lamb, be the blessing, and the honour, and the glory, and the dominion, for ever and ever.
[[People]] Unto the Lamb be glory!
Worthy art thou, for thou wast slain, and didst purchase unto God with thy blood men of every tribe, and tongue, and people, and nation.
[[People]] Unto the Lamb be glory! Salvation unto our God which sitteth on the throne, and unto the Lamb. Blessing, and glory, and wisdom, and thanksgiving, and honour, and power, and might, be unto our God for ever and ever. Amen.

Or another hymn may be sung.

If there has been no special service before the celebration of the Lord's Supper, one or more of the passages on pp. [[205-7]] may be read here.

The Liturgy of the Church of South India

Then shall the presbyter say:

Brethren, we have come together to hear God's most holy Word, and to receive the body and blood of the Lord. Let us, therefore, kneel and examine ourselves in silence, seeking God's grace that we may draw near to him with repentance and faith.

All shall kneel. After a short silence the presbyter shall say:

Ye that do truly and earnestly repent you of your sins, and are in love and charity with your neighbours, and intend to live a new life, following the commandments of God and walking from henceforth in his holy ways, make your humble confession to Almighty God, that you may be reconciled anew to him through our Lord Jesus Christ.

The deacon leading, all shall say together:

Heavenly Father, we confess that we have sinned against thee and our neighbour. We have walked in darkness rather than in light; we have named the name of Christ, but have not departed from iniquity. Have mercy upon us, we beseech thee; for the sake of Jesus Christ forgive us all our sins; cleanse us by thy Holy Spirit; quicken our consciences; and enable us to forgive others, that we may henceforth serve thee in newness of life, to the glory of thy holy name. Amen.

¶ *Or the presbyter may use certain other forms.*[1]

Then the presbyter shall stand and say:

Hear the gracious Word of God to all who truly turn to him through Jesus Christ.

Come unto me, all ye that labour and are heavy laden, and I will give you rest.

God so loved the world, that he gave his only-begotten Son, that whosoever believeth on him should not perish, but have eternal life.

Faithful is the saying, and worthy of all acceptation, that Christ Jesus came into the world to save sinners.

If any man sin, we have an Advocate with the Father, Jesus Christ the righteous: and he is the propitiation for our sins.

---

[1] [[The following are recommended: Psalm 51. 1-3, 9-12 (said or sung); One of the Confessions in the Book of Common Prayer; a hymn; extempore prayer by the presbyter.]]

After a short silence, the presbyter shall say:

Almighty God, our heavenly Father, who of his great mercy has promised forgiveness of sins to all who forgive their brethren and with hearty repentance and true faith turn unto him; Have mercy upon you; pardon and deliver you from all your sins; confirm and strengthen you in all goodness; and bring you to eternal life; through Jesus Christ our Lord.
〚*People*〛 Amen. Thanks be to God.

The presbyter may say 'us' and 'our' for 'you' and 'your'; if so, the prayer shall precede the reading of the Gracious Word of God.

THE MINISTRY OF THE WORD OF GOD
The Lord be with you;
〚*People*〛 And with thy spirit.

Let us pray
Here shall follow the Collect of the Day, or another short prayer.

The people may stand for the reading of Scripture, or at least for the reading of the Gospel. Before each lesson the reader shall say: Hear the Word of God, as it is written in [*the name of the Book*], in the . . . chapter, beginning at the . . . verse; *and after it he shall say:* Here ends the lesson.

The lesson from the Old Testament shall be read, and after it the people shall say:
Thanks be to thee, O God.

A psalm or hymn may be sung.

The Epistle shall be read, and the people shall say:
Thanks be to thee, O God.

The Gospel shall be read, and the people shall say:
Praise be to thee, O Christ.

Then the sermon shall be preached, the people sitting.

Then the Nicene Creed shall be said or sung by all, standing:
I believe in one God . . . 〚CF 4〛 . . . to come. Amen.
〚But reading 'Holy Spirit', 'the Holy Spirit, The Lord, The Giver of life', 'One, Holy, Catholic'〛

Or the Apostles' Creed may be used.[1]

Announcements may be made here, and the collection may be taken. A hymn may also be sung.

Biddings for prayer may be made, and then, all kneeling, one of these litanies may be said or sung, the deacon leading; or the presbyter may offer intercession in his own words for the Church and the world.

Let us pray

Almighty God, who hast taught us to make prayers and supplications, and to give thanks, for all men; hear us when we pray: That it may please thee to inspire continually the universal Church with the spirit of truth, unity, and concord:
[[*People*]] Hear us, we beseech thee, O Lord (*and so after each petition*).

That it may please thee to grant that all they that do confess thy holy Name may agree in the truth of thy holy Word, and bear witness to it with courage and fidelity:

That it may please thee to lead the nations in the paths of righteousness and peace:

That it may please thee to guide with thy pure and peaceable wisdom those who bear authority in the affairs of men, especially the President of the Indian Republic . . . and those who rule over us; that we and all men may be godly and quietly governed:

That it may please thee to give grace to all bishops, presbyters, and deacons, especially thy servants . . . our Moderator and . . . our bishop, that by their life and doctrine they may set forth thy true and living Word, and rightly and duly administer thy holy Sacraments:

That it may please thee to guide and prosper those who are labouring for the spread of thy Gospel among the nations, and to enlighten with thy Spirit all places of education, learning, and healing:

That it may please thee that through thy heavenly benediction we may be saved from dearth and famine, and may with thankful hearts enjoy the fruits of the earth in their season:

That it may please thee to give thy heavenly grace to all thy

---

[1] [[Baptism may be administered after the Creed.]]

people in their several callings, and especially to this congregation here present; that, with meek heart and due reverence, they may hear, and receive thy holy Word; truly serving thee in holiness and righteousness all the days of their life:

That it may please thee of thy goodness, O Lord, to comfort and succour all them, who in this transitory life are in trouble, sorrow, need, sickness, or any other adversity:

And we praise thee for all thy servants departed this life in thy faith and fear, beseeching thee to give us grace that we may follow their good examples, and with them be made partakers of thy heavenly kingdom:

The second litany:

For the peace that is from above, and for the salvation of our souls, let us pray to the Lord.
[[*People*]] Lord, have mercy (*and so after each bidding*).

For the peace of the whole world, for the welfare of God's holy Churches, and for the union of all, let us pray to the Lord.

For our bishops and all other ministers (especially . . . our Moderator and . . . our bishop), that with a good heart and a pure conscience they may accomplish their ministry, let us pray to the Lord.

For the rulers of our country and all in authority, let us pray to the Lord.

For the sick, the suffering, the sorrowful, and the dying, let us pray to the Lord.

For the poor, the hungry, orphans and widows, and them that suffer persecution, let us pray to the Lord.

For ourselves and all who confess the name of Christ, that we may show forth the excellencies of him who called us out of darkness into his marvellous light, let us pray to the Lord.

That, with all his servants who have served him here and are now at rest, we may enter into the fulness of his unending joy, let us pray to the Lord.

The Liturgy of the Church of South India

[1]*After either Litany the presbyter shall say:*
>Let us pray

Almighty God, the fountain of all wisdom, who knowest our necessities before we ask, and our ignorance in asking; We beseech thee to have compassion upon our infirmities; and those things, which for our unworthiness we dare not, and for our blindness we cannot ask, vouchsafe to give us, for the worthiness of thy Son Jesus Christ our Lord. ℟ Amen.

Or this:

Almighty and everlasting God, by whose Spirit the whole body of the Church is governed and sanctified, receive our supplications and prayers, which we offer before thee for all estates of men in thy holy Church, that every member of the same, in his vocation and ministry, may truly and godly serve thee; through our Lord and Saviour Jesus Christ. ℟ Amen.

The presbyter shall then give the first benediction:

The grace of the Lord Jesus Christ, and the love of God, and the fellowship of the Holy Spirit, be with you all. ℟ Amen.

He may say 'us' instead of 'you'.

Those who leave[2] shall leave now.

THE BREAKING OF THE BREAD

All shall stand, and the presbyter shall say:

   Behold, how good and joyful a thing it is, brethren, to dwell together in unity.
   We who are many are one bread, one body, for we all partake of the one bread.
[*People*] I will offer in his dwelling an oblation with great gladness, I will sing and speak praises unto the Lord.

The 'Peace' may be given here.[3]

---
   [1] [Confirmation may be administered after the Intercession.]
   [2] [Including any who are excommunicate or under discipline.]
   [3] ['The giver places his right palm against the right palm of the receiver, and each closes his left hand over the other's right hand. . . . The presbyter gives the Peace to those ministering with him, and these in turn give it to the congregation. It may be passed through the congregation either along the rows, or from those in front to those behind. It is suggested that each person as he gives the Peace, may say in a low voice, "The peace of God", or "The peace of God be with you".' [from the INTRODUCTION].]

A hymn shall now be sung, and the bread and wine for the Communion, together with the alms of the people, shall be brought forward and placed on the Table. Those who bear the offertory shall stand before the Table during the following prayer.

All standing, the presbyter shall say:

Holy Father, who through the blood of thy dear Son hast consecrated for us a new and living way to thy throne of grace, we come to thee through him, unworthy as we are, and we humbly beseech thee to accept and use us and these our gifts for thy glory. All that is in heaven and earth is thine, and of thine own do we give to thee. R/ Amen.

The bearers of the offertory shall now return to their places.

The presbyter and people shall kneel, and say together:

Be present, be present, O Jesus, thou good High Priest, as thou wast in the midst of thy disciples, and make thyself known to us in the breaking of the bread, who livest and reignest with the Father and the Holy Spirit, one God, world without end. Amen.

The presbyter shall now stand.

[[*Presbyter*]] The Lord be with you;
[[*People*]] And with thy spirit.
[[*Presbyter*]] Lift up your hearts;
[[*People*]] We lift them up unto the Lord.
[[*Presbyter*]] Let us give thanks unto our Lord God;
[[*People*]] It is meet and right so to do.

It is verily meet, right, and our bounden duty, that we should at all times, and in all places, give thanks unto thee, O Lord, Holy Father, Almighty and Everlasting God;
   [1]Through Jesus Christ thy Son our Lord, through whom thou didst create the heavens and the earth and all that in them is, and didst make man in thine own image, and when he had fallen into sin didst redeem him to be the first fruits of a new creation.

[[*Presbyter and People*]] Therefore with angels and archangels and with all the company of heaven, we laud and magnify thy

---

[1] Instead of the words 'Through Jesus Christ . . . a new creation', another Preface proper to the season of the Christian Year may be said. [[For Proper Prefaces, see Appendix A.]]

glorious name; evermore praising thee, and saying, Holy, Holy, Holy, Lord God of hosts, heaven and earth are full of thy glory. Glory be to thee, O Lord most high.

[*Presbyter and People*] Blessed be he that hath come and is to come in the name of the Lord, Hosanna in the highest.

[*Presbyter*] Truly holy, truly blessed art thou, O heavenly Father, who of thy tender love towards mankind didst give thine only Son Jesus Christ to take our nature upon him and to suffer death upon the cross for our redemption; who made there, by his one oblation of himself once offered, a full, perfect, and sufficient sacrifice, oblation, and satisfaction, for the sins of the whole world; and did institute, and in his holy Gospel command us to continue, a perpetual memory of that his precious death, until his coming again: Who, in the same night that he was betrayed, took bread,[1] and when he had given thanks, he brake it, and gave it to his disciples, saying, Take, eat, this is my body which is given for you: do this in remembrance of me. Likewise after supper he took the cup,[2] and, when he had given thanks, he gave it to them, saying, Drink ye all of this; for this is my blood of the new covenant, which is shed for you and for many for the remission of sins: do this, as oft as ye shall drink it, in remembrance of me.

[*People*] Amen. Thy death, O Lord, we commemorate, thy resurrection we confess, and thy second coming we await. Glory be to thee, O Christ.

[*Presbyter*] Wherefore, O Father, having in remembrance the precious death and passion, and glorious resurrection and ascension, of thy Son our Lord, we thy servants do this in remembrance of him, as he hath commanded, until his coming again, giving thanks to thee for the perfect redemption which thou hast wrought for us in him.

[*People*] We give thanks to thee, we praise thee, we glorify thee, O Lord our God.

[*Presbyter*] And we most humbly beseech thee, O merciful Father, to sanctify with thy Holy Spirit, us and these thine own gifts of bread and wine, that the bread which we break may be the communion of the body of Christ, and the cup which we bless the

---

[1] [*The Presbyter takes the paten with the bread into his hand.*]
[2] [*The Presbyter takes the cup into his hand.*]

communion of the blood of Christ. Grant that being joined together in him, we may all attain to the unity of the faith, and may grow up in all things unto him who is the Head, even Christ, our Lord, by whom and with whom, in the unity of the Holy Spirit, all honour and glory be unto thee, O Father Almighty, world without end. ℟ Amen.

Here the presbyter may kneel.

As our Saviour Christ hath commanded and taught us, we are bold to say:

〚*Presbyter and People*〛 Our Father, who art ... 〚CF 1〛 ... and ever. Amen.

Then shall silence be kept for a space, all kneeling.

〚*Presbyter and People*〛 We do not presume to come to this thy Table, O merciful Lord, trusting in our own righteousness, but in thy manifold and great mercies. We are not worthy so much as to gather up the crumbs under thy Table. But thou art the same Lord, whose property is always to have mercy: Grant us therefore, gracious Lord, so to eat the Flesh of thy dear Son Jesus Christ, and to drink his Blood, that our sinful bodies and souls may be made clean by his most precious Body and Blood, and that we may evermore dwell in him, and he in us. Amen.

Then the presbyter shall rise, and break the bread, saying:

The bread which we break, is it not the communion of the body of Christ?

Or this:

The things of God for the people of God.

Or he may break the bread in silence.

The ministers and people shall now receive the bread and wine.[1]

---

[1] 〚'Communion may be administered in the place and manner customary in the congregation. It is however recommended that communion may be given by "tables", i.e. the people come forward to receive in front of the holy Table, and each row remains kneeling till the presbyter dismisses them with a blessing such as "The grace of the Lord Jesus Christ be with you all". When this is done, it is convenient that there should be "stewards". A spoon may be used for administering the wine' [INTRODUCTION].〛

The following words of administration may be used:
The body of our Lord Jesus Christ, the bread of life.
The blood of our Lord Jesus Christ, the true vine.

Or certain other words may be used.[1]

During this time these words may be said or sung:
O Lamb of God, that takest away the sin of the world, have mercy upon us.
   O Lamb of God, that takest away the sin of the world, have mercy upon us.
   O Lamb of God, that takest away the sin of the world, grant us thy peace.

Or some other hymn may be sung.

When all have partaken, the presbyter shall say:
Having now by faith received the sacrament of the Body and the Blood of Christ, let us give thanks.

Then one of the following prayers shall be said or sung by the presbyter alone, or by all together:
O almighty God, our heavenly Father, who hast accepted us as thy children in thy beloved Son Jesus Christ our Lord, and hast fed us with the spiritual food of his most precious Body and Blood, giving us the forgiveness of our sins and the promise of everlasting life; we thank and praise thee for these inestimable benefits, and we offer and present unto thee ourselves, our souls and bodies, to be a holy and living sacrifice, which is our reasonable service. Grant us grace not to be conformed to this world, but to be transformed by the renewing of our minds, that we may learn what is thy good and perfect will, and so obey thee here on earth, that we may at the last rejoice with all thy saints in thy heavenly kingdom; through Jesus Christ our Lord, who liveth and reigneth with thee and the Holy Spirit, one God, for ever.

---

[1] [The following alternatives are recommended in the INTRODUCTION:
   1. As in the Book of Common Prayer [CF 11].
   2. 'The Communion of the Body of Christ.' 'The Communion of the Blood of Christ.'
   3. 'Take ye, eat ye; this is the body of Christ which is broken for you: this do in remembrance of him.' 'This cup is the new covenant in the blood of Christ, which is shed for many unto remission of sins: drink ye all of it.']

Or this:

Almighty and everlasting God, we most heartily thank thee, for that thou dost vouchsafe to feed us, who have duly received these holy mysteries, with the spiritual food of the most precious Body and Blood of thy Son our Saviour Jesus Christ; and dost assure us thereby of thy favour and goodness towards us, and that we are very members incorporate in the mystical Body of thy Son, which is the blessed company of all faithful people; and are also heirs through hope of thy everlasting kingdom, by the merits of the most precious death and passion of thy dear Son. And we most humbly beseech thee, O heavenly Father, so to assist us with thy grace that we may continue in that holy fellowship, and do all such good works as thou hast prepared for us to walk in. And here we offer and present unto thee ourselves, our souls and bodies, to be a reasonable, holy, and living sacrifice unto thee, through Jesus Christ our Lord, to whom with thee and the Holy Spirit be all honour and glory, world without end.

[[*People*]] Amen. Blessing, and glory, and wisdom, and thanksgiving, and honour, and power, and might, be unto our God for ever and ever. Amen.

The presbyter shall then give the second benediction:

The peace of God, which passeth all understanding, keep your hearts and minds in the knowledge and love of God, and of his Son Jesus Christ our Lord: and the blessing of God Almighty, the Father, the Son, and the Holy Spirit, be amongst you and remain with you always. ℟ Amen.

The presbyter may say 'our' *and* 'us' *instead of* 'your' *and* 'you'.

A hymn of praise and thanksgiving, or a part of Psalm 103, or the Nunc Dimittis, *may be sung after the benediction.*

After the benediction the ministers shall go out, carrying with them the Bible, the gifts of the people, and the vessels used for the Communion. Any bread or wine set apart in the Service which remains over shall be carried out to the vestry, and may there be reverently consumed.

The Lord's Prayer may be said before the Thanksgiving, and the Gloria in Excelsis *after it, if they have not previously been used.*

PART III

APPENDIX A

PROPER PREFACES

IN this Appendix are printed (with the exceptions noted below) the Proper Prefaces ordered or permitted to be used in all the liturgies included in this volume. Many of the modern Prefaces are intended for use upon various occasions. The Prefaces have therefore been arranged in liturgical order: *temporale, sanctorale,* commons, and votives; and each occasion of use has been cross-referenced to the text of the Preface, which has of course been printed only once.

The following points should be noted:

1. In the Scottish and Indian Prayer Books all the Prefaces may be used both with the 'national' liturgy and also with the local recension of **1662**.

2. In the case of the Indian Liturgy, the Prefaces included are those of the Indian Prayer Book (1961), which are not so numerous as those of the *Proposed Prayer Book* (1951).

3. The Bombay Liturgy, before its incorporation into the *Proposed Prayer Book*, had its own Proper Prefaces. In the 1951 revision it shared those of the Indian Liturgy, and its original Prefaces are not included here. The text given in the 1961 Supplement [see page 94] refers to the use of Proper Prefaces, but gives neither texts nor a reference to those of **IndR**. Presumably, any of the Prefaces given in **IndR** may be used, as was expressly provided in the *Proposed Prayer Book*.

4. The Liturgy of the C.S.I. permits the use of the Proper Prefaces of **1928** or of the *Proposed Prayer Book*. [See p. 238.]

5. The Swahili Mass uses the Prefaces of the *English Missal*. But that book prints all the **1662** Prefaces, together with English versions of all those of *Missale Romanum*. It is not clear (*a*) which Preface is used when the **1662** and Roman texts differ, or (*b*) how extensive is the Kalendar, and therefore how many of the 'extra' Roman Prefaces are used. For this reason the Swahili Mass is ignored in this Appendix. But it may be pointed out that most of the Roman Prefaces are in use in some part of the Anglican Communion; and some are used universally. They are indicated

here by the sign '[R]' below the name of the liturgical day at the right of the page.

6. In this Appendix, except by citing **1549** and **1552**, no attempt is made to give an historical edition such as has been attempted with the liturgies themselves.

7. The printed text is that of **1662**, when the Preface occurs in that book. In all other cases the printed text is that of the first book in the list above the text of the Preface.

8. An asterisk* indicates that the use of a Preface is optional. It should be added that the Scottish Prayer Book has a rubric saying that 'Proper Prefaces other than those for the Great Festivals are for permissive use only'; the writer does not feel competent to interpret this rubric in terms of asterisks. In the West Indian Liturgy the following Prefaces appear in a distinct group, which may be intended to imply that they are optional: Christ the King, Feasts of the Blessed Virgin Mary, St. Joseph, and Apostles (nos. 31, 56, 41, 61[1]).

9. The notes to this appendix follow the lines of a traditional critical apparatus, since their purpose is to illuminate the text of the Prefaces and not the history of the several liturgies. Abbreviations will be found on pp. xv, xvi and are given here, with the exceptions noted in paragraph (7) above, in alphabetical order.

10. No notice has been taken of the votive use of the Prefaces, e.g. of that of Whitsun for occasional use 'of the Holy Ghost'.

1 **Scot, Cey, Jap*, WInd**   Advent (*a*)

Because thou hast given salvation unto mankind through the coming of thy well-beloved Son in great humility, and by him wilt make all things new when he shall come again in his glorious majesty to judge the world in righteousness.

Jap: PREF And especially do we praise thee · through ... righteousness] by the Advent of thine only Son; who, when he shall come again in great glory to judge the world with righteousness, shall make all things new.

2 **BCO***   Advent (*b*)

We praise thee for Jesus Christ, thy Son, our Saviour, by whom thou hast sent a new light to shine upon the world, that we who rejoice in that light may be found cleansed from our sins and without fear when he shall come again to judge the world in righteousness.

---

[1] The only one of these Prefaces to appear in the Jamaican edition is no. 61.

Proper Prefaces

3 On the Day only, **1549**.   Christmas (a)
    On the Day and seven days after, **1552, 1662, Amer, Can, CanR, Ire, Jap, Rhod**
    Until the Epiphany, **1928, Afr, Cey, Ind, Jap*, Kor, Nyas, Scot, WInd**
    Also Maundy Thursday, **Rhod**
    Also Corpus Christi, **Kor, Nyas, Rhod, WInd*** (except Jamaica)
    Also the Purification, **1928, Afr, Jap*, WInd**
    Also the Annunciation, **1928, Afr, CanR, Cey, Ind, Jap*, Scot**
    Also the Transfiguration, **Kor**
    Also Feasts of our Lady, **Ind, Kor, Nyas, Rhod, Scot*, WInd***

Because thou didst give Jesus Christ thine only Son to be born as at this time for us; who by the operation of the holy Ghost, was made very man of the substance of the Virgin Mary his Mother, and that without spot of sin, to make us clean from all sin.

<small>at this time] this day **1549, 1552**   as at this time] OM **Cey, Jap**; [[**Scot** follows text in Christmastide but reads 'as on this day' on the Feast]]   for us] for our salvation **Cey** [[also **Ind** out of Christmastide]]   Ghost] Spirit **CanR, Ind,** Virgin] Blessed Virgin **Scot**   [[In these notes no account is taken of adjustments of 'as at this time' to enable the Preface to be used out of Christmastide]]</small>

4 **BCO***   Christmas (b)

Especially at this time, we praise thee, because thou didst give Jesus Christ thine only Son to be born for us of Mary, that through him we might have power to become the sons of God.

5 **Amer**   Purification, Annunciation and Transfiguration
   CanR   After Octave of Christmas to Epiphany
                                 and on Purification and Transfiguration

Because in the mystery of the Word made flesh, thou hast caused a new light to shine in our hearts, to give the knowledge of thy glory, in the face of thy Son Jesus Christ our Lord.

6 **Scot, 1928, Afr, Amer, BCO*, Can, CanR**   Epiphany
    Cey, Ind, Jap*, Kor, Nyas, Rhod, WInd
    All include Octave except **BCO**
    Also Transfiguration* in **Jap**

Through Jesus Christ our Lord; who, in substance of our mortal flesh, manifested forth his glory, that he might bring us out of darkness into his own marvellous light.

Through] We praise thee for **BCO**; ADD thine only Son **Jap** our Lord] OM **Jap** in substance ... flesh] in the likeness of men **BCO** his glory] thy glory **BCO** us] all men **1928, BCO, Cey, Ind, Jap, WInd**; all men everywhere **Afr, Nyas** darkness] ADD and perplexity **Jap** own] OM **BCO** marvellous] glorious **Amer, Jap, Kor**

7 **Scot, Cey, Kor** [[cf. no. 10]] Lent (*a*)

Because thou hast given us the spirit of discipline, that we may triumph over the flesh, and live no longer unto ourselves but unto him who died for us and rose again.

thou hast ... we may] through our bodily abstinence thou dost enable us to **Kor**

8 **WInd, Nyas** Lent (*b*)
[R]

Who by bodily fasting dost restrain the vice that is within us, dost raise our minds to things above, and dost bestow upon us virtue and heavenly rewards, through Christ our Lord.

[[The translation of **Nyas** varies in detail from the text above]]

9 **Jap**★ Lent (*c*)

Through Jesus Christ our Lord; who, when he had fasted forty days and forty nights, was hungry; and, being tempted of the devil, was victorious over him; that, by his merits, we, when we are tempted, may come with boldness to the throne of grace, there to receive mercy and to obtain grace and power.

10 **BCO**★ [[cf. no. 7]] Lent (*d*)

We praise thee for Jesus Christ our Lord, who was in all points tempted like as we are, yet without sin; by whose grace we are enabled to subdue the sinful desires of the flesh, and live no longer unto ourselves, but unto him who died for us and rose again.

11 **Scot, Kor** Passiontide (*a*)
Also Feasts of the Holy Cross, **Kor**

Because thou didst give thine only Son, our Saviour Jesus Christ, to redeem mankind from the power of darkness; who, having finished the work thou gavest him to do, was lifted up upon the cross that he might draw all men unto himself, and, being made perfect through suffering, might become the author of eternal salvation to all of them that obey him.

Because] Who **Kor** up upon] up on **Kor** that he might draw] drawing **Kor** of them that] who **Kor**

Proper Prefaces

12 **Cey, Jap***   Passiontide (*b*)
Through Jesus Christ our Lord; Who, being found in fashion as a man, humbled himself and became obedient unto death, even the death of the Cross, that, being lifted up from the earth, he might draw all men unto him.

<small>that, being lifted ... might] that he, being lifted up, might, **Jap**</small>

13 **CanR**   Passiontide (including Maundy Thursday) (*c*)
For the redemption of the world by the death and passion of our Saviour Christ, both God and Man; who did humble himself, even to the death upon the Cross for us sinners, who lay in darkness and the shadow of death; that he might make us the children of God, and exalt us to everlasting life.

14 **WInd:** also Holy Cross   Passiontide (*d*)
Nyas: also Sacred Heart, Precious Blood, and Holy Cross   [R]
Who by the tree of the Cross didst give salvation to all mankind, that so whence death arose thence life also might rise again, and that he who by a tree once overcame might also by a tree be overcome, through Christ our Lord.

<small>⟦The translation of **Nyas** varies in detail⟧</small>

15 **BCO***   Passiontide (*e*)
We praise thee for Jesus Christ our Lord, who the night before he suffered did institute this holy Sacrament, to be a pledge of his love and a memorial of his passion, that we being partakers of these holy mysteries, might receive the benefits of his redemption.

16 **Scot, 1928, Afr, Cey, Ind, Jap*, Nyas** Maundy Thursday (*a*)
Also at Thanksgiving for Holy Communion, **1928*, Cey, Jap***
Through Jesus Christ our Lord; who having loved his own which were in the world, loved them unto the end, and on the night before he suffered, sitting at meat with his disciples, did institute these holy mysteries; that we, receiving the benefits of his passion, and being quickened by his resurrection, might be made partakers of the divine nature.

<small>which were] that were **1928, Cey, Ind, Jap**   before he suffered] in which he was betrayed **Jap**   sitting...disciples] OM **Afr, Nyas**   receiving...passion] redeemed by his death **1928, Cey, Ind**; redeemed by his passion **Jap**   being] OM **1928, Cey, Ind, Jap**   made] OM **1928, Cey, Ind, Jap**   the divine] his divine **1928, Afr, Ind, Jap**   nature] ADD and be filled with all the fulness of God **Afr, Nyas**</small>

17 See nos. 3 and 13   Maundy Thursday (*b*)

18 On the Day only, **1549, BCO***   Easter
On the Day and during the Octave, **1552, 1662, Amer,**   [R]
   Can, Ire, Jap
Until the Ascension, **1928, Afr, CanR, Cey, Ind, Jap*, Kor, Nyas, Rhod, Scot, WInd**
Also at 'Memorial Services' **CanR**

⟦**Kor** begins the use of this Preface at the Easter Vigil⟧

But chiefly are we bound to praise thee for the glorious Resurrection of thy son Jesus Christ our Lord, for he is the very paschal Lamb which was offered for us, and hath taken away the sin of the world, who by his death hath destroyed death, and by his rising to life again hath restored to us everlasting life.

for he] who **BCO**   restored to] brought to **BCO**; given **Jap**   to us] unto us **Kor**

19 On the Day only **1549**   Ascension (*a*)
On the Day and during the Octave, **1552,**   [R]
   1662, Amer, Can, Ire, Jap, Nyas, Rhod
Until Whitsun, **1928, Afr, CanR, Cey, Ind, Jap*, Kor, Scot, WInd**

Through thy most dearly beloved Son Jesus Christ our Lord, who after his most glorious resurrection manifestly appeared to all his Apostles, and in their sight ascended up into heaven, to prepare a place for us; that where he is, thither we might also ascend, and reign with him in Glory.

dearly] dear **1549, 1552**   Apostles] disciples **1549**   to prepare] and now prepares **Kor**   might also] shall also **Kor**

20 **BCO***   Ascension (*b*)

We praise thee for Jesus Christ our Lord, who ascended up on high, the one Mediator between God and man; who abideth for ever in that glory which he had with thee, and in that nature which he took of us, that he might bring us to the fellowship of his Godhead.

21 On Whitsunday only, **1549**   Whitsuntide (*a*)
On Whitsunday and six days after, **1552, 1662,**
   Amer, Can, CanR, Rhod, Scot ⟦with no. 22 as alternative⟧
Also at Ordinations and Synods, **CanR**

Through Jesus Christ our Lord, according to whose most true promise, the holy Ghost came down, as at this time, from heaven

Proper Prefaces

with a sudden great sound, as it had been a mighty wind, in the likeness of fiery Tongues lighting upon the Apostles to teach them, and to lead them to all truth, giving them both the gift of divers languages, and also boldness with fervent zeal, constantly to preach the Gospel unto all Nations, whereby we have been brought out of darkness and error into the clear light and true knowledge of thee, and of thy son Jesus Christ.

Ghost] Spirit **CanR** as at this time] this day **1549, 1552** 〚**Scot** follows text in Octave but reads 'as on this day' on the Feast〛 with a sudden . . . tongues] OM **Amer, CanR** Apostles] disciples **Amer** to all truth] into all truth **Amer, CanR, Rhod** both . . . and also] OM **Amer, CanR** divers languages] tongues **Can, CanR, Scot**; utterance **Rhod** have been brought] are brought **1549, 1552** 〚In these notes no account is taken of adjustment to enable the Preface to be used out of Whitsuntide〛

22 On Whitsunday and six days after, **Scot** Whitsuntide (*b*)
〚alternative to no. 21〛, **1928, Afr, Cey,** [R]
Ind, Ire, Jap, Kor, Nyas, WInd

〚**Kor** begins the use of this Preface on the Vigil〛

Through Jesus Christ our Lord; who after that he had ascended up far above all the heavens, and was set down at the right hand of thy Majesty, did as at this time pour forth upon the universal Church thy holy and life-giving Spirit: that through his glorious power the joy of the everlasting Gospel might go forth into all the world; whereby we have been brought out of darkness and error into the clear light and true knowledge of thee, and of thy Son our Saviour Jesus Christ.

up] OM **Kor** the right . . . Majesty] thy right hand **Ire** thy Majesty] the Father **Jap** as at this time] OM **Cey, Jap, Kor** upon the universal Church] upon the children of adoption **Afr, Ire, Nyas**; upon the Church **Cey**; OM **Kor** and lifegiving] OM **Jap** glorious] OM **Cey**; mighty **Jap** joy of the] OM **Cey, Jap** go forth] come abroad **Ire, Jap** true] OM **Nyas** our Saviour] OM **Kor** Christ] ADD our Lord **Kor**. 〚In these notes no account is taken of adjustments to enable the Preface to be used out of Whitsuntide〛

23 **BCO*** Whitsuntide (*c*)

We praise thee for Jesus Christ our Lord, who having ascended up on high, and sitting at thy right hand, sent forth the promise of the Holy Spirit upon the whole Church, that the everlasting Gospel should be preached among all men to bring them out of darkness into the clear light of thy truth.

24 On Trinity Sunday only, **1549, 1552, 1662, Can**   Trinity (*a*)
Also on three following days and any Sunday★
  not provided for, **Jap**
Also on Feasts of our Lord not provided for, **Rhod**

Who art one God, one Lord, not one only person, but three persons in one substance. For that which we believe of the glory of the Father, the same we believe of the Son, and of the holy Ghost, without any difference or inequality.

<small>Who art] which art **1549, 1552** and the Holy Ghost, **Jap, Rhod**   Who] ADD , with thine only-begotten Son or inequality] of equality **Jap**</small>

25 On Trinity Sunday only, **Scot, 1928, Afr,**   Trinity (*b*)
  Amer 〚with no. 27 as alternative〛**, Cey, Ind, Ire**   [R]
Also on Sundays not otherwise provided for, **Kor, Nyas, WInd**
  〚cf. no. 33〛

Who with thine only-begotten Son and the Holy Ghost art one God, one Lord, in Trinity of Persons and in Unity of Substance; for that which we believe of thy glory, O Father, the same we believe of the Son, and of the Holy Ghost, without any difference or inequality.

<small>Ghost] Spirit **Ind**   O Father] OM **Cey**   the same] ADD also **Kor**   the Son] thy Son **1928, Cey, Ind, Kor, WInd**   Ghost] Spirit **Ind**   or inequality] of inequality **Amer**</small>

26 **CanR:** Trinity Sunday only   Trinity (*c*)

Whom with thy co-eternal Son and Holy Spirit we confess as one God, in Trinity of Persons and in Unity of Substance. For that which we believe of thy glory, O Father, the same we believe of the Son, and of the Holy Spirit.

27 **Amer:** 〚cf. no. 25〛 Trinity Sunday only   Trinity (*d*)

For the precious death and merits of thy Son Jesus Christ our Lord, and for the sending to us of the Holy Ghost, the Comforter; who are one with thee in the Eternal Godhead.

<small>〚This alternative Preface goes back to 1790. Until the last revision it was alternative to the **1662** text of no. 24.〛</small>

28 **BCO**★   Trinity (*e*)

We praise thee for Jesus Christ our Lord, who, with thee and the Holy Spirit, art one God, the same in substance, equal in power and glory.

29 See no. 3   Corpus Christi

Proper Prefaces

30 See no. 16   Thanksgiving for Holy Communion

31 **WInd, Nyas**   Christ the King
                                                                                [R]

Because thou hast anointed thine only-begotten Son Jesus Christ our Lord with the oil of gladness to be a Priest for ever and to be King over all mankind: that when he had offered himself a spotless sacrifice of peace upon the altar of the Cross, he might fulfil the mystery of our redemption, and having brought all creatures under his governance, might present unto thine infinite Majesty a kingdom universal and everlasting, a kingdom of truth and life, a kingdom of sanctity and grace, a kingdom of justice, love, and peace.

[[**Nyas** has a translation differing in detail]]

32 **1928**   Sundays (*a*)

Through Jesus Christ our Lord; for he is the true High Priest, who hath washed us from our sins, and hath made us to be a kingdom and priests unto thee our God and Father.

33 **Afr** [[cf. no. 25]]   Sundays (*b*)

Who, with thine only-begotten Son and the Holy Ghost art one God, one Lord, in Trinity of Persons and in Unity of Substance, who hast created all things through thy eternal Word.

34 **Cey**   Sundays (*c*)

Through Jesus Christ our Lord; Who on the first day of the week did rise from the dead, that we might live in him by the power of the Holy Ghost.

35 See nos. 24 and 25   Sundays (*d*)

---

36 **Scot** (see no. 52)   St. Kentigern

37 **Scot*, Cey, Rhod**   Presentation or Purification (*a*)

Because thy blessed Son Jesus Christ our Lord, born of a woman, born under the Law, was, as on this day, presented in the Temple, and revealed to thy servants as a light to lighten the Gentiles and the glory of thy people Israel.

as on this day] OM **Cey**

234   The Liturgy in English

38 **Amer:**   Purification (*b*)
   also Annunciation, Transfiguration

Because in the Mystery of the Word made flesh, thou hast caused a new light to shine in our hearts, to give the knowledge of thy glory in the face of thy Son Jesus Christ our Lord.

39 See nos. 3 and 5   Purification (*c*)

40 See no. 52   St. Patrick

41 **WInd, Nyas**   St. Joseph
                                                              [R]

And that in the festival of Joseph the blessed, we should praise, bless, and tell forth thy wonders: who being a righteous man, was espoused to the Virgin Mother of God by thine appointment: a faithful and wise servant made ruler of thy household: that in the office of a father he should guard thy only-begotten Son, conceived by the overshadowing of the Holy Ghost, even Jesus Christ our Lord.

⟦The translation in **Nyas** differs in detail⟧

42 See nos. 3 and 38   Annunciation

43 **Nyas:** including Octave   St. John Baptist (*a*)

And especially on this day, whereon we celebrate the birth of thy servant John Baptist, who before his birth rejoiced in the presence of his Saviour, and whose office it was to bear witness to him whom the Prophets had foretold as the redeemer of the world; even Jesus Christ our Lord.

44 See no. 53   St. John Baptist (*b*)

45 See no. 52   St. Columba

46 See no. 53   St. Mary Magdalen

47 **Scot**   Transfiguration (*a*)

Because thou hast made known to us the honour and glory of thy beloved Son, to whom before his passion thy voice bare witness on the holy Mount.

48 **1928, Afr, Cey, Nyas, WInd**   Transfiguration (*b*)

Because the divine glory of the Incarnate Word shone forth

Proper Prefaces

upon the Holy Mount before the chosen witnesses of his majesty: And thine own voice from heaven proclaimed thy beloved Son.

divine] OM **Afr, Nyas**   the Incarnate] thine Incarnate **Afr, Nyas**   shone] did shine **Afr, Nyas**   before... witnesses] unto eyewitnesses **Afr, Nyas**   chosen] OM **Cey**   And thine... Son] and did manifest the power and coming of his Kingdom with his Saints in light **Afr, Nyas**

49 See nos. 3, 5, 6, and 38   Transfiguration (c)

50 See no. 52   St. Ninian

51 See nos. 11 and 14   Holy Cross Day

52 **Scot:** All Saints, St. John Baptist,   All Saints (a)
    St. Columba, St. Kentigern, St. Patrick,
    St. Ninian, St. Margaret of Scotland
  Amer: All Saints' Day and the Octave
  CanR: All Saints' Day and other Festivals of Saints
  Rhod: All Saints' Day

Who in the multitude of thy Saints hast compassed us about with so great a cloud of witnesses, to the end that we, rejoicing in their fellowship, may run with patience the race that is set before us, and together with them receive the crown of glory that fadeth not away.

to the end] OM **Amer, CanR**   receive] may receive **Amer, CanR**

53 All Saints, Apostles, Evangelists, and St. John   All Saints (b)
    Baptist, **1928, Afr, Cey, Kor**
  All Saints, St. John Baptist, and St. Mary, Magdalen, **WInd**
  All Saints and Octave, **Ind, Nyas** 〚also any Saint, **Ind**〛
  〚**BCO** has some similarity with this form. See no. 54 below〛

Who in the righteousness of thy Saints hast given us an ensample of godly living, and in their blessedness a glorious pledge of the hope of our calling: That, being compassed about with so great a cloud of witnesses, we may run with patience the race that is set before us: And with them receive the crown of glory that fadeth not away.

the righteousness of] OM **Afr, Nyas, WInd**   ensample] example **Afr, Nyas, WInd**   living] life **Afr, Nyas, WInd**   in their blessedness] OM **Afr, Nyas, WInd**   being] OM **Afr, Nyas, WInd**   with patience] OM **Kor**   with them receive] receive with them **Afr, Nyas, WInd**   crown... away] never fading crown of glory **WInd**

54 **BCO*** All Saints (c)

We praise thee for Jesus Christ our Lord, who in the blessedness of thy saints has given us a glorious pledge of the hope of our calling; that, following their example and being strengthened by their fellowship, we may exult in thee for thy mercy, even as they rejoice with thee in glory.

55 See no. 52 St. Margaret of Scotland

56 **WInd** Our Lady (a)
[R]

And that in the ... of Blessed Mary ever Virgin, we should praise, bless, and tell forth thy wonders: in that by the overshadowing of the Holy Ghost, she conceived thy only-begotten Son, and the glory of her virginity still abiding, brought forth for man the Light eternal, even Jesus Christ our Lord.

57 See no. 3 Our Lady (b)

58 **Scot, Rhod** Apostles and Evangelists (a)
Nyas: including Octaves

Through Jesus Christ our Lord, who did vouchsafe to choose thy servant Saint N. [*or* thy servants Saint N. and Saint N.] to be of the company of the Apostles [*or* to be an Evangelist], by whose ministry thine elect might be gathered in from every nation, and thy Church instructed in the way that leadeth unto everlasting life.

did] didst **Nyas, Rhod** company] number **Nyas** [[**Nyas** has no provision for more than one Saint]] everlasting] eternal **Nyas**

59 See no. 53 Apostles and Evangelists (b)

60 **Jap*** Apostles and Evangelists (c)

And especially do we praise thee because through Jesus Christ thy Son, our Lord, thou didst call Saint ... to be an Apostle [Evangelist]: that we, holding fast the faith which he taught, may fearlessly preach the Gospel to all men.

61 **WInd** Apostles
[R]

And that we should humbly entreat thee, O Lord, the everlasting

Shepherd, to leave not thy flock untended, but to keep it by thy blessed Apostles under thy continual protection, that it may be governed by those same rulers, whom in thy stead thou hast chosen for thy work as shepherds of thy people.

62 **Jap**★ [[cf. no. 53]] Any Saint
[[See also nos. 52 and 53]]
Who in thy Saints hast given us an ensample of godly living and a firm pledge of the hope of our calling; that we, being compassed about with so great a cloud of witnesses, may run with patience the race that is set before us; and with them receive the crown of glory that fadeth not away.

---

63 The three Orders and Ember Days, **Scot, Cey** Ordination (*a*)
Ordination, **Nyas**

Through Jesus Christ our Lord, the great Shepherd of the sheep; who for the feeding and guidance of his flock, did appoint divers orders of ministers in his Church.

64 See no. 21. Ordination (*b*)

65 Day of Dedication and anniversary, **Scot** Dedication (*a*)
'Upon the Dedication', **Rhod**
Who in temples made with hands buildest up for thyself a spiritual temple made without hands.

66 (i) Day of Dedication and anniversary, Dedication (*b*)
   1928, **Afr, Cey, Jap★, Nyas, WInd**
Anniversary and Octave, **Ind**
[[**BCO** has some similarity with this form. See no. 67 below]]

Who, though the heaven of heavens cannot contain thee and thy glory is in all the world: Dost deign to hallow places for thy worship, and in them dost pour forth gifts of grace upon thy faithful people.

Dost . . . worship] yet dost accept the earthly habitations dedicated to thy name
Afr, Nyas, WInd

66 (ii) [[**Kor** has a version of this text so diverse as to require separate printing]]

Who, though thy glory is in all the world, and thy greatness is unbounded, dost vouchsafe to hallow for thy Name places meet for thy worship; and through them to stir up in the hearts of thy people the spirit of grace and of supplication.

67 **BCO**★   Dedication (*c*)

We praise thee, O God, whom the heaven of heavens cannot contain, much less this House that our hands have builded; but who hast promised that in all places where thou dost record thy name, there wilt thou meet with thy people to bless them.

68 See no. 21.   At a Synod

69 **Afr, Cey**   Of the Departed (*a*)

Through Jesus Christ our Lord: who hath brought life and immortality to light, that we, who are burdened by the weight of sin and death, may grieve not as those who have no hope: because we know that when our earthly tabernacle is dissolved we have a better habitation.

may grieve not] might not sorrow **Cey**

70 **WInd, Jap**★**, Kor, Nyas**   Of the Departed (*b*)
                                                                                                [R]

Through Jesus Christ our Lord; In whom hath shone forth unto us the hope of a blessed resurrection, that they who bewail the certain condition of their mortality may be comforted by the promise of immortality to come. For to thy faithful people, O Lord, life is changed, not taken away; and at the dissolution of the tabernacle of this earthly pilgrimage a dwelling place eternal is made ready in the heavens.

⟦The translations of **Jap, Kor,** and **Nyas** vary from the text above and from one another in detail⟧

71 See no. 18   Of the Departed (*c*)

⟦In the *Book of Common Worship* (1963) of the Church of South India, Proper Prefaces are provided. Three (Palm Sunday and two for use at ordinations) are new texts. The remainder are nos. 2, 4, 6, 10, 12, 16, 18, 20, 21, 28, 53, and 66 (i) of those printed above; but in most cases some change has been made in the wording.⟧

APPENDIX B

OFFERTORY SENTENCES

THE Roman Rite, as Cranmer celebrated it, included a chant to be sung at the Offertory. Long before his time this had been reduced on most days to a brief anthem; and at Low Mass it was read, as it is still read, by the celebrant alone. The text of the chant varied according to the day or the season and was not chosen on account of its suitability to the act of 'offering'. The 1549 Prayer Book took over this feature of the liturgy but transformed its character. A collection of 'Sentences of Holy Scripture' was provided, one or more of which was to be sung or one to be said. If it was sung, it was to accompany the people's offering (of money); if it was said, it was to precede the offering. But the Sentences no longer varied with the season, nor were they connected with the Christian mysteries. They were an encouragement to generosity.

The anthology of Sentences remained unaltered up to 1662 (inclusive); but from 1552 their singing was given up, and the celebrant was told to read 'one or more . . . as he thinketh most convenient'. According to the rite of 1552 this reading was to precede the collection of the alms; since 1662 it has been ordered to accompany it.

Revisers of the Prayer Book have usually reduced the number or changed the contents of the 1549 collection of Sentences, influenced by the desire to reduce its financial flavour and to increase the element of self-offering. But some revisers have also added a fresh collection of sentences concerned not with offering but (as in the Roman Rite) with the season.

Those that have contented themselves with revising the non-seasonal anthology of 1549 are: the English (1928), Scottish, American, and Canadian (1917) rites. The recension of 1662 in the Scottish Prayer Book makes no change in the selection of Sentences, except that it adds one. Seasonal sentences have been added by Ireland*, Ceylon*, South Africa, Japan*, India, Canada (1959), and the West Indies.

* (as in Appendix A) indicates optional use.

The Sentences that are used are set out in the two tables below. Table I gives the 1549 set of twenty Sentences, followed by the sixteen Sentences of a non-seasonal character that have been added in various liturgies. Table II gives the seasonal Sentences which are found in the liturgies mentioned above. No attempt has been made to indicate changes in the order of the Sentences which have been introduced in various liturgies; nor has any indication been given of changes or variations in the translation of the Bible from which the Sentences are taken.

Something should, however, be said of the history which lies behind the Scottish and American selections, for the tables note only the current (1929, 1935) revisions of those Prayer Books.

The Scottish Liturgy of 1637 contained half of the 1549 Sentences together with five others. Three of these five appear in Table I (*b*). The Liturgy of 1764 had the same selection but for one omission. The American Liturgy contained simply the 1549 selection until 1892, when five sentences were added, three of which appear in Table I (*b*).

The Irish Prayer Book assumes that two Sentences will be used, the first 'general' (Table I) and the second 'proper' (Table II).

There are no Offertory Sentences in **Bom** or **Kor**. But, in the latter, the Offertory may be accompanied by a psalm or a hymn; and there is a prayer *super oblata*.

TABLE I

SENTENCES FOR GENERAL USE

(*a*) *The English selection of 1549–1662*

1. Let your light . . . is in heaven (Matt. 5. 16) **1928, Afr, Amer, Can, Ind, IndR, Ire, Jap, ScotE** [[cf. Table II. 3 (*c*)]]
2. Lay not up . . . break through and steal (Matt. 6. 19) **1928, Afr, Amer, Can, Ire, ScotE**
3. Whatsoever ye would . . . the Prophets (Matt. 7. 12) **1928, Afr, Can, Ind, IndR, Ire, ScotE, WInd** [[cf. Table II. 10 (*e*)]]
4. Not everyone that saith . . . is in heaven (Matt. 7. 21) **1928, Afr, Amer, Can, Ind, IndR, Ire, Jap, Scot, ScotE, WInd.**

Offertory Sentences

5. Zacchaeus stood forth ... restore fourfold. (Luke 19. 8) **Can, ScotE**
6. Who goeth a warfare ... the flock (1 Cor. 9. 7) **Can, ScotE**
7. If we have sown ... worldly things (1 Cor. 9. 11) **1928, Can, Ire, ScotE**
8. Do ye not know ... of the Gospel (1 Cor. 9. 13 f.) **1928, Can, Ire, ScotE**
9. He that soweth ... cheerful giver. (2 Cor. 9. 6 f.) **1928, Amer, Can, Ire, ScotE** [[cf. Table II. 23]]
10. Let him that is taught ... he reap (Gal. 6. 6 f.) **1928, Afr, Can, Cey, Ire, ScotE**
11. While we have time ... household of faith (Gal. 6. 10) **1928, Afr, Amer, Can, Ind, IndR, Ire, Scot, ScotE** [[cf. Table II. 1 (b)]]
12. Godliness is great riches ... anything out (1 Tim. 6. 6 f.) **1928, Can, Ire, ScotE**
13. Charge them who are rich ... eternal life (1 Tim. 6. 17–19) **1928, Amer, Can, Ire, ScotE**
14. God is not unrighteous ... do minister (Heb. 6. 10) **1928, Can, Ire, Jap, ScotE**
15. To do good ... is pleased (Heb. 13. 16) **1928, Amer, Can, CanR, Ire, Scot, ScotE, WInd**
16. Whoso hath this world's ... God in him (1 John 3. 17) **1928, Amer, Can, Cey, Ire, ScotE**
17. Give alms ... away from thee (Tobit 4. 7) **Can, ScotE**
18. Be merciful ... of necessity. (Tobit 4. 8 f.) **1928, Amer, Can, ScotE**
19. He that hath pity ... paid him again (Prov. 19. 17) **Can, Ire, ScotE**
20. Blessed be the man ... time of trouble (Ps. 41. 1) **1928, Afr, Can, CanR, Ire, ScotE, WInd**

(b) *Additions and alterations to the 1549 selection*

21. Remember the words ... than to receive. (Acts 20. 35) **1928, Afr, Amer, Can, CanR, IndR, Ire, Jap, Scot, ScotE, WInd**

22. All things come . . . given thee (1 Chron. 29. 14) **1928, Afr, Amer, Can** [[cf. **Ire** no. 32]]
23. Lift up your eyes . . . to harvest. (John 4. 35) **1928, Ire**
24. Offer unto God . . . most Highest (Ps. 50. 14) **1928, CanR, Cey, IndR, Scot** [[cf. Table II. 11 (c)]]
25. I will offer in his dwelling . . . the Lord (Ps. 27. 6) **1928, Cey, IndR, Jap, Scot, WInd**
26. Melchizedek king of Salem . . . high God (Gen. 14. 18) **1928, Afr, Cey**
27. Ye shall not appear . . . given thee (Deut. 16. 16 f.) **Amer, Ire**
28. And they came . . . Lord's offering (Exod. 35. 21) **Can, CanR**
29. And the King shall answer . . . unto me (Matt. 25. 40) **Amer**
30. How then shall they call . . . without a preacher (Rom. 10. 14 f.) **Amer**
31. Jesus said . . . labourers into his harvest (Luke 10. 2) **Amer**
32. Thine, O Lord . . . head above all (1 Chron. 29. 11) **Amer, Ire** [[incl. v. 14]] [[cf. no. 22]]
33. Walk in love . . . sweet-smelling savour (Eph. 5. 2) **Afr**, [[cf. Table II. 5 (c)]]
34. I beseech you therefore . . . reasonable service (Rom. 12. 1) **Afr, Cey** [[cf. Table II. 4 (b)]]
35. I will offer to thee . . . all his people (Ps. 116. 15 f.) **Afr, Cey, Scot, WInd**
36. Give the Lord the glory . . . his courts (Ps. 96. 8) **CanR, IndR, Scot** [[cf. Table II. 12]]

TABLE II
SEASONAL SENTENCES

1. ADVENT
    (a) Rejoice greatly, O daughter . . . unto thee (Zech. 9. 9) **Afr, Cey, Jap***
    (b) While we have time . . . household of faith (Gal. 6. 10) **CanR, WInd** [[cf. Table I. 11]]

2. CHRISTMAS
    (a) Ye know the grace . . . might be rich (2 Cor. 8. 9) **CanR, Ire, WInd**
    (b) Unto us a child . . . son is given (Is. 9. 6) **Afr, Cey, IndR,**
    (c) Let the heavens rejoice . . . Lord cometh (Ps. 96. 11, 13) **Jap**

Offertory Sentences

3. EPIPHANY
    - (a) All kings shall fall . . . him service (Ps. 72. 11) **Afr, Cey, IndR**
    - (b) All the earth shall worship . . . my soul (Ps. 66. 4, 16) **Jap**
    - (c) Let your light . . . in heaven (Matt. 5. 16) **CanR, WInd** [[cf. Table I. 1]]

4. LENT
    - (a) Rend your heart . . . and merciful (Joel 2. 13) **Afr, Cey, Jap**
    - (b) I beseech you, brethren . . . reasonable service (Rom. 12. 1) **CanR, WInd** [[cf. Table I. 34]]

5. PASSIONTIDE
    - (a) Thy rebuke hath broken . . . comfort me (Ps. 69. 21) **Afr, Cey**
    - (b) Reproach hath broken . . . found none (Ps. 69. 20) **Jap**
    - (c) Walk in love . . . sacrifice to God (Eph. 5. 2) **CanR, WInd** [[cf. Table I. 33]]

6. MAUNDY THURSDAY
    - (a) He shall feed me . . . comfort (Ps. 23. 2) **Cey, IndR**
    - (b) For as often as ye eat . . . blood of the Lord (1 Cor. 11. 26 f.) **Jap**
    - (c) A new commandment . . . one another (John 13. 34) **CanR**

7. EASTER
    - (a) Christ our passover . . . the feast (1 Cor. 5. 7 f.) **Ire**
    - (b) Christ is risen . . . that slept. Alleluia (1 Cor. 15. 20) **Afr, Cey, IndR, Jap**
    - (c) Worthy is the Lamb . . . blessing. [Alleluia] (Rev. 5. 12) **CanR** [[also festivals]], **WInd**

8. ASCENSION
    - (a) When he ascended . . . unto men (Eph. 4. 8) **IndR, Ire, Jap**
    - (b) Lift up your heads . . . come in. Alleluia (Ps. 24. 7) **Afr, Cey**
    - (c) Lay up for yourselves . . . heart be also. (Matt. 6. 20) **CanR, WInd**

9. ROGATION DAYS
    Verily, verily, I say unto you . . . in my name (John 16. 23) **Cey, WInd**

10. WHITSUNDAY
    (a) God hath sealed us ... our hearts (2 Cor. 1. 22) **Ire**
    (b) I will pour out my spirit upon all flesh. Alleluia (Joel 2. 28)
        Afr, Cey, IndR
    (c) Thy God hath commanded ... presents unto thee (Ps. 68,
        28 f.) **Jap**
    (d) He that soweth to the Spirit ... everlasting (Gal. 6. 8)
        WInd
    (e) Whatsoever ye would ... and the Prophets (Matt. 7. 12)
        CanR [[cf. Table I. 3]]

11. TRINITY SUNDAY
    (a) Now unto the King ... ever and ever. Amen (1 Tim. 1.
        17) **Ire**
    (b) Who shall not fear ... only art holy (Rev. 15. 4) **Afr, Cey,
        IndR, Jap***
    (c) Offer unto God the sacrifice ... Most High (Ps. 50. 14)
        WInd [[not Jamaica]] [[cf. Table I. 24]]
    (d) Not everyone ... in heaven (Matt. 7. 21) **CanR** [[cf.
        Table I. 4]]

12. CORPUS CHRISTI
    Ascribe unto the Lord ... into his courts (Ps. 96. 8) **WInd**
    [[cf. Table I. 36]]

---

13. PRESENTATION
    I will fill this house ... Lord of hosts (Hag. 2. 7) **Cey**

14. ANNUNCIATION
    How beautiful ... God reigneth (Is. 52. 7) **Cey**

15. TRANSFIGURATION
    We all, with unveiled face ... the Spirit (2 Cor. 3. 18) **Cey**

---

16. FEASTS OF THE BLESSED VIRGIN MARY
    (a) Mary said: Behold the handmaid ... word (Luke 1. 38)
        WInd
    (b) Mary said: My soul doth magnify ... my Saviour (Luke
        1. 46) **WInd**

Offertory Sentences

17. APOSTLES AND EVANGELISTS
    Instead of thy fathers ... ever and ever (Ps. 45, 17 f.) **Jap**

18. SAINTS' DAYS
    (*a*) All thy works praise ... unto thee (Ps. 145. 10). **Afr, Cey, IndR, Jap, WInd**
    (*b*) The Lord preserveth the souls ... the ungodly (Ps. 97. 10) **WInd**

19. DEDICATION OF A CHURCH
    The glory of this latter ... Lord of Hosts (Hag. 2. 9) **Cey, IndR, Jap, WInd**

20. EMBER DAYS
    The harvest is plenteous ... into his harvest (Luke 10. 2) **Cey, WInd**

21. THE DEPARTED
    (*a*) None of us liveth ... are the Lord's (Rom. 14. 7 f.) **Afr, Cey, WInd**
    (*b*) Blessed are the dead ... their labours (Rev. 14. 13) **Jap**

22. FOR MISSIONS
    Go ye and make disciples ... end of the world (Matt. 28. 19 f.) **Cey**

23. ROGATION AND HARVEST
    He that soweth ... cheerful giver (2 Cor. 9. 6, 7), **CanR** [[cf. Table I. 9]]

24. [[UNNAMED]]
    Thine, O Lord ... have we given thee (1 Chron. 29. 11, 13, 14) **Ire** [[follows the collection of Proper Sentences]]

APPENDIX C

POST-COMMUNION COLLECTS

THE Mass-propers of the Roman Rite contain a chant, the 'Communion', which is sung during the Communion or (at Low Mass) read by the celebrant after it; this chant is followed by a Collect, the 'Post-communion', which is read by the celebrant after the 'Communion'. The liturgy of the 1549 Prayer Book took over the name 'Post-communion'; but applied it to a Sentence of Scripture, which the clerks were to sing (see pp. 22 ff.). But these 'Post-communion Sentences' had no seasonal connexion and were more concerned with the righteousness of Christian men than with the work of God in the Sacrament. Being a chant, the Sentence more closely resembled a slightly delayed 'Communion' than a 'Post-communion'; the place formerly occupied by the 'Communion' having been given to *Agnus Dei*. Instead of a variable Post-communion Collect, there was a fixed prayer (see p. 24). This was substantially the 'Prayer of Thanksgiving' of the 1662 rite, but it was given no title.

In 1552 the 'Post-communion Sentences' were abolished, and the fixed post-communion prayer of 1549 became alternative to the 'Prayer of Oblation', which (with the Lord's Prayer) was removed from a place before to a place after the Communion. This arrangement was retained in 1662. But the Scottish and American liturgies have never had the 'Post-communion Sentences', have always retained the 'Prayer of Oblation' and the Lord's Prayer before the Communion, and (save in the proposed American Amended Book of 1786) have always had the Prayer of Thanksgiving as the one fixed post-communion prayer.

The only revival of a proper anthem or Sentence in connexion with the Communion in modern times[1] is the use of an anthem in the ancient place—that is to say, during the Communion—at the Coronation of Queen Elizabeth II. In this case the choice of text, 'O taste and see . . .', is dictated simply by the connexion with the Communion and not with the circumstances in which it was being celebrated. The Communion anthem prescribed

[1] Except that **Nyas, Rhod, Zan**, and **WInd** have restored a 'Communion' of the Roman kind.

by *Liber Regalis*, which was last used at the Coronation of Charles II, was *Intellige clamorem* (Ps. 5. 2), which is 'proper' to a Coronation in that it reminds the king and his people of a greater kingship than his own. Thus, although the anthem used in 1953 occupies the ancient place of the 'Communion', it does not fulfil the same function; nor, on the other hand, does it correspond with the 'Post-communion Sentences' of 1549. It is unique.

The revival of Post-communion *Collects*, on the other hand, is by no means unusual in recent revisions; and of course it will be claimed that upon certain occasions they have never been absent from the Anglican liturgies. But they are no longer in their ancient place; nor do the texts provided have that close link with the Sacrament which was characteristic of the ancient forms. It is not proposed to print the texts, which are all optional; but some account of the present situation (May 1963) and an investigation of the historical background seem to be required.

The Prayer Book of 1549 made no provision for ordinations. But this deficiency was supplied at the end of the year (March 1549/1550); and, of course, these services were designed to be fitted into the 1549 liturgy. No proper Post-communion Sentence was provided, so that one of the ordinary collection must have been used. But a prayer suited to each Order was to be said 'after the last collect, and immediately before the benediction'. This rubric has been continued, though the prayers prescribed have been modified, into the 1662 liturgy; and priests and bishops have the 'proper' prayer and also 'Prevent us, O Lord . . .'. But, although the rubric is unchanged, its circumstances are not. Since 1552 the precise position referred to, 'after the last collect, and immediately before the benediction', has been occupied by *Gloria in Excelsis*. The rubric can therefore no longer be carried out strictly. The prayers in the Ordination services can be read *either* 'after the last collect' *or* 'immediately before the benediction'— but not both. In practice, it appears that it is usual to read the prayers between *Gloria in Excelsis* and the Blessing. This is probably the less satisfactory way of interpreting the rubric from the pastoral point of view, though a lawyer would no doubt lay great weight on the word 'immediately'.[1]

---

[1] It should be noted that in the Scottish Prayer Book, where Ordinations may occur either in **Scot** or in **ScotE**, the rubric has been altered to require the position immediately before the Blessing.

But the Ordination rites no longer stand alone in this matter, for the practice of inserting prayers after *Gloria in Excelsis* has spread to the Coronation rite. In the rite used for Charles I the act of Communion was followed by an anthem while the King returned to his throne. Then there is a rubric: '*After the Anthem the Archbishop reads the last Prayers. The Quire singeth* Glory be to God on high etc. *and so the Communion endeth.*' The text of the *last Prayers* is not specified; but two things are clear: there was probably another prayer or prayers between the Oblation or the Thanksgiving and *Gloria in Excelsis*, and there were no prayers between this hymn and the Blessing.

Of the Coronation of William and Mary sixty years later the full text is available. After the act of Communion, '*The Archbishop goes on to the Postcommunion*'. This rubric is followed by the cues of the Lord's Prayer and the Prayer of Oblation. Then '*The Quire sing* Glory be to God on High etc.', while the King and Queen return to their thrones: '*and the Archbishop reads* THE FINAL PRAYERS.' The prayers referred to are two collects, one proper and one general in character. A similar arrangement is to be found in the rite used for Victoria and for Elizabeth II. For Edward VII, George V, and George VI no extra prayers after the Communion were used.

If the 'last prayers' of Charles I, like the 'final prayers' of William and Mary, included one or more collects in addition to the Prayer of Oblation or the Prayer of Thanksgiving, then it seems probable that the custom of placing the extra prayers after *Gloria in Excelsis* dates from the Restoration. That is the first extension outside the Ordination rites of the muddle arising from the leaving of the 1549 rubric with doubt as to its interpretation.

For a long period it remained the only such extension, and the question of the position of Post-communion Collects was of little interest to the generality of the clergy or to the laity. But the revival of proper Post-communion Collects in some recent revisions has brought the use of these prayers after *Gloria in Excelsis* (for that is where they are invariably placed) into the experience of a large number of Anglicans. All these additions are, however, optional; and it would be difficult to discover how generally they are used in the several liturgies that allow them.

Post-communions in the 'post-Restoration' position are permitted in the following liturgies: 1928, South African, Indian (1960), Irish, Japanese, and Scottish.

Post-communion Collects

The Scottish Liturgy (whose Post-communions may also be used with the **ScotE**), provides collects proper to Advent, Christmastide, Epiphany, Lent, Passiontide, Eastertide, Ascensiontide, Whitsuntide, Trinity Sunday, and 'Saints' Days, except All Saints' Day'. There are also two Post-communion Collects for general use; and there is a further set of nine Collects which may be used either after the Collect of the Day or before the Blessing. The nine Collects include four of the **1662** set for use after the Offertory when there is no Communion.

The Irish Prayer Book allows the use of the **1662** 'Offertory set' before the Blessing and adds two additional general prayers, one for Embertide, and one for use at Ordinations.

The South African Prayer Book allows the use of the **1662** 'Offertory set' before the Blessing and adds a further three general prayers.

The 1928 Prayer Book has simply this rubric in connexion with the Alternative Order of Holy Communion: *And whenever this Service is used, Collects, contained in this Book, or sanctioned by the Bishop, may be said after the Intercession, or before the Blessing.*

The Indian Prayer Book (1961) does not permit the use of the **1662** 'Offertory set' as Post-communions; nor is there any such provision at all in its recension of the **1662** rite. But the 1960 liturgy is provided with Proper Collects which may be said before the Blessing on the following occasions: Christmastide, Epiphany, Maundy Thursday, Eastertide, Ascensiontide, Whitsuntide, Trinity Sunday, All Saints' Day and the Dedication Festival. There are also two general collects. The *Proposed Prayer Book* (1951) made much more generous provision.

The Japanese Liturgy provides a Post-communion Collect for every occasion that has a Proper Preface, namely: Advent, Christmastide, Epiphany, Lent, Passiontide, Maundy Thursday, Eastertide, Ascensiontide, Whitsuntide, Feasts of Apostles and Evangelists, Saints' Days, Dedication of a Church, Commemoration of the Departed, and one for use 'upon any other occasion'.

The Swahili Mass, **Nyas**, and **Rhod** provide for variable Post-communion Collects immediately before the Blessing, although the two last allow them to be followed by some form of the **1662** 'Prayer of Thanksgiving'. The Korean Liturgy includes a set of five additional Post-communion Collects; since this rite has *Gloria in Excelsis* at the beginning, these fit into the '1549' position.

It is plain that the 'Post-communion' has suffered its full share of those 'changes and chances of this mortal life' which are referred to by one of the prayers that are now being used as Post-communion Collects. It has also, in what has been called its post-Restoration form, grown from being an infrequent and exclusively pontifical element in the liturgy to become a normal part of the experience of worshippers in many parts of the Anglican Communion.

APPENDIX D

INTROITS AND GRADUALS

ANGLICAN liturgies have in the past provided for no chant at the beginning of the rite or between the lessons. The only exception to this rule before the present century was the ordering of proper psalms for the Introit in the First Prayer Book. And the only rite among the moderate revisions of **1662** given in Chapter III of the present volume to include such chants is the Coronation Order, to which an Introit psalm was restored for King Edward VII and a Gradual psalm for Queen Elizabeth II. From the Coronation of George IV to that of Queen Victoria the Sanctus had been sung in place of an Introit. The provisions of **IndR** may, however, be used with **Ind**.

But in recent times the use of Introits and Graduals, at least as an optional feature of the rite, has become widespread. Of the twentieth-century Anglican liturgies which are printed in full above, only four make no such provision: the Scottish, the South African, the Northern Rhodesian, and the proposed English revision of 1928. The situation in respect of the remainder is as follows:

INTROIT
    No provision at all   **Amer, Bom**
    Unspecified Introit   **Nyas, Zan**
    Unspecified psalm or hymn   **Cey★, Jap★, Kor★**
    Unspecified psalm   **IndR★** [in certain circumstances: see p. 115, no. 9]
                                          WInd★
    Psalm appointed for the day   **CanR**

GRADUAL
    Unspecified Gradual   **Nyas, Zan**
    Unspecified psalm or hymn   **Jap★, Kor★, WInd★**
    Unspecified hymn or anthem   **Amer★**
    Unspecified psalm   **Cey★**
    Unspecified hymn   **Bom** [but a proper psalm between OT lesson and Epistle]
    Psalm appointed for the day   **CanR**

      ★ (as in Appendix A) indicates optional use.

APPENDIX E

SUPPLEMENTARY CONSECRATION

THE accident that a priest should have set apart insufficient bread or wine (or both) for the number of communicants was not provided against in the Book of Common Prayer before the revision of 1662. This is surprising in view of the provision for a supplementary consecration of wine in the *Order of Communion* (1548), in which the priest was instructed simply to repeat the second half of the institution narrative over the refilled chalice. It seems probable that this instruction was inserted in view of the small size of many of the chalices then in use, which had been designed for the Communion of the celebrant alone. It seems unlikely that the situation can have improved greatly by 9 June 1549, for it was not until Elizabeth's reign that pressure was brought to bear upon the clergy and churchwardens to procure 'decent Communion cups' instead of continuing to make do with the surviving 'popish chalices'; though it is, of course, true that the new pattern of cups began to be made under Edward VI.

When, in 1662, instructions for supplementary consecration were restored, the method of the *Order of Communion* was revived but was applied to both species severally or together: that is to say, the institution narrative (or the relevant portion thereof) was to be recited, together with the performance of the new manual acts prescribed by the rubrics of the Prayer of Consecration. This arrangement is retained unaltered in the following liturgies: South African (as an alternative method only), Canadian (1918) Indian (the 1662 Order and the Indian Liturgy), Irish, and the Scottish recension of **1662**. In most cases this is what would be expected, for the liturgies in question are conservative revisions of **1662** and contain no alterations to the Prayer of Consecration. In the case of the Indian Liturgy of 1960, however, the retention of the 1662 form of supplementary consecration suggests that the compilers regard the form which they have given to their revised anaphoras as of small theological significance.

But **1928**, the South African Liturgy, the Scottish Liturgy, the Japanese Liturgy, the American Liturgy, the West Indian Liturgy,

Supplementary Consecration

the Canadian Liturgy (1959), and that of Ceylon have followed their revised anaphoras with revised methods of supplementary consecration.

Some have found the 1662 method unsatisfactory on two grounds:

1. It allows consecration in one species alone.
2. It uses the institution narrative as a quasi-magical formula, without the thanksgiving or blessing prescribed by the Lord and without the petition for consecration that Christians have commonly added thereto.

Both these practices are abandoned by America, Ceylon, Japan, and Scotland. South Africa makes a new arrangement but allows the 1662 method as an alternative.

The forms used vary as follows:

Afr From *Hear us, O merciful* ... to the end of the epiclesis.
Amer From *All glory* ... to the end of the epiclesis.
Cey The Institution and the epiclesis.
Jap A version of *Hear us, O merciful Father* ... to the end of the Institution.
Scot The Institution and the epiclesis.

Others have revised arrangements, but allow consecration in one kind alone.

CanR *Hear, O merciful Father, we beseech thee, the prayer and thanksgiving which we offer through Jesus Christ our Lord,* with the relevant portion of the Institution.
WInd *Hear us, O merciful Father* ... (see p. 182, no. 23), followed by the relevant portion of the institution narrative. This liturgy allows consecration in one species. According to the text, if more of *both* species is to be consecrated, *none* of the institution narrative is used; but this is presumably an error of drafting.
1928 *Hear us, O merciful Father* ..., followed by the relevant portion of the institution narrative.

The remaining Anglican liturgies contain no provision for supplementary consecration; and the same may be said of the Book of Common Order and the Congregationalist liturgy.

The Liturgy of the Church of South India permits a second consecration by one of two methods:
1. By taking more of either element and saying: *Obeying the command of our Lord Jesus Christ, we take this bread [wine] to be set apart for this holy use, in the name of the Father and of the Son and of the Holy Spirit. Amen.*
2. By repeating the institution narrative only. This method is not defined in detail, although it raises questions concerning the performance of manual acts.

PRINTED IN GREAT BRITAIN
AT THE UNIVERSITY PRESS, OXFORD
BY VIVIAN RIDLER
PRINTER TO THE UNIVERSITY